GHOSTS, MURDERS AND SCANDALS
of Worcestershire

GHOSTS, MURDERS AND SCANDALS
of Worcestershire

by

Anne Bradford

Illustrated by Glenn James

Hunt End Books

... her husband was the person who had executed the king.
(Cookhill priory, page 176)

HUNT END BOOKS
66 Enfield Road, Hunt End, Redditch
Worcestershire, B97 5NH, England
Telephone: 01527 542516
e-mail: annebradford@tiscali.co.uk

31 October 2005
ISBN 0-9549813-0-8

Printed in Great Britain
by SupaPrint (Redditch) Limited
www.supaprint.com

ILLUSTRATIONS

CONTENTS

denotes not real name

1. WORCESTER

he great Cathedral of Worcester rises majestically from the river Severn. It is blessed with a wealth of fine architecture, chiefly a blend of Norman and Perpendicular and possesses many treasures, for example, in the chancel is the oldest royal effigy in England, that of King John, who was buried in a monk's cowl (over his embroidered robe) between Saint Oswald and Saint Wulstan, so that he could slip unnoticed into heaven. The delicate fan vaulting of Prince Arthur's chantry is a superb work of art - the prince's death, at Ludlow, changed the history of England, for his brother went to the throne as Henry VIII.

There have been Christian buildings on the site since about 680 and there was a Bishop of Worcester before there was a King of England. In 1084 Saint Wulstan began to build a new cathedral to replace an old one, and amazingly, a part of it still survives, in the lovely simple Norman crypt. When he died, no expense was spared for his shrine but unfortunately, half a century later, the precious metals had to be melted down to pay the monastery's fine for taking the side of the French in an Anglo/French war. In about 1218, a new and gorgeous shrine was built but the body of St Wulstan was too long to fit in it. The Bishop, 'with his own hand' cut up the body. It is said that divine retribution took its toll and six weeks later the Bishop was dead.

The Cathedral's library has a priceless collection of books and manuscripts, once housed in the charnel house together with unwanted human bones. The charnel house was next to the north porch, now the main entrance. The upper room of the charnel house was, in 1636, converted into a school but the smell from the bodies was so great the school had to be moved to, what is now, the school hall. The area around the present main road was once an enclosed burial ground. So many bodies had been placed there, layer upon layer, that the ground had risen by four feet and it was necessary to go down a flight of steps to enter the Cathedral. The extra ground was removed and levelled by the Victorians.

Trouble in the churchyard

Throughout the centuries the churchyard has suffered from fights, and the occasional murder and has been 'reconciled from bloodshed' several times. A monastery was attached to the Cathedral until 1540, when Henry VIII dissolved the religious houses, and even the monks are known to have been involved in a scrap or two. Attracted, no doubt, by the monks' wealth and status, various orders of friars began arriving at Worcester from 1239. There was no love lost between the monks and the Friars. Matters came to a head in 1289, when the Franciscan Friars and the monks of Worcester both claimed the body of Henry Poche, a citizen of Worcester. The sacristan of Worcester Priory snatched the body and there was a skirmish as friars tried to reclaim the corpse. A crowd gathered, there was a lot of pushing and shoving and the friars fell into some dung heaps. They appealed to the Archbishop of Canterbury who took up their cause, and told the prior of Worcester to exhume the body and return it to the friars within two weeks. The monks agreed, providing that it was taken away quietly. However, the friars collected it with great pomp and uproar, inviting everyone to the spectacle. They carried the body away, singing, 'amidst an uproarious scene'.

There were also squabbles between the Prior and the Bailiffs of the city. Bailiffs twice removed from the Cathedral someone who was seeking sanctuary there, disregarding the authority of the Prior. In 1349 a serious riot took place between the monks and townsmen in which bailiffs and citizens 'comming in warlike manner with arms' attacked the church and priory, broke the priory gates, made assault on the prior's servants and beat them and 'with bows and arrows and other offensive weapons', pursued the prior and the monks, and tried to set fire to the monastery.

However, the greatest conflict which ever took place at the foot of the Cathedral and round about, was the Battle of Worcester, between the Royalists and the Parliamentarians. The son of Charles I returned from exile abroad to be crowned Charles II in Scotland. He raised a Scottish army and marched through England, hoping to gain extra support. On August 22nd, 1651, his tired army of 15,000 or 16,000 entered the staunchly Royalist town of Worcester and set up camps near Powick bridge and on both sides of the river Severn, relying heavily on the rivers Teme and Severn for protection.

Oliver Cromwell's Protestant army was estimated at 28,000. Bridges across the river had been demolished but the Protestants managed to form a bridge by lashing 20 boats together. Many soldiers from the Scottish army were forced back into the centre of Worcester so that some of the heaviest fighting took place in Sidbury, at the foot of the Cathedral, where there was a gate in the city wall. Fighting continued here even after the Scottish army had surrendered elsewhere. Charles looked down on the fighting from the tower of Worcester Cathedral and when he saw that the battle was turning against him, he ran down and joined in the fighting. The story goes that one of Cromwell's troopers recognised the king and rode at him. Close by was a team of oxen attached to an ammunition wagon that had come to a halt when the driver had been killed. William Bagnall, a Worcester citizen, seized the leading bridle and draw the oxen across the road so that Charles could slip away through a narrow space between the entrance to the Commandery, the city walls and the oxen. Charles managed to reach his quarters and escape through the back door while his enemies entered the front. The Commandery is still there, so is 'King Charles' house', his quarters in New Street.

After the battle, an estimated 3,000 of the Scottish army lay dead. A letter of the time says that 'the dead bodies lay in the way from Powick bridge to the town, and on the ground either side of it, and in almost every street of the town. Many lie killed in the houses, in the College and Church, on the Green, and in the cloisters, and quite through Sidbury and about a mile that way'. Bodies were stacked up against Sidbury Gate. There were said to be 10,000 prisoners, common prisoners were put in the Cathedral (later disinfected with 'pitch and rosen') and about 1,000 of them were transported.

While trying to rally his troops near Perry Wood, the Duke of Hamilton fell, shot in the leg. He had been billeted in the Commandery which was being used as a hospital and so he was carried there. The King's surgeon was present, who said that the Duke's leg must be amputated, but Cromwell had sent his own surgeon, who said that amputation was not necessary. While they were arguing, the Duke died. On the ground floor of the Commandery was a red stain, said to be the blood of the Duke, which no amount of scrubbing could remove.

The Duke's family wanted his body returned to his stately home, but the victorious Council ruled that he should be buried in Worcester and nowhere else, so he was wrapped in lead and placed on the north side of the Cathedral, within the altar rails. Two hundred years later, in 1862, the altar pavement was being renovated when a pickaxe went through the body of the Duke.

The grey lady of the Commandery

The Commandery is thought to have been founded by Bishop Wulstan to offer help to the elderly, the poor and needy, and to travellers in about 1085, although most of the present building dates back to the 14th and 15th centuries. It is said that it took its name from the early nurses who were called 'Commanders'. Its early years seem to have been more of a battle against poverty and corruption. Successive Bishops of Worcester complained about its poor state and in 1321 an investigation was held into the 'dishonourable lives of the brethren'.

When Henry VIII appropriated all the churches' possessions, the Commandery was sold as a private house. Perhaps past occupants have returned to protest about falling into secular hands because, for many years, the building has had the reputation of being haunted.

Henry Badham is now in his nineties but he still remembers clearly how, when he was a young man, he twice saw the grey lady:

Round about 1935 I lived in the first house on the Commandery drive which is now part of the shop. Mr Littlebury then lived in the Commandery. I saw the grey lady on two occasions. She appeared to come out of the cottage on the opposite side of the drive (where Miss Davies, the famous painter, used to live) then she started going down the pathway towards my front door. She was very clear. It became deadly cold, like an ice box.

The strange thing is, that each time I saw the grey lady, it was the same time at night - about ten o'clock, and on both occasions she looked exactly the same. She was wearing long clothes that could have been any period. There was a cowl over her head so that you couldn't see any features. She was old, about 60, and floating very slowly, it took quite a while for her to go down the drive. She made no noise. As she got close to me she just evaporated. It was very eerie.

I wasn't scared - she couldn't harm me. I was just cold. At the time I tried to find some kind of explanation but I couldn't find a history of anyone who had died or had been killed. I suppose she could have come from a long time ago.

Mary and her friend went on a tour of the Commandery at the end of the 1990s. The great stairs were made in 1600 but no-one knows where. They were moved to the Commandery a hundred years later.

I'm interested in history and old buildings and so, during the half-term of October 2003, I went with my best friend to the Commandery. We paid our money and asked the lady on the desk how long it would take to go round, she said, 'About an hour'. No-one else was in the building, we were the only ones there. We went up the main staircase and when we reached the top, we stopped. We couldn't go on. We felt that it wasn't a very pleasant atmosphere and that we were being watched, we were unwanted. We both felt it at the same time.

We came down the stairs and decided, instead, to go into the great hall. My friend said she could smell a strange, sweet perfume but I smelt a horrid, bad smell. We went into a little room where children can practice writing with quill pens and there is a set of old-fashioned shirts hanging on a rail for dressing up. As there were some chairs there, we decided to sit down, have a brief rest and recover from the earlier rather unsettling incident. Suddenly, my friend went hot and clammy. I could see beads of perspiration on her forehead, and at the same time, I went freezing cold, as if I had walked into a freezer. Although the doors and windows were closed, it seemed as if swirly cold draughts were going round. We felt as if there was a strange entity with us.

My friend said out loud, 'If you are there, make something happen!'. Suddenly, the shirt in the middle of the rail started to move by itself. It seemed as if someone had their finger on the hook and was slowly moving it forwards and backwards an inch either way. It was gently swaying on the rail. All the clothes on either side were stationary. We sat there for about five minutes, watching it and it carried on all the time and we could both still feel the swirling cold.

I 'phoned up BBC Hereford & Worcester when they were appealing for ghost stories about the Commandery, but I was busy teaching when they wanted to interview me so I couldn't talk to them.

A guide remarks, 'One of the guides had a little white dog. This little dog would go everywhere, but it wouldn't go into the room where Captain Hamilton had died'.

The Garibaldi Murder (The Old Magistrate's Court)

Up until 3 or 4 years ago Courts were held at the magistrates' Court, Deansway and this is where Roger Shotton made his first encounter with 'what I believe to be a 'ghost'.'

I was finishing off my Court paperwork in Court 1 at approximately 4 pm on a December afternoon in 2000. No-one else was in the Court room - well, no-one that was living!

I noticed a figure moving in the secure balcony at the rear end of the Court room. It appeared on the right-hand side and moved three-quarters across the balcony and then vanished. 'Very odd', I thought, and tidied up my desk and left the Court.

The next morning I was again in Court 1, when I happened to mention my experience to Jill, one of our cleaners. She asked me to describe what I had seen, which I did as follows:

'The figure seemed to have dark cape on and was approximately six feet tall. It seemed to appear on the right-hand side wall and move three-quarters across and vanish'.

Jill replied, 'Oh that's the ghost of the Police Officer who murdered the landlord, his wife and child at a pub in 1912 whilst he was on duty.

I relayed my experience to a member of the *Worcester Evening News*, and they reported on it 26 January 2001, expanding upon Jill's story. *The Daily Telegraph* also reported on their findings.

Of the more recent accounts of the murder, perhaps the best is in *Midland Murders and Mysteries* by Barrie Roberts, of which the following is a summary:

Leading off Sidbury is a tiny street known as Wylde Lane. Along here on the left was, until recently, a public house known originally as the Garibaldi, then the Lamplighter, then the Welcome Inn. Ernest Laight was licensee of the Garibaldi in 1925 and he became friendly with the local policeman, Herbert Burrows. After an amiable evening at the pub, Burrows battered to death the landlord, the wife and the baby, leaving a six year old girl sound asleep upstairs. He gave himself away the next morning by announcing, as soon as he got to work at the police station, 'What about those terrible murders at the Garibaldi?'. The Inn had not yet been opened up and no-one had discovered the bodies. Despite medical evidence that Burrows had syphilis (which causes general paresis of the insane) he was found sane enough to hang.

For many years afterwards, local people said that the ghost of a woman and child had been seen in there, and Andy, the last barman prior to its closure, said that he could hear bumps and thuds upstairs when no-one was there.

Ghost stories and stores

In Crowngate is a large Departmental Store. When clothing arrives at the store it's usually creased, and so Gill*, one of the sales staff, has the job of ironing it before it goes on display. Gill says, 'I know there's a ghost up there on the first floor. The staff have experienced all kinds of strange things, stock has been thrown around and some things have disappeared entirely and reappeared in a strange place. While I'm ironing I can see, out of the corner of my eye, a woman standing there and watching me'.

A few years ago the Mayor reported that one of the shops in Reindeer Court in Malcheapen Street was haunted. He said, 'You go in the entrance and it's the first place on the left. The sales staff used to find that the washing up had been done. The girls used to argue about it, 'You must have washed up', 'Oh, no, I didn't'. One of the girls used to wear a lot of jewellery. She had to take it off one day for some reason and it disappeared. It was found later outside on the window ledge.

The shop uses the room on the first floor, but you can go up another stair-case and the room there was used as a temporary courtroom.'

Oh hullo there! (London Road)

Sidbury continues into the London Road which was heavily involved in the civil war. Cromwell was about to attack the city from the south, and so an elaborate series of earthworks were constructed across the London Road and covering the south side of the town. Charles divided his army into two halves, one half was sent to the junction of the Teme and the Severn but the larger half was kept within the city to man the walls and the new fortifications.

No wonder that the housewife in the next story, who lives on the London Road, feels 'a presence'.

When we moved here, 18 years ago, I was fairly quickly aware of what I can only describe as a presence. I have never seen a shape or an aura or detected a smell or anything like that but there has always been a presence, not in the house but outside in the garden. Quite regularly I have had the feeling that somebody is there. I can feel a pair of eyes on my back. It has been so strong that I have sometimes thought it was my husband coming home from work. I have opened the back door and looked out and been surprised when nobody was there. I have thought 'Where's he gone?'. It wasn't an unpleasant feeling, I knew that it was quite friendly.

One day, I was getting something out of the car and I was half in and half out of the car when I distinctly heard this voice say, 'Oh, hullo there'. Again there was this feeling of a presence. We have a very thick hedge running along one side of the garden so I went to the gate and looked back along the hedge, thinking that there was someone on the other side. Nobody was there, not a soul.

The only time I have had this feeling of a presence indoors was when I was unwell. I was lying on top of the bed and I had one of my cats with me. Her back legs were on the bed and her front paws were on my body so that she was lying diagonally across me, when suddenly she began to stare upwards. Her eyes were absolutely fixed. It was as though she was looking at someone standing on the far side of the bed. She stayed like that for several minutes.

The processions to the gallows used to go past our house to a place outside the city walls and nearby was the Jennet Tree where the gallows used to be. There's a seedling from it in one of the gardens in London Road. However, I don't think the presence is associated with this because that would be a frightening presence and this is quite friendly. The area around here is where the civil war was fought and I think it's more likely to be associated with that. My family think I'm nuts.

Psychic granny (Woolhope Road)

Between the London Road and the Bath Road, south of Sidbury, is Woolhope Road. During the 1970s Darren's grandmother lived in Woolhope Road in a house which had been built about 1930. Darren says that she seemed to be psychic:

I remember my father giving her a present once - it was just a little box so it could have been anything, but she knew before she opened it that it was a silver toothpick. My father was amazed, they hadn't been talking about it beforehand or anything.

His father, Roy, regarded his mother's abilities as a bit of a joke:

She used to tell us these tales that when she was lying in bed, an old woman used to appear and stay there for several minutes, smoothing her bedclothes. My mother did quite a lot of research into it but never found it who it was, she only knew it wasn't anyone from the family who had previously lived here.

Anyway, I realised one evening that we hadn't heard about this apparition for some time so I remarked to my mother, 'What happened to the old woman who used to pay you a visit?'. She said, 'Oh she's gone'. Evidently, each time she appeared she was further and further up the bed and when she nearly reached the pillow my mother decided that she had had enough and told her to go away, which she did.

The old lady of Castle Street

By 1069 the Sheriff of Worcestershire had built a castle, with motte and bailey, to protect Worcester from the Danes and the Welsh who had a nasty habit of sailing down the Severn and attacking the town. It was probably only a wooden fortress because it has completely disappeared. The site was levelled in 1833 and is now the terraced gardens between the King's School and the river.

Although Castle Street leads in the direction of the castle, it was not named after it but originally known as 'Salt Lane'. It was just a rough track across the fields leading to the Severn. If merchants took their salt into the city, they had to pay tolls, so they made this track to load the salt on to barges. The name was changed to Castle Street when the prison was built there in 1813 in the style of a medieval castle. Public hangings and whippings took place on the roof of the prison gatehouse until 1863. It was quite a spectacle. There would be a procession of under-sheriff and officers, with six javelin men in front and six warders behind. The infirmary gates nearby offered a good vantage point, crowds gathered in front of them and treated the occasion with noisy hilarity. The prison fell into disuse in the 1914-18 war and was closed in 1922.

Over the years there were many suicides within the dark walls of Worcester prison. In 1916, a particularly contemptible criminal took his own life. In a drunken rage, 24-year old Michael Cook, of Fockbury, had knifed his baby daughter to death (see chapter on Bromsgrove).

At the inquest the cell was described as having a window, a door and an iron gate, but the door was usually left open and there was a light in the cell all night. One warder was on duty each night who was supposed to visit each cell every fifteen minutes. The warder for the night in question was William Lovatt, who said that at 5.15 am Michael appeared to be asleep in bed. The warder was assisted by the night watchman who, after lighting up, looked into the cell at 5.30 am and saw Michael fully dressed, standing at the window 'in a stooping position'. He called out 'Are you alright', and receiving no answer, went to find the warden who had the keys.

Prisoners had the option of either sitting in their cells doing nothing or taking on some kind of work, and Michael had asked to be employed in mail bag making. He had hung himself from the window with a piece of string used in his work. No-one applied to take the body for burial.

Joyce told this story at Perdiswell Matures Club:

There used to be a row of old houses in Castle Street. Most of the houses have been demolished and a police station built, but I think that the one where I worked as a cleaner is still standing. I saw an old lady at the bottom of the stairs. Another lady was working with me, I thought it was her sister. I said to her, 'Your sister is downstairs'. She said to me, 'No, I don't think so'. This lady had a felt hat and a coat and had a basket on her arm. We both saw her walk out of the door and up the passage where there's no outlet. I saw her as plain as plain.

When I told our supervisor she said, 'You have seen the old lady'. There used to be coaching inn here and the passageway was the entry. She used to keep the inn. Our supervisor said that we were very privileged to see her.

Hauntings at Henwick (YMCA)

At Henwick was a holy well, producing what was said to be the purest water in Worcestershire. It was thought to have medicinal properties and cured diseases to the eyes. The water was piped to the cathedral but the pipes were blown up during the civil war of the seventeenth century and the lead from the pipes was used to make bullets.

In Henwick Road is one of the most impressive Victorian buildings in Worcester. Now the YMCA, it was originally the Royal Albert Orphanage. Richard Padmore gave £4,000 in 1869 towards its costs, an enormous amount in those days. The architect was William Watkins from Rushock, near Droitwich and the building was designed to hold 38 boys and 38 girls.

A young man by the name of Simon recounts events which took place one evening at around 9.30 pm sometime in May of 2003.

I used to play drums with a group of friends in a band called, 'The Murder of Rosa Luxembourg'. We were, and they still are, quite a popular band nationwide and also in Europe. At the time of these events we were in rehearsals before we recorded our second record, our first full-length album. I have now left the band because of the pressure of 'A' levels but at that time there were six members in the band.

We used to rehearse in a converted wing of the old YMCA building in Henwick Road in Worcester. It's quite a forbidding, forlorn-looking building, it looks like something from the set of an old horror film. The main part of the building still serves as a YMCA. At some point in the mid 1990s the back of the north wing was bought by a business man and renovated to provide rehearsal studios for musicians to practice.

We had all gathered there one evening to rehearse new material that we were writing for our album. We were in the room that we had used regularly every week for months, it's a well-lit room with two windows, both of which were covered by blinds. I had set my drums up at an angle offset in the corner opposite the door of the room, while one of our guitarists Thomas Bush, had set up his amplifier next to my drums and stood at right angles to me facing the door. We had a normal evening of practice until around 9.30. We were halfway through playing a song when suddenly, what I could only describe as a fabric-like black shape came right through the solid wood of the door! I stopped playing immediately as this happened, not believing what I had just seen. I looked directly at Tom our guitarist. He had a pale, horrified look on his face, and he said to me, 'Did you just see that?'

Seconds after this, I felt something touching me, putting pressure on the left side of my body and I felt incredibly uncomfortable. I could feel something behind me. The only way I could describe that feeling, was as if there was a great mass of energy directly behind me. None of the other four members saw what Tom and I saw, although they all saw Tom and me react at exactly the same time at the point. They just stood there looking confused. For the remaining half an hour that we rehearsed, everybody felt very uncomfortable and unnerved. We moved to a rehearsal studio across the river after this! Perhaps we had annoyed a spirit by playing our music too loud!

What I found most interesting about the whole experience was to come two days after the occurrence. I told a friend at college what had happened, and he was intrigued. As we were on the subject of ghosts he mentioned by chance that he had with him a book about ghosts around the Worcestershire area called 'Haunted Worcestershire'. So out of interest we started having a read through some of the stories and I stumbled upon a story from the YMCA in Henwick Road. The story really unnerved me as it had extremely strong similarities to what we had experienced in that room. The account documented in the book talked about a man staying at the building in the 1960s. Before he went to bed he went to go to the bathroom but his way through the doorway to the bathrooms had been blocked by a tall man wearing a black cloak tied at the neck. He had to walk underneath the man's arm to get through the doorway. He felt icy cold as he ducked under the man's arm. When he turned round the man had vanished! It so happens that I know that our rehearsal room was on the spot where the bathrooms once were. The black cloak sounded awfully familiar as well! Until my experience I had always been interested in ghosts and hauntings, but now having actually experienced this situation my interest has grown rapidly!

...what I can only describe as a fabric-like black shape came right through the solid wood of the door! (Henwick, Worcester).

The last game (Worcestershire Golf Course)

Two years ago, a tragedy occurred on the local golf course. The following account comes from a club member:

A chap collapsed while he was playing golf and died. A few days later, two young lads in their early teens came into the club house and said that they had seen an apparition of a man on the course. When they described the person they had seen, somebody said, 'That's the chap who died'. For the next few days, most of the talk in the golf club was about it.

A week or two later, about four or five of us were in the club house late at night. We were standing around, having a drink and talking, and the question arose whether one should believe these stories or not - you know, the old type of discussion. Some people were saying it was rubbish while others thought there was something in it. My own point of view was that you really shouldn't scorn these things without a proper examination. As we were talking this bulb in the wall light jumped out and flew across the room. One or two said, 'What the hell's that?'. Everybody went very quiet afterwards. The discussion dropped.

The phantom horse (Claines)

There has been a church in the centre of Claines for more than a thousand years. The present church of St John the Baptist was built in the 1400s. The picturesque, half timbered public house standing next to it was built about the same time, and is the only public house in England standing on consecrated ground. The 'Mug House' features in *Haunted Pubs and Hotels of Worcestershire and its Borders* and in Bill Gwillam's *Old Worcestershire Inns*. Ghostly footsteps walk up and down the stairs, doors open and close at night and glasses jump off shelves. The traditional ghost walks to the door, cries 'Beware' then drifts into the church to play the organ.

West of Claines is the river Severn. Mike has a shop in Droitwich High Street but his story comes from Claines:

About fifteen to eighteen years ago, my wife and I were sitting on the Worcester Road side of the River Severn at Claines, and I was fishing. We heard the noise of a galloping horse, we looked up and saw that on the other side of the river, going from left to right, was a white horse. It looked very normal, galloping away. We watched it for about ten or twelve seconds then suddenly it disappeared. One moment it was there, the next it had gone.

I looked at my wife and she looked at me and about ten minutes later, she said, 'Did you see that horse disappear?'. It didn't run off or anything, it just went. Although the river Severn at Claines is now a peaceful spot, there have been many events which could have produced a terrified horse. The old main road from Worcester to Birmingham passed through North Claines. Perhaps it was fleeing from the battle of Worcester. To the north of the parish of Claines is Hindlip Hall, home of the Habington's, associated with both the Babington Plot and the Gunpowder Plot. Bevere, nearby, was once an island where terrified citizens twice took refuge, from the Danes in 1041 and from the plague in 1637.

(... and the phantom burglar)

A retired businessman in Claines was terrified to hear and see a burglar entering his bedroom:

> I suppose it must have been the middle of the night. I know that I had been in a deep sleep and I had the impression that I had woken up and was lying there awake. The bedroom door was open and I could see into the hallway. We have quite a lot of windows round the hall and the street lighting outside means that the hallway is never quite dark.
>
> I could see someone coming along the hall towards the bedroom. It was a dark, male figure that you might associate with a burglar. I couldn't see any facial features, he was a solid shape, just a silhouette, of more or less average shape and build. He came to the bedroom door.
>
> When I tried to do something about it I found that I couldn't move. I was paralysed. It's very frightening to see someone there and you can't do anything. I panicked, and it must have been the panic that woke me up, because I suddenly realised I was awake. I could see the same view but without the person. It had only lasted for a minute or two, quite a short time. It was quite a surreal experience.
>
> This has happened five or six times over the past twelve months, and each time I have seen a person. I put it down to burglary being on my mind, although I must admit that I haven't been thinking about burglaries lately. However, since the Martin case everybody has been talking about what they would do if they found a burglar in their house and it may have been embedded in my subconscious.

The black friars of Warndon

Warndon was a quiet little village until 1962, when the M5 was built nearby. Now it's a large, new housing development. The Church has a timber-framed tower, a 13th century window and other Norman gems. Next to the church is a seventeenth century house, known as Warndon Manor or Warndon Farm.

Anne now lives in Evesham but 40 years ago, when she was travelling through Warndon, she saw an unusual character:

This happened in about 1961, when I was 22. My boyfriend was a builder, working on different sites, and one winter evening we arranged that, after work, we would go out and look at one of sites. I was in the Territorial Army, so at about nine o'clock he came to collect me in his car from Lansdowne Road in Worcester, where the territorial barracks were, and we drove straight out to Warndon. The big roundabout wasn't there then.

We were going along the road where the church is, when all of a sudden, somebody was in front of our car and we hit him. We both saw this tall, thin, youngish person and we both felt the bump. It was a man - he was wearing a big, wide-brimmed man's tweed hat and a tweedy, cloak-type, loose coat, It frightened us to death. My boyfriend pulled up, we got out of the car and looked everywhere but we couldn't find anybody. We were so certain that a body would be around somewhere that we went to the police station and reported it. They said that a number of people had reported a similar thing.

The whole body was there, it wasn't as if it was a piece of paper blowing about or anything. It was most strange. It must have been a ghost, there was no mark on the car. I often think about it.

The more traditional Warndon ghost is a hooded silhouette of a monk, and several times over the last few years a dark monk has been seen running through Warndon Long Meadow. Part of Warndon was owned by the Black Friars of Worcester who wore a black cloak and hood over a white habit.

About two years ago a member of Warndon WI was driving back home after a meeting when:

As I was driving along Claines Lane I saw a dark shape in the middle of the road. I said to myself, 'That person is going to have to get off the road'. It was a cold, wintry evening and a wet night. It was just a human shape, there was no depth to it, I couldn't see whether it was male or female, but he or she was very upright. I thought, 'I'm going to have to brake in a moment' but when I got closer nothing was there. It frightened me so much that I won't drive along there now.

One Red Light

Phil was a recovery driver for the AA in the mid 1980s. Between junction 7 & 8 on the M5 would bring him somewhere near Warndon.

I had been to Cornwall to pick up a passenger whose car had broken down so I had him in the car with me. I was going down the M5 between junction 7 and 8, I was just south of Worcester when, in front of me, I could see one red light. At first I thought it was a motor bike, but when I nearly got to it I saw that it was an old Rolls Royce with an open top. Sitting in the car

...I looked in the mirror and to my surprise, the lights had gone.
(Between junctions 7 and 8 on the M5).

was a gentleman and a lady with a big bonnet. I assumed they were going to a rally or something. I put my indicator on and as I went past I could see that the car was all new and glittering. I looked in the mirror and, to my surprise, the lights had gone. I looked round and nothing was there. I thought they had had an accident and gone off the road. I pulled up into the slow lane and stopped at a police box. The police patrol car came and had a look along the embankment. He couldn't find anything. He had my name and address and said, We'll have another look round tomorrow in the daylight and we'll ring if we find anything'. But nothing came of it.

The Powick poltergeist

Powick has one of the few bridges across the River Severn, consequently its history has been extraordinarily eventful. In the 1200s, Simon de Montfort captured Henry III at Powick and made him prisoner.

The first and last battle of the English Civil War took place at Powick. At the outbreak of war in 1642, Charles I, who was at Shrewsbury, sent Sir John Byron to Oxford to collect money and other supplies. Prince Rupert was sent to help guard him on his return. This came to the ears of the Parliamentarians, so that Colonel Fiennes and his soldiers placed themselves at Powick, hoping to intercept Byron. The two armies accidentally met at Powick Bridge. Prince Rupert was an experienced soldier, and immediately charged the enemy. About fourteen were killed, and Fiennes was so terrified that he made his horse gallop for nine miles to Pershore. When he reached Essex's bodyguard and told them the story, they also fled.

The first bridge was built early in the 15th century with three arches over the river Teme and two on the Worcester side. The latter two were broken down in the civil war. The cast iron bridge was built in 1837.

The Price* family lived in Powick Village for several years with their three teenage children, two girls and a boy:

So many things happened that I can't remember them all. I can only give you a few examples. We regularly heard footsteps and small items went missing, like keys and jewellery. My daughter had a Gate bracelet for Christmas. She thought she had lost it, we hunted for it high and low. Two weeks after Christmas there it was in the middle of the dining room carpet. We had cats and people suggested that a mischievous cat had taken it away and brought it back, but too many things happened like that for it to be cats.

I put some very important paperwork on top of my handbag. Then it was gone. We hunted for several days. We had a small business, the keys to the premises were hanging up on a row of hooks in our house and they disappeared. It cost us £320 to change the locks. We wanted to claim on the insurance but we couldn't say that the ghost had taken the keys! The missing items were usually back a few days later but not in the same place, they could be anywhere. He was like a mischievous child. We called him Mr Nickitt. We had a lady come round who was psychic and she said the ghost's name was Cedric.

We had strange sensations. On one occasion both my cousin and I lent forward towards each other and put our hands out as if to catch something, then we looked at each other, realised what we had done and felt so stupid. At another time my daughter was eating crisps and she felt that my other daughter, who was in another room, was pinching them.

On a still summers day we heard a window slam. We thought it was my daughter larking about but with hindsight it was impossible to slam the window from the inside

My son hated one part of his bedroom. He said it was dark but it was right beside the window. One afternoon I left him in the house while I popped out for a few minutes, and when I was coming home I saw him running down the road to meet me. He said that he had seen someone sitting in the dining room in an orange costume.

While I was in the conservatory I thought I saw my husband walk past the other end. I spoke to him but he didn't answer. I thought, 'Why doesn't he answer?' and I went to go after him to see if he felt ill or something. Then he walked in from the opposite direction.

The funny thing was, it wasn't frightening or intimidating at all. Nothing ever felt threatening, it was just a way of life.

Someone told me that ghosts are attracted by the colour blue, and the house was painted right through in blue and white, even the ceilings were blue. A friend of a friend said that a lady who lived there previously threatened to leave her husband if the family didn't move to another house. We don't know whether this was because of the ghost. The people after us moved out very quickly and we wondered why.

Monks and nuns (Callow End)

Follow the B4424 south of Powick for half a mile and you reach Callow End. South of the village along the Upton Road at Stanbrook is St Mary's Benedictine monastery. A nunnery for English ladies had been founded in France in 1625, but they were expelled for political reasons in 1808. They settled at Salford Priors then moved into a new monastery, built by the famous church architect Pugin, in about 1880.

Back in 1950 or 1951, John had a motorbike:

My girlfriend, Pauline, lived by the hospital at Callow End and I had strict instructions that she had to be home be ten o'clock.

One evening, I was taking her home and I got down to Powick village when the chain broke on my motor bike. I pushed it to the Red Lion and then had to walk her back home. I was a little bit late taking her home so it must have been about eleven o'clock when I was walking back towards the large house, The Wheatfield. It was moonlight and everything was perfectly visible. I had just got round the bend and was walking along Ferry Lane when out of the wall opposite the Wheatfields, came this figure, shrouded like a monk, with a grey-black hooded cloak that went down to the ground. He was about five feet six inches in height, the face was blurred and his back was bent so that he would be fairly old. He floated across the walk and then along the pathway next to me. I was standing on the edge of the pavement and it floated half through me. As it did so, I went very cold. I spoke to it, I said, 'Good evening' or something but there was no reply. It went towards the left and over a bank. A large pear tree was there then which was gradually dying and was half hollow, it went through the pear tree. By the tree was a gateway, I looked over the gate but nothing was there. It really shook me, I had hair then and it stood on end.

I have now bought a house nearby but the thought of the apparition doesn't bother me.

John should have seen a nun, not a monk, but no doubt monks did, and still do, visit the abbey. Niklaus Pevsner, the architectural historian, describes The Wheatfield as a 'substantial Italianate villa, in style c1850'.

Arthur* lives in Callow End and says that his small nephew saw his great grandmother two days after she died:

He didn't understand that she had died. When his mother went to tuck him up in bed at night he said, 'I just saw gran' and he described her sitting in the small armchair in his bedroom. He said that she didn't say anything.

His grandmother was in her nineties. She wasn't someone you could mistake for anyone else. She had long grey hair in a plait and she was always dressed in black. She lived about 25 miles away and I don't think she had even visited the house. It wasn't as if she was a regular there. His mother was slightly taken aback.

2. ALCESTER AND STUDLEY (WARWICKSHIRE)

lcester flourished in Roman times, being situated on a Roman road, 'Icknield Street'. Considering that it has been cursed twice, it seems to have survived very well as a historic, and attractive little town. The central streets are full of houses from the 17th and 18th century and between the free car park and the High Street is a lively antique centre. East of the town is a picturesque spot where the river Arrow joins the river Alne. The first curse is said to be from Saint Chad, who became Bishop of Mercia in a about 700 AD. When he came to preach Christianity to the Alcester residents, they made such a clatter with their hammers that he could not be heard. He left them with a curse. Nevertheless, a great meeting of church leaders took place in 709 'at a celebrated place called Alne'. Historians believe that this may have been Alcester.

The second curse came from a monk, 'Anselm'. A Benedictine Abbey was founded in 1140, during the civil war between King Stephen and Empress Matilda, a time of terrible upheaval and anarchy. It stood near the present Alcester Grammar school playing fields. King Stephen wanted to get the support of the monks, and so he gave generous endowments, but then he quarrelled with the monk Anselm and ordered his murder. With his dying breath, Anselm cursed the country, the king and the town. Two hundred years later, he appeared to a group of monks in the church and asked them to find his bones and bury them in consecrated ground as his curses had been fulfilled. The abbey closed in 1545.

For whom the bells tolls

The church of St Nicholas is unmissable at the end of the High Street. It has a 14th century tower and a windows, and a doorway going back to 1500. Inside is the alabaster effigy of Fulke Greville who died in 1560, clad as a knight in armour. His ghost has been seen several times in the church. The ghost of his grandson, who haunts a tower of Warwick Castle, is better known.

One of the bellringers says:

We were waiting for the last chap to come before we could start ringing bells. We heard footsteps coming up the stair and expected the missing person to walk in, but instead the footsteps went straight on up to the belfry at the top of the tower. We waited for someone to come down but nobody appeared. We thought we had better go and have a look, somebody might be stuck up there. We went up, but nobody was there.

The Angel and the Devil

The church divides the High Street and to the right, it becomes Church Street. A blue and white plaque on the wall of a house opposite the church marks the Angel Inn, where a notorious murderer was, himself, murdered. The story begins in London in the late 1600s where Captain Richard Hill fell in love with a beautiful actress, however, she preferred a young man by the name of William Mountford. One dark night, Captain Hill stabbed Mountford with the help of Lord Mohun. The Captain then fled to Mohun's relatives at the castle of Moons (Mohun's) Moat and perhaps murdered Mariolle Mohun while he was there. He then turned up at The Angel where, after a party, he disappeared. From that time onwards, 'The Angel' was said to be haunted. In 1937 'The Angel' was refurbished and when an old oven was removed, several items were found that could only have belonged to Captain Hill. More details can be found in *A Taste of Murder* by Barrie Roberts and *'The Story of the Angel Inn'* by Aubrey Gwinnett. The latter is available from Alcester library.

Eavesdropping in Butter Street

To the left, the High Street becomes the narrow passageway of Butter Street. In the early 1990s one of the residents said that she had found evidence that a lady had burned to death in one of the houses. The current belief is that a baby was killed there:

A friend of mine lives in Butter Street. From time to time the front door opens and there's a noise as if someone has come in but nobody is there.

There is no division between their eaves and the next-door the neighbours' eaves so that sounds carry easily from one house to the other. Their neighbours asked them what was wrong with their children, they said that the children kept crying and keeping them awake at night. My friend doesn't have any children and she hasn't heard any children crying.

My friend went into the next door neighbour's house to feed their cat for them while they were away. The walls are whitewashed, and while she was putting the food down for the cat she saw a large shadow of a man loom up on the wall. She turned round but no-one was there. She made a very hasty exit.

They have done some research on the property and discovered that a baby was burned to death in a fire. They believe that the mother comes looking for her baby.

Is anybody there?

On the far side of the church is the lovely old town hall, completed in 1641 and originally a market house. The lower half is of stone colonnades and the upper half is half-timbered. The Town Hall was by the Town Gaol, now demolished. The Court Leet of the manor is still held in the town and a head bailiff appointed, continuing a tradition that began in 1299. The town hall was bought by the town in 1919 as a war memorial.

In the middle of the 1970s a choir was rehearsing at the Greig Hall nearby and a member says:

We needed a rostrum from the town hall. Jim offered to go and get it. We said to him, 'Are you alright going by yourself, don't you want somebody to come with you', because the town hall had the reputation of being haunted. A good many people have gone into the Town Hall and got a strange feeling. He said, 'No, I'll be alright'. Afterwards, he came back and he had definitely seen something. He was in quite a state. He would never go back there again.

In 1979 my husband was in the kitchen at the Town Hall building cupboards. He heard footsteps and called out, 'Is that you, Lawrence' because he was expecting the High Bailiff to come and see what he was doing. Nobody came and he went into the hall to have a look and see what was going on. It was a large hall and as he stood and listened he could hear the footsteps going right across it.

The night visitor

Margaret* and her husband used to live in Allwoods Close, Alcester:

One night, something woke me up, very suddenly. Immediately, I sat up in bed, wide awake and bolt upright. In the hazy darkness I could see a man standing on my side of the bed, on the left. He was short, thick-set and dark - not from the colour of his skin but because he was in silhouette. I couldn't see his features but he seemed to be middle-aged. I woke up my husband who couldn't see anything. He had to get out of bed and switch the light on, when the man disappeared. The house is built on the site of a carpet factory and I thought it might be something to do with that.

Her husband says:

If you wake up in the middle of the night and somebody says to you when you are half asleep that there is a man standing by the side of the bed, it's a bit scary. It was only when the light came on that she was convinced that nobody was there.

The ghost on the zimmer frame

Until recently, Lucy* was working as a care assistant in a retirement home near Alcester.

A lot of people have seen or experienced strange things there. Two or three of us were sitting on the sofa in the lounge and suddenly it was knocked sideways violently as if someone had given it a good kick. I was woken up one night by a lady stroking my hair! After one lady passed away, there was a tremendous smell of flowers in her room for a week. Several of us remarked on it.

Upstairs was a room that was really haunted. You could hear banging and hammering coming from there as if someone had been locked in, but no-one was in it . The manager put our beds in there but we wouldn't sleep in them, we said that we would rather sleep on the sofa downstairs!

One dear elderly lady was very little trouble when she was alive but she gave us a lot of problems after she had died. Several people saw her in various places round the home and for about a month afterwards we would hear her zimmer frame coming down the hall.

The secret tryst (Kings Court Hotel)

Leaving Coughton by the A435, a mile or two further on is a large detached half-timbered house known as Kings Court Hotel. A senior member of staff says that it used to be a farm and:

There's an old legend that there was a young lady in love with a Cavalier who was much older than she was, and so her parents disapproved of the relationship. They used to meet in the courtyard after dark. They both died suddenly in mysterious circumstances.

The other week three members of staff, including myself, had strange experiences. I stood in the dining room at about ten to twelve and, out of the corner of my eye, I saw somebody walk in. When I looked up, whatever it was, had gone. I knew that the doors were shut but I could hear the swish of a door swinging to and fro.

A couple of days later in the evening there was all the members of staff standing by the bar when the manageress jumped and said that something had just brushed past but she couldn't see anything.

The head chef has accommodation on the road side of the hotel, in the old part. He was in his room late one night when he heard footsteps coming up the stirs towards him, then he felt somebody in his room. He said that he felt very frightened.

We don't usually have this kind of thing happening and these three events happened within a few days of each other. We wondered if it was some kind of anniversary for the couple in the yard.

The glass eye (Coughton Court)

Coughton Court is an early 16th century mansion. For nearly six centuries, it has been the seat of the Throckmorton family, one of the foremost families in the Midlands and vigorous upholders of the Catholic faith. Many a secret plot was hatched by the Throckmortons to place a Roman Catholic king on the throne. In 1583 they were at the head of a plot to depose Elizabeth I and replace her with the Catholic Mary, Queen of Scots. In 1605 Sir Everard Digby was living at Coughton and it was here that Lady Digby waited with two Catholic priests to hear whether or not parliament had been blown up.

In 1688 an anti-Catholic mob from Alcester burned the house and pulled down the east wing. The house was transferred to the National Trust in 1945 but the contents remain the property of the Throckmortons.

As an electrician, Brian Orme spent three months at Coughton Court early in 1956, helping with renovations:

The whole place had just been taken over by the National Trust. The Throckmortons lived in the north wing, at that time they were Sir Robert and Lady Isobel. Lady Isobel bred dogs and had quite a successful business. I used to do a little bit of shopping for Sir Robert. He had got war injuries and I used to get embrocation oil and Neatsfoot oil for him from a saddler's firm.

The housekeeper was Miss Thomson and the butler was Mr Wells. He had been Sir Robert's father's batman in the First World War. He told a story about Sir Robert's father who was killed in Gallipoli in about 1915.

The family crest was carried above the main entrance door. One night, the face slipped off and smashed to the ground. Sir Robert's mother said that this meant something terrible has happened. Two days later she got the telegram saying that her husband had been killed. They worked out that it must have been just at the same time that the face fell of the family crest. I heard that story from both Miss Thomas and Mr Wells.

Brian has a couple of other entertaining stories about Coughton Court:

If you look at the front of Coughton Court there are two towers in the centre block. In the one tower, a worker shone a torch through cracks in the floorboards and found an eye looking up at him. It gave him quite a shock. They took up the floorboards and found a secret priest's hole into which the glass eye of a stuffed tiger had rolled. The historians reckoned that at least two priests had hidden down there. They found a little stool, a bible and, I believe, a shoe.

The historians reckoned that the priests moved from one location to another by crawling along the two-foot gap between the ground floor and the first floor. We used this floor space for the rewiring. While I was there, one of the painters got a stocking and some white sheets, crawled between the floorboards to an adjoining room and appeared to a young apprentice technician who was making some terminals for the rewiring. I have never seen anyone so frightened as the young apprentice. His legs would not hold him up. He fell outside into the snow. The painter got a ticking-off.

Who goes there!

The old Roman road, Icknield Street (A435) runs past Coughton Court and the Kings Court Hotel. The road seems to be infested with a ghostly assortment of white ladies, females on bicycles, glowing men, and horse and carriages, described in previous books such as *Midland Spirits and Spectres* and *Strange Meetings.*

It is said that the Romans built Icknield Street along the line of an earlier road which could go right back to the Bronze Age. People at this time could have had skills which we have now lost, they may have been able to tap into the earth's energy lines and therefore build pathways along them, now known as Ley Lines. It has been suggested that Icknield Street could have been an old Ley Line.

The first policeman to be killed on active duty was murdered in Icknield Street, about a quarter of a mile from Weatheroak. PC Davis was killed in 1885 by an itinerant poacher, Moses Shrimpton.

Margaret's husband, John, who has now passed away, was a descendent of PC Davis. John's mother died when he was three and he had been through the war so, says Margaret:

He was not one to be easily shaken, but in the early autumn of 1950, when he was about 25, he had an experience that really frightened him. He was riding his motor-bike home to Redditch from Alcester at about 9.30 in the evening when it was beginning to get dark, and he was on the Coughton Straight, just past the King's Coughton Hotel, when suddenly, he saw a man walk out into the road in front of him. He couldn't avoid him and he knew that he hit him. He went back expecting to find a body but nothing was there. That shook him as much as anything. Thinking back, later, he remembered that there had been no bump. He told me about it the following day, he said, 'I know I hit him and I was certain that I had hurt somebody. I'm not going that way again'.

Another anecdote comes from Mark who lives in Redditch:

This happened, I think, in 1996. I was playing in a band at the time, called Gust Fontaine or something like that, after a well-known footballer. In the summer, we were playing in a gig in the gardens of Salford Priory. We finished in the early evening and I packed away all the gear in my car and headed for home. I was driving and there were three lads in the car. Although it was evening, the visibility was really good. I had got to Coughton First school, just approaching the cross roads where the one branch goes to Coughton Ford and the other to Astwood Bank, when suddenly, a car appeared in front of me coming out of the lane on the left. It didn't give me much time to think. It was a long, maroon car with a running board - old fashioned-looking. It was a little bit like a Bewick, an American car, a gangster type of thing. I didn't have much time to look at it. The bonnet was poking out into the road and I smashed right into it sideways, I caught the front.. One of the lads shouted 'Look out!' and I heard this almighty crash. Another of the lads said, 'Well done, you missed it'. I stopped the car and got out. I thought I had written my car off, but when I looked at it, there was no damage. I just collapsed. I couldn't drive after that. One of the other lads had to drive us home. Of the four of us in the car, two saw it (me in the front and one in the back) and two didn't. I went back the next morning and there was no glass on the road or anything.

I don't drive that way now, I go the long way round to get home.

The dog in the night time

Young Clare can't remember how long ago the following happened, but it was just before the speed cameras were installed outside Coughton Court:

I had been with two friends to a bonfire party at Hampton-in-Arden and was coming home, travelling towards Alcester along the A435. It wasn't tremendously late, about 9.30. I was in the front of the car with the driver and we had a chap in the back.

We were just approaching the slight dip where the camera is now, when another car came from the opposite direction, flashing its lights, horn blaring and going like mad. I said, 'Oh my God, what's happened!'.

We got into the dip and the chap who was driving slowed right down. Bear in mind that everywhere was quite foggy because of the smoke of the bonfires, I saw what I thought was a dog in the middle of the road. It was quite a large dog but not as big as a Labrador and it was jumping around, so that I could see it above the bonnet of the car. It didn't look like a proper dog at all, it was dark and fuzzy. When I looked at the side of the road the dog had disappeared but the mist had parted in a straight line between the trees straight up to Coughton Court, as if something had passed through it.

It really shook me up. I said to the driver, 'Did you see that?' but he said he hadn't seen anything. To this day I think he saw something but wouldn't say, otherwise why did he slow right down? What I would like to know is, what had the car seen that was coming the other way? Why was he flashing his lights?

The ghost of Washford Mill (Studley)

Icknield Street continues towards Birmingham into Studley. Although one of the largest villages in England, it has managed to retain open countryside on its eastern side. This is the home of needle-making that arrived here in the early 1600s and, by the 20th century, its Needle Industries was the largest needle manufacturing plant in the world. Very little needlemaking now remains and many of the old mills have been converted for other uses. Washford Mill, for example, was once a scouring mill, where needles were covered with abrasive substances, wrapped in hessian and set under runners to be rubbed to and fro for days or even weeks. When it closed it became semi-derelict, then it was bought by an Irish family who modernised the living area and bravely set up a small needle museum. Redditch new town began in the 1960s, and a new owner pleaded for it to be kept out of the development on the grounds that it was an ancient mill. Walter Stranz writes in *Me and My Town,* 'Cynics may observe that soon afterwards the owner turned the needle mill into a public house and painted it in mock Tudor fashion black and white and put on a mock Norman date, 1066 AD'.

Staff report that a ghost has been seen there many times, contentedly smoking a churchwarden's pipe and rocking to and fro in a high chair. The ghost has been claimed by Rita Williamson as that of her great grandfather, George Hartles:

> He lived from 1823 to 1899 and was a seventh child. They are always said to have strange powers. In his later years he was employed as a needle scourer at Washford Mill. His wife died in 1883 but he was cared for by his two sons and their families. The family have told me that he was very little trouble and sat in his chair, gently rocking to and from, wearing his velvet jacket and smoking cap with his long churchwardens pipe in his mouth. He died from cirrhosis of the liver and exhaustion.

The dark horse (Sambourne)

From Studley, a quiet country road branches off westward past Sambourne's Oak Farm. Some historians believe that Sambourne was the cradle of needle-making, as the wealthy Richard Hemming learned the art at a local horse-mill in the early 1700s and his apprentices are thought to have established the trade in the area. Perhaps Susan* saw someone who was once involved in the needle trade, a traveller selling wire, or a local needlemaker taking his finished goods to the needle factor:

> My husband and I were travelling back home towards Studley along the B4092, otherwise known as Jill Lane. We had come down from Astwood bank at about 6.45 pm, it was between dusk and dark and therefore we

needed the headlights. We have travelled this road a lot and at various times and I have never seen anything like this before or since.

We had just passed the Troy Industrial Estate and were coming up to the house/farm that is now used by various businesses, the property is behind wooden rail fencing. Coming towards us was a coach, just passing the Sambourne turning on its way to Astwood Bank. I was extremely concerned at this point because as the coach was coming towards us, I saw that it was going to be impossible for my husband to pull out for passing. I had seen in front of us a man on a horse, walking slowly. I was worried because my husband was going too fast to slow down, and I was sure that we were going to drive into the back of them. I felt a little 'Hyacinth Bucket (Bouquet)' saying to my husband 'Mind the horse and rider!'.

The figure was a male wearing a light-coloured coat which split across the horse's rear and his collar was up around his neck. The horse was a 'cob' type, stocky with feathers around its hooves and an extremely wide rear. It was certainly not a thoroughbred. On reflection I thought it was the type used just for plodding from one place to another. The rider was not wearing a hat - I could only see him back view. There was no urgency in the horse's movements. As I said, having told my husband to drive with caution, I looked back immediately but no horse and rider was there. It was only a very short time from seeing it to not seeing it.

I felt incredibly stupid, my husband had not seen it and thought I had completely flipped. He insists on calling me 'barmy' now. I do really believe that what I saw was there. I'm not one for tall stories or seeing things but it does make you wonder about your own sanity! I am certain I saw it, however stupid I now feel trying to explain it.

The ghost that smoked (Mappleborough Green)

The old route of the old Icknield street (A435) disappears soon after it leaves Studley village, and the road veers to the east. Along here, just over a mile from Studley, is the ancient village of Mappleborough Green, mentioned in the Domesday Book as part of the Manor of Beoley, held by Pershore Abbey. Until the 1970s it was a tiny rural village but now the houses of Redditch have now crept to its doors. The Dog restaurant has a reputation for excellent, affordable carveries and a young lady went with her husband to sample its delights on Sunday, 9 December 2001:

I started with a chilli dip and my husband had a prawn cocktail, then we went to collect our meal. My spectacles were reflecting the light in my eyes so that I could see one or two strange blurs, but then I realised that I could see cigarette smoke. I said to my husband, 'I thought it was no smoking in here'. He said, 'Yes, what of it', and I said, Well, there's a chap over there smoking a pipe'. He turned round but he couldn't see anybody. This chap was in his seventies with grey hair, he was wearing a herringbone jacket, dark-coloured trousers and shoes with the laces tied round each leg. He was one of those elderly people you feel you would like to cuddle because they look so sweet, he had a very pleasant face.

I smoke myself, so I nipped off to the toilet for a cigarette. When I went back, he was still there although my husband couldn't see him. I mentioned it to the bar lady, I said, 'I can see an elderly man smoking a pipe over there and I haven't had too much to drink, I don't drink'. She said, 'Funny you should say that, for the last couple of nights we have had a really strange smell of tobacco in the bar, like pipe smoke'.

One of the staff took me over to where he was sitting. I said, 'He's actually looking round at you. Why don't you put an ashtray there and see if he fills it?'. The lady said she couldn't do that because it would encourage people to smoke. She asked, 'What happens if somebody wants to sit there, will they sit on his lap?'. I told her, 'Take no notice, I'm sure he'll move to one side'.

She said, 'I feel quite spooked and I have got to sleep in this place to-night'. I told her, 'Normally I would feel spooked if somebody told me about it but he's such an affectionate-looking gentleman I wouldn't worry about it if I were you'. He looked so relaxed with a pipe in his mouth'.

The whole experience was just very weird.

Fitting for a Princess (Ragley Hall)

Ragley Hall is the seat of the Marquess of Hertford. The manor of Ragley originally belonged to Evesham Abbey but, in the 1400s, it was sold to John Rous who built a castle on the site. By 1680 the castle had fallen into disrepair and the present splendid residence was begun by the mathematician and scientist, Robert Hooke. Of all the houses he designed, only Ragley Hall survives. In the late 1600s the owners married into the Seymour family and Lady Jane Seymour, Henry VIIIs first wife, would have spent many happy hours there.

After the death of the sixth Marquess in 1912, Ragley Hall was neglected. It was used as a hospital during the 1914-18 war, but continued to be in poor condition until the eighth Marquess, who succeeded to the title in 1940 at the age of nine, took up residence in 1956. He spent his lifetime restoring the house and now visitors can see the state dining room, the bedroom in which the Prince Regent slept in the 1800s, and many other treasures.

Next to the Garden House is a cottage, once occupied by the parents of the narrator in the following story:

To reach it, you go in through the main gates, past the Lodge, then you turn right and continue down that driveway. The cottage was very old, and if you looked out of the window on the living room side you could see that it was partly underground. It used to be the gardener's cottage and there was a lovely walled garden outside.

The Princess Brenda De Chimay lived in the Garden House, she was the former Lady Hertford's mother who married Prince Alphonse De Chimay. My mother was her cook and companion for five years. The princess died, I think, in April 1985 or 1986, and my mother died in the November. The princess is buried with her husband in Arrow churchyard.

I was staying at the cottage in November 1986 as my mother had been moved to Myton Hospice. Something woke me up in the early hours. I was in the middle bedroom, I could hear my father snoring in one bedroom and the dog snoring in the bedroom on the other side. Then I was aware that someone was walking backwards and forwards at the foot of the bed, to and fro, walking just a short distance, about a yard and a half. There was nobody living above us; I suppose it could have been someone walking under the window outside but no-one would have been about at that time of night. I didn't see anything, I didn't look, but I had this feeling that it was something to do with my mother. I thought that perhaps she had come to say goodbye. I wasn't frightened at all, in fact I felt quite comforted.

The next day her condition deteriorated and she died from lung cancer three days later. She was only 59 years old.

The white lady springs eternal

The entrance and exit gates of Ragley hall are a mile apart, and halfway between the two is a stile and water trough known as 'The Springs'. Folk used to stop and water their horses there. Almost every book of paranormal tales published has an anecdote about the white lady of the springs. Even the Marquis of Hertford has a story. He says that a little old lady would sometimes stop a passing vehicle and ask to be taken to Dunnington Cross roads, but when the driver would turn to help her down, she had disappeared. The ground around the springs was excavated, the bones of a little old lady found and she was interred in Arrow churchyard. The phantom hitch-hiker had disappeared, but a variety of apparitions have taken her place. In 2005, a lady at an Alcester meeting told how her uncle saw the white lady when he was coming back from fishing, one evening at dusk. Pete has another story:

When I was courting my wife I lived at Littleton and my wife was at the Queen Elizabeth hospital, training to be a nurse. I was driving back home one night at about 2.30 in the morning past the Ragley hall estate, and I was just before the sharp turn at the bottom of the hill, when I saw a horse and rider coming towards me. I slowed right down and looked out of the side window as I went past the rider; nothing was there. When I had gone past I looked in both car mirrors and again, nothing was there. I thought, 'Blimey, I must be tired - my mind is playing tricks'. Looking back no-one would have taken a horse out at that time of night.

I have seen nothing else strange since.

The bloodstain

The tiny town of Alcester is surrounded on all sides by farmland and woodland. During the 1970s Cynthia* lived on a farm not far from Alcester, on the borders of Warwickshire and Worcestershire:

We had 200 acres of arable and sheep and the farmhouse dated back to the 1600s. Going up the centre of the farmhouse was this massive staircase and on the stairs was a large dark indelible stain. My father used to say that it was blood.

My son came in one evening and he looked as white as a ghost. He said, 'I have just had such a funny experience'. He had been putting his motor bike together in a shed next to the house when he heard the garden gate open and he saw the silhouette of an elderly man going past his window. This shape went past the window a second time, going back the way it had come. He thought it was his grandfather but nobody came in and when he went to look, no-one was there. When my son repeated this story to his father, his father said, 'Don't worry, I have seen it as well'. The shed had once been an old coach house and we wondered if it was an old coachman.

The shed was very near to one of the corners of the lounge. I had a corner unit there and a huge vase on the floor. Most nights at about nine o'clock, the dog would bark and we would hear a bump in that corner. My husband would say, 'The coachman's doing his rounds'.

Another night we were just off to bed when we heard the noise of a baby crying. It was the sound of a small baby, about three or four months old. My husband said, 'Somebody has left a baby on our doorstep'. We had a look but nothing was there. We heard it for about ten minutes until it stopped. It was very clear. It seemed to be coming from that one corner.

3. BEWDLEY

f all the Worcestershire towns, Bewdley has the most romantic and eventful history. On its western side is a remnant of Tickenhill Palace, where the eldest son of the king, the young and handsome Prince Arthur, romped with his teenage bride, Catherine of Aragon. The whole country was in deep mourning when he died of tuberculosis at the age of 15. Henry VIII inherited the throne and Catherine became his first bride. Tickenhill is now a retirement home.

Bewdley, of course, stands on the river Severn, and before Stourport was built in the 1770s, it was an important transport interchange. Most of the Severn goods arrived at Bewdley, either by packhorses to be transferred to boats or by boats to be transferred to packhorses. There were often as many as 400 packhorses stabled there. When the Staffordshire and Worcestershire canal opened, Bewdley was by-passed and the rows of stables for pack-horses were empty. The town had 700 poor inhabitants and the wealthy were having to pay taxes of 52p in the £ to support them.

There's an entertaining story about Bewdley's participation in the Civil War of 1641-1646. One of the Parliamentarian heroes was Tinker Fox, a brave and inspired leader, said to have been a tinker but probably a manufacturer of knives, swords and other metal objects. He took part in the battle of Stourbridge Heath in 1644 and was very upset when he lost Stourton Castle. He decided that he should redeem himself in some way. One of the king's favourites was Thomas Lyttelton, governor of Bewdley, who was living in Tickenhill Palace, and Fox decided to try and capture him. One dark night, in April 1644, he set out with about 60 men and rode to Bewdley. He knew that one of the Royalist leaders, Prince Rupert, had passed nearby and so Fox pretended to be a detachment of Rupert's stragglers. The guards were half asleep and half drunk as they let him across the bridge. Amazingly, Fox and his comrades were also allowed into the town by a second set of soldiers who were guarding a chain across the road. Fox's men captured the sentries, murdering half-a-dozen, and put guards on the billets where the enemy were sleeping. He then took a posse to Tickenhill Palace, dragged Thomas Lyttelton out of bed and raced with him to Coventry. Lyttleton was taken to the Tower of London whence he was soon out on bail. However, he was re-arrested and spent some years in gaol. He was released for a second time, but died soon afterwards, in 1650, and is buried in Worcester Cathedral.

South of Bewdley and across the river is the cave in Blackstone rock, where legend tells of a hermit. Before he took holy orders, the hermit was to be married to a certain young lady but at the wedding she was snatched by an unknown young man and carried off on horseback. When the villain found that the rescue party was gaining on him, he threw the young lady into the river where she drowned. The hermit waited patiently in his cave, giving absolutions and hoping for the day that he could take his revenge. There are many versions of this legend, but they all conclude with the villain finally coming to confess his sins and the monk throwing him from the cave into the river below.

The white lady of the Severn

For generations, local folk have talked about the white lady of the Severn. Phil once saw her; he now works for the BBC at Pebble Mill but he was a patrolman with the AA:

I was doing some night fishing in Bewdley, when I was about 15. It was about three o'clock in the morning. A lot of people go night fishing, it's a good time to catch eels and that sort of thing. You choose a dark spot in the river, then you twist a piece of shining silver paper on the end of the line. You put a torch on the rod so that you can see if you have caught anything.

I was over there one Friday night, there were about twelve of us. It was tipping down, the rain stopped us fishing so we were sitting in a circle under the oak tree by Styles Warehouse, telling jokes. The chap facing me had his back to the path to the river. Then over my mates' shoulder, I saw this white shape heading towards us, walking up the river. I said, 'Can anybody else see what I can see?'. The others looked round, then they just ran. Up until then, I didn't believe in ghosts.

Bewdley battles

Down the centuries the men of Bewdley have had the reputation of being unusually militant. In the time of Henry IV, the rivermen were annoyed by the number of boats passing freely through Bewdley so in 1411, they tied a number of huge boats (trows) together and blocked the river. No-one was allowed through unless they paid outrageous charges. The Bewdley men heard that at boat was coming through for Gloucester, laden with wood and other fuel. They lay in wait and when in arrived, they jumped out on it and said that, if the owner of the boat didn't cut it into pieces, all the men on board would have their heads cut off. Understandably, the boat was pulled apart.

A few years later Bewdley became the refuge for thieves, vagabonds and other criminals. In 1425 Bewdley became the property of Richard, Duke of York. Under his patronage, it prospered and changed from a little village into

...over my mates' shoulder, I saw this white shape heading towards us, walking up the river. Bewdley.

a flourishing town with an annual market and fair. Then tragedy struck. Richard was killed during the Wars of the Roses and all his property was confiscated. However, the townsfolk remained loyal to Richard. When his son, Edward, was facing the Lancastrians at the battle of Mortimer's Cross, the townsfolk supported him and no doubt many Bewdley folk joined his army. Edward crushed the Lancastrians and, in 1461, at the age of 19, became Edward IV. In gratitude he gave the town many privileges including that of becoming a sanctuary town.

Across the river in Wribbenhall is the hamlet of Catchem's End, the last place that the bailiff's men could arrest a fugitive, and also Whispering Street, where the fugitives hid until night fell and they could creep across the bridge under cover of darkness. The respectable citizens lived near the river, the rogues lived on the fringe of the town, well out of reach of the arm of the law. Bewdley had another advantage in that no-one had decided whether it was in Shropshire or Worcestershire. Therefore, if a bailiff's men from Worcestershire came to arrest someone they would say they came from Shropshire, and vice versa.

There were physical battles over the politics, for example, polling days usually ended on a free-for-all between the occupants of Bewdley and Stourport-on-Severn. In the 1700s, Bewdley was in the unusual situation as having two rival corporations 'who fullminated against each other like rival Popes'. This was because, in a charter granted to the town by James I, Bewdley was to be ruled by a bailiff and twelve eminent citizens known as 'capital burgesses'. However, this was supposedly superseded by another charter in 1685 giving additional privileges. A dispute arose as to whether or not this second charter was legal. So there was one Corporation set up under the James I charter and another under the 1685 charter. Matters came to a head when two rival MPs were elected, Salwey Winnington and Henry Herbert. Herbert was a Whig and as the Whigs were in power, they decided that he should be the MP.

There were battles over religion. In the centre of Load Street (the main street), dividing the road into two, is the old church of St Annes. There were once shops and market stores filling the centre of this street but they have now been cleared away. We shall meet Richard Baxter, the great preacher who established Puritanism in the county, many times in this book and, in 1646, he paid a memorable visit to St Annes. John Toombes was then the curate and he made no secret of his objection to infant baptism, so a great debate was arranged between Baxter and Toombes. It began at nine in the morning and finished at five in the afternoon. Contemporary reports say that the two sides 'became like two armies' and 'the civil magistrate had much to do to quieten them'. The church had a heavy bill for repairing the furniture. John Toombes continued as curate, but at the same time, in the same year, founded the Baptist community.

The last stand (Wribbenhall)

The Saxon name for Bewdley was Wribbenhill which the Normans found difficult to say as they had no letter W and said GW instead so in 1215 the name was changed to Beaulieu which means beautiful place. The original name remains in that part of Bewdley which is across the river, known as Wribbenhall.

 Before this century, you could cross from Bewdley to Wribbenhall at low tide. The first bridge was built in 1447 when the Bishop of Worcester granted an indulgence of 40 days to all those who contributed to the work. It was destroyed during the Wars of the Roses, rebuilt, then destroyed again during the civil war between the Royalists and Parliamentarians. A timber bridge was built which was swept away in a great thaw.

 The present bridge was built by the great engineer, Thomas Telford. To the amazement of the locals, he was able to complete the bridge in one season. They remarked that it had been built 'as if by enchantment'.

 In this area, near Catchems End and Whispering Street, where fugitives hid for their lives, is Hoarstone Farm. If you go into WH Smith in Union Street, Birmingham, to buy a book, Maggie herself will tell you her story:

My eldest brother - by 19 years - married into a farming family out that way in 1963 and after a few years moved to a lovely old fortified manor-turned-farmhouse in Trimpley Lane near Wribbenhall, which at one point had been owned by relatives of the Lyttleton family (Gunpowder, Treason and Plot!) - but which had been owned in the 14th century by a chap called Richard who had been Gentleman of the Bedchamber to the unfortunate Richard II. So you can see it had a fair grounding in history. It was called Hoarstone Farm and is mentioned in Dugdale's history of Worcestershire. Hoarstone, as far as I know, means a boundary stone.

Every holiday my brother and I had the good fortune to stop with my eldest brother and his wife, together with my nieces and nephews who were pretty close to me in age. The house had a distinct atmosphere and at the back there was an old buttery with the original shelves through which one had to pass to go to the modern bathroom. This place made your hair stand on end. I used to psych myself up to run through it because I knew 'something' was coming to get me. 'It' was lying in wait for me - I knew! Bear in mind that this was 1969 when I was only about ten or eleven. Also off the huge kitchen was a door behind which was a staircase leading to the old servant's rooms and attics. I was terrified of the staircase because footsteps came down it when no-one was there and I had to run because I *knew* that if I waited I might see something I would not like.

I refused to sleep in the upper bedroom on my own and my lovely brother and sister-in-law always indulged me and made me a bed in the front room because something systematically went through the house at night. You could hear the doors opening and closing one by one. One night I actually saw that happen and I heard the old oak floor boards creak in unison! Probably some former resident checking the place out way back in his own time - or maybe searching for someone.

Lose a cow and find a knight (North Wood)

On the same side of the river as Wribbenhall but about a mile further north is North Wood. A house was acquired there by the Prior of Great Malvern in 1318, but half a century later, in 1362, it was granted to John Attwood (or Attewood) who was Usher of the King's Chamber. A local legend says that he, like all brave and noble men of his time, became a Crusader and fought in the holy land. He was gone for so many years that his wife was being forced into another marriage, against her will. However, a milkmaid went on an errand to find a lost cow and found instead a ragged and battle-scarred male in iron chains and fetters, who declared that he was John Attwood. He was recognised by nobody except his faithful dog, who ran to him, licking him. Fortunately, before he had set off for the crusade, he and his wife had broken their wedding ring in two and he was still in possession of his half, hung round his neck. He was therefore able to prove his identity. He arrived home just in time to save his wife from the second marriage.

He declared that he was brought home by a swan which has been included in the Attwood coat of arms. His iron fetters were preserved for many centuries, and the person who looked after them was given a meadow in Wolverley rent-free, still known as 'The Knight's Meadow'. He owned property in both Wolverley and North Wood, and the old, worn effigy in Wolverley Church is said to be that of John Attwood.

Habington writes in the 1500s (gyves were iron fetters used in prisons):

> But there was one Sir John Attwood who, being imprisoned by the infidels, was miraculously carried from that far remote dungeon of his captivity to Trimpley, losed of his gyves and restored to liberty, the same is so public the chapel builded in remembrance thereof so notable, the gyves themselves reserved as a trophy of this glorious redemption so clear a testimony as none but wilful obstinate can deny it.

It therefore seems that the first church at Trimpley was built by John Attwood as a 'thank you' to the Almighty for his safe return. The decorative little church has now been rebuilt but is said to be a copy of the original Romanesque design.

Local people say that the neighing of the horse and the rattling of the iron fetters can still be heard on dark nights near North Wood.

4. BROMSGROVE

romsgrove is so old that its origins are lost in the mists of time. The daughter of King Alfred (of the burned cakes fame) built a wooden fort here and that was probably on the hill where the church stands. The High Street is an incredibly ancient trackway, probably pre-Roman and on the main route from Worcester to Birmingham. Folk have been walking along it for more than 2,000 years. No wonder many of the shopkeepers have heard phantom cutomers. Often, when a sales assistant is working in a back room, he or she hears someone come into the shop but when they go to serve the customer, no-one is there. Other shops have reported mild poltergeists causing things disappear and reappear in strange places.

The oldest building in Bromsgrove is the church of St John's. It was built mainly in the 1200s and the splendid spire, seen from many directions, goes back to the 1300s. St John's is thought to have replaced an even earlier church.

Bromsgrove churchyard has well-known headstones to two 'engineers' (railway engine drivers) who were killed in 1840 by an exploding boiler of a tank engine named, rather aptly, 'Surprise' on the Birmingham and Gloucester Railway. Both headstones have pictures of old engines and that of Thomas Scaife reads:

> My engine now is cold and still
> No water does my boiler fill:
> My coke affords its flame no more,
> My days of usefullness are o'er
> My wheels deny their noted speed,
> No more my guiding hands they heed;
> My whistle too, has lost its tone
> Its shrill and thrilling sounds are gone;
> My valves are now thrown open wide
> My flanges all refuse to guide,
> My clacks also, though once so strong,
> Refuse to aid the busy throng
> No more I feel each urging breath
> My steam is now condens'd in death.
> Life's railway o'er, each stations past,
> In death I'm stopped and rest at last.
> Farewell dear friends and cease to weep
> In Christ I'm SAFE, in Him I sleep.

There was also a witty memorial about a man by the name of Knott:

Here lies a man that was Knott born,
His father was Knott before him.
He lived Knott, and did Knott die,
Yet underneath this stone doth lie;
Knott christened,
Knott begot,
And here he lies,
And yet was Knott.

Bromsgrove was once an important adminstrative centre for the royal forest of Feckenham. The Court Leet still meets annually for an election of officers.

For over a hundred years, during the 1700s and 1800s, nail-making was Bromsgrove's staple industry. As late as 1906, nail-making was the major occupation in the town.

Out of the mist

More important then Bromsgrove was Grafton Manor on its the south-western outskirts, home of some of the most important people in England since the 1300s, although the present house only dates back to 1710.

Sir Humphrey Stafford of Grafton Hall was famous enough to be immortalised by Shakespeare in the second part of Henry VI (Act IV, scenes I and II). He died in 1450, killed in Jack Cade's rebellion, and he lies in Bromsgrove Church together with his wife, Eleanor. Sir Humphrey may be responsible for that symbol of Bromsgrove, the Bromsgrove Boar, incorporated into the town's coat of arms. Various ballads written in the time of Henry VIII refer to Sir Ryalas, 'the jovial hunter' thought to be the pseudonym of Sir Humphrey. One ballad is in the British Museum and states that Sir Ryalas was out hunting when he came across a distraught woman who said a wild boar had killed her husband and thirty of his men. Sir Ryalas blew his horn to all four points of the compass, the boar appeared and after a fierce battle, Sir Ryalas killed the boar. Instead of being grateful, the woman flew at him in anger and said that the boar was her son. She had changed him into a boar so that he could kill Sir Ryalas. With that, he recognised her as a witch and chopped her in two.

The white lady of Grafton Manor is traditional enough to have appeared in the very respectable magazine of the Bromsgrove Historical Society, *The Rousler*. A local farmer has a story about a white figure in the 1990s, and, in 1995, Jon Bond saw an apparition very similar to the one described below (see *Haunted Pubs and Hotels of Worcestershire*).

Then we started seeing a woman coming out of the mist.
(Grafton Manor, near Bromsgrove).

I'm twenty-one this year and this happened when I was about fifteen. I used to stay with my cousins in Sidemoor and we used to go down to the countryside near Grafton Manor, firing stones at the birds with our catapults. It would have been in the autumn and about six o'clock in the late afternoon, the nights had just begun to draw in. We were not used to dusk coming so early and had lost track of time.

About eight of us were round by the big lake, messing about in the water, there were my two cousins and the rest were friends. We started hearing funny noises as if badgers were moving in the undergrowth but we couldn't see anything. We noticed a mist moving on the still lake. Towards the edge is an old tree, partly in the water, and the mist was across there. Then we started seeing a woman coming out of the mist. She was oldish, with long straggly hair, and a tatty old gown and she was all one colour, dark grey. She glided across the lake towards us. We all saw her and we jumped up and started to run off down the lane. She came on to the grass and followed us as we were running. She disappeared at the gate to Grafton Manor which is some way from the lake.

Please note that Grafton pool belongs to the hotel and permission has to be obtained before visiting it.

Schoolmasters abroad

Bromsgrove school is so old no-one knows when it began. In 1548, during the reign of the tragic Edward VI, its lands were confiscated but the fixed payment of £7, already in place, was continued to a priest who was 'bound to keep the school' and assist the local curate. Iin about 1556, 'Bloody Mary' put the school on a more stable footing when she re-endowed it as a 'free grammar school of King Philip and Queen Mary' and entrusted the running of the school to six men of the town.

The school was upgraded in 1693, when Sir Thomas Cookes of Bentley bequeathed £50 annually. £20 was for a master to teach twelve poor boys living in Bromsgrove or adjoining parishes. Cookes also rebuilt the school, the oldest part dating from that time and containing the original schoolroom.Three years later Cookes gave £10,000 for a building at Oxford University, plus an endowment for its upkeep. The building was to be for boys from Bromsgrove and Feckenham, and especially for any of his relatives. Gloucester Hall at Oxford was converted into Worcester College for this purpose. Unfortunately for Worcester, these rights were withdrawn in 1857 except for students from the Bromsgrove School.

Down the centuries Bromsgrove School has had its ups and downs and has even been closed occasionally. The period from 1816 to 1819 was one of its worst, when the Reverend Thomas Davies was appointed as master but the next year was taken off to Fleet prison for debt. He was also guilty of 'frequent inebriation in public as well as private' and 'the use of language not the most decorous'. The Bishop of Worcester was asked to interfere and managed to procure Rev John Topham of St John's College, Cambridge. The school has continued to progress from that time onwards and is now one of the top ten public schools in the country. Among its famous pupils was the poet Alfred E Housman who won a foundation scholarship at the age of eleven. His statue now stands in the High Street.

Anthony Wright was at Bromsgrove School from 1963 to 1965.

I don't know if Broome House is still there, but in those days the building was what was called, 'a waiting house'. If you were a boarder and there was not a place at your intented house, you stayed there for a couple of terms or so. The housemaster in those days was Mr Taylor. His wife kept seeing a ghost. One night, we heard a commotion, and in the morning we said, 'What was all that about?'. We were told that it was Mrs Taylor, she had seen the ghost. Evidently the ghost was male but that's all we could find out about it as they didn't want to frighten us.

What a pity we don't have a more detailed description of this ghost. Could it have been the generous benefactor, Thomas Cookes? Or perhaps it was the colourful Reverend Thomas Davies, returning from a spell in jail to resume his work as Master.

The phantom beast

Bromsgrove's pride and joy is the Dolphin Centre, with its large swimming pool plus chute, a small paddling pool, a cafeteria and a gym. To the right of the Centre is Bromsgrove Methodist Church, and to the rear is a large sports ground, where young Darren* had a terrifying experience:

About nine years ago, before the new houses were built on the site, I was at the back of the Dolphin Centre with my uncle. We used to go every night with the dog looking for the rabbits. One night we heard panting and growling behind us and when we turned round we couldn't believe our eyes - bushes were being bent over to the ground but nobody was there. The scuffling sound began to get really fast and was coming towards us, following us. As we ran towards the gate where the brook starts, it disappeared. Suddenly the gates were flung wide open all by themselves. We couldn't wait to get home.

Gentleman in a White Nightgown

Not far from the centre is a late Georgian Dower-house, said to have been built by the Earl of Shrewsbury for a Dowager Duchess. Its present occupier says:

In later years it became a girl's school, Elgar gave music lessons here. During the second World War it was acquired by the army or the air force and after the war it remained derelict for many years. When my husband and I moved in five years ago it had been partly renovated and we put the finishing touches to the alterations. As soon as we moved in I had a feeling that somebody was here. I knew that there was someone in the bedroom and in the lounge. I have had this sensation before in other places but usually I don't have to stay there. In this case I would be spending the rest of my life in the house and I knew that I would have to conquer the feeling.

About ten days later, I was fast asleep when I was aroused by somebody sitting on my bed. I opened my eyes and saw this old gentleman with a full white beard and thinning hair. He was quite small and very frail and he seemed to be wearing a long white nightgown. It was as if he was coming to see who had moved in. He never stirred but just sat there. I was really frightened. Later, when I mentioned it to my husband he said that he had once seen the door handle turn but the door hadn't opened and nobody had come in.

This went on for a couple of months then one night I plucked up courage. I sat up in bed and said, 'Look, don't frighten me. If you frighten me I will leave. Please don't frighten me'. Then I lay down, closed my eyes and turned over. My heart was in my throat and I could feel it pounding. When I opened my eyes he had gone. After that, I wasn't scared any more.

Although I haven't seen him since that night I can still feel that he is around. Sometimes, when I go past the kitchen, I feel a 'brushing chill', and I check round to see if I have left a window open. But now, he gives me pleasant sensation. I stop in the house on my own a lot and I feel quite comforted by his presence. He gives me a warm feeling.

The haunted quarry

Hill Top and Rock Hill were chiefly red sandstone and were peppered with quarries. The largest was on Rock Hill, owned by Jonathon Brazier (1827-1895) the son of a nailmaker. The haunted quarry is a remnant, now covered with trees, garages and houses.

Kirk is now twenty but when he was in his early teens he used to go with his 'mates' in the evening to play in Bromsgrove quarry with torches. The reason that he has given this story is that a similar experience was featured in *Unquiet Spirits of Worcestershire.*

*I opened my eyes and saw this old gentleman with a full
white beard and thinning hair.*

We were there one night when suddenly all our torches went off. Over the hedge at the top of the bank used to be an old mine shaft. I went towards it and I saw an old man standing on the beam. He had a kind of glow on him. He was wearing black trousers, a brown leather apron, hob-nailed boots and a white shirt. He had white hair and a white beard and moustache. He just stood there. I started crying. I couldn't move I was so pertrified. My mum had to come and fetch me. I still feel terrified when I think about it and I still dream about it at night.

The voice (Broad Street)

Broad Street is on the north-western side of the town. One of its residents, a very sane and sensible middle-aged lady, once had a very weird experience:

I was doing some washing up at the sink when I heard someone come into the kitchen behind me. I thought it was my husband so I was chatting to him. I happened to look out of the window and saw that it was raining. I heard a voice behind me saying, as clearly as anything, 'It's really going to rain now' but as the voice was not my husband's, I turned round. Nobody was there.

Nell Gwynne of the Birmingham Road

Fred is a well-known retired businessman and charity worker in Bromsgrove: About 15 years ago, he and his wife were living in a large house on the Birmingham Road at Marlbrook. Fred says:

The house was built, probably in the early 1930's but there had been a house on the site before then. I was working in front of the garage, cleaning the car or the mower, something like that, when I saw an apparition. She would be approximately 20 feet away. She walked across the drive, right across the end of the car park and into the garden. I saw her very clearly. She was dressed in medieval costume, rather like Nell Gwynne. She had fair hair which, as far as I can remember, was hanging straight down, and she was middle-aged. She was dressed in pastel colours, pale green and pinks. My first reaction was a double take. You see her, turn round and look back again very quickly. You think, 'Did I see it or didn't I see it?'.

I saw her again perhaps about six months later, when I was out on the car park. Three other people also saw her. A friend of mine was here one day and he couldn't believe his eyes. A couple of years later we had some work done on the house and the two workmen on the roof of the house spotted her.

My wife never saw her. It was very strange.

Touch not the cat

The M42 divides the few houses of Blackwell from the Lickey Hills. Its country roads are busy at the weekends because of two popular garden centres. The housewife in the next story lives near to one of these centres:

> We have a mischievous ghost. I'm just recovering from an accident, so I was in bed during the day and, to my surprise, I felt something jump on my bed and snuggle down, completely out of the blue. At first I thought it was the cat, but when I looked across, nothing was there. It's happened several times and is coming to the stage where it's nearly coming into bed with us!
>
> It's done it to my daughter as well. She was going to bed a couple of nights later. She said, You'll never guess, it's coming to sit on my bed now. My daughter is in her twenties and six feet tall, not the kind of person to be easily intimidated but it's starting to really upset her. She's quite frightened.

A phantom cat on the bed is a very common ghost. There was a house in Studley where the children could even hear it purring! In fact some people get quite fond of their mysterious pet!

Murder at Fockbury

Michael Cook was 24 years of age and living with his wife and three-month old baby (both named Elizabeth) at Stone Cottage, Fockbury, which is about $2^1/_2$ miles from Bromsgrove. He must have been quite an intelligent young man because he was employed as a 'motor driver' which in those days meant mechanic/engineer at a company in Selly Oak. On the evening of Saturday, 29th July 1916, Michael Cook and his wife walked into Bromsgrove, pushing the baby in a 'cart'. The wife returned soon afterwards, but Michael went into the George Inn at 8.10 pm, and by 9.30 he was seen leaving the Queen's Head Inn and heading for home.

Stone Cottage was owned by James Smith of Valley Farm and it abutted their long garden. Late that evening, Mrs Smith was tending to his horses in the stable when the maid rushed in saying, 'Come quick', Mrs Cook wants to see you'. Mrs Cook was standing in the passage-way, and cried out 'Run at once for mother and father to protect me'. Michael was standing at the gate with the baby in the perambulator. Mrs Cook's mother tried to take the baby from him but he hit the mother twice, knocking her to the ground. He then grabbed the baby, who started to scream, and ran off across a field and over a stile. A witness said that he staggered in his walk as he passed him. Mr Smith informed the police who looked for him, together with several neighbours, until two o'clock in the morning, without success.

The search was resumed the next day. Holborn Wood was a mile way and two youths reported finding a baby's bonnet and a man's hat there. A gruesome trail of bloodstained clothing led the police to the barn of Warbage Lane Farm, Dodford. Police-constable Hayes moved some loose hay and found the naked body of the baby Elizabeth. The removal of more hay revealed Michael Cook. PC Hayes said, 'I have been looking for you, Mike' to which Michael replied, 'Where am I? What have I done?'. When he was shown the body of his baby daughter, bruised and with her throat cut four times, he cried, 'Good God Sergeant, have I done that? Let me kiss her, I must have been mad', and he kissed the baby.

He was tried at Bromsgrove and incarcerated in August, in Worcester prison. Soon aftewards, he committed suicide (see the chapter on Worcester).

Stone Cottage is now occupied by Geoff Webb, who supplied this story. He adds, 'Fortunately, the murder was not perpetrated in the house but across the fields near a footpath (which is still there)'.

The haunted hall (Avoncroft)

Avoncroft is a museum that suits everyone from two to ninety-two. It covers 15 acres so there is plenty of room for even the most active members of the family to run around and explore. Some of the most interesting parts are in the open air, so that on a wet day it's a good idea to take macs and umbrellas, however, there are more than 24 historic buildings, all rescued and carefully rebuilt on site, in which to shelter. They include timber-framed buildings, a working windmill, a wartime prefab, and a firm favourite - a row of prison cells.

The fine timber roof of the Gueston Hall at Avoncroft comes from a building of the same name at the rear of Worcester Cathedral. Some of the ruins are still there. Built by Prior Wulstan de Bransford in 1320 for his guests, no expense was spared. Here, people of rank and wealth enjoyed sumptuous banquets and were entertained by the best minstrels and musicians in the land. Among those who knew it well were Catherine of Aragon, the first wife of Henry VIII, and Mary, his daughter.

Worcester Cathedral has a traditional spectre. It has been seen several times and especially in the Gueston Hall. The ghost is thought to be that of Thomas Morris, whose tombstone is set in the floor outside the Cathedral gift shop, bearing the one word 'MISERRIMUS', meaning 'O miserable one'. Thomas was a minor canon at the Cathedral and vicar of Claines. He refused to swear an oath of allegiance to William and Mary in 1689 and so he was never promoted. Before he died, he said, 'I have been walked over in life, I will be walked over in death' and he asked to be buried at the foot of the steps leading from the south door with the one word on his tombstone. The story goes that if you tread on his slab, you invoke his ghost. Among those who have seen Thomas was a young man and his girlfriend who were courting late one evening outside the ruins of the Gueston Hall. They looked up, and through the ruined window they could see a cleric looking down at them with an expression of extreme disapproval. He was so clear that they could see a gold tooth in his head. It was not until the next day the young man discovered that the wall below the ruined window was covered in moss and no-one had been up there for years.

The question is, has Thomas Morris moved with the roof? The Enterprises Manager of Avoncroft is suspicious:

Last February my colleague, Andrea, and I, were at an 18th birthday party in the Gueston Hall. I went to sit by her and I noticed that she was looking really white. I thought she might be feeling unwell or something, so I asked her, 'What on earth's the matter?'. She told me that a few minutes beforehand she was certain that I was standing behind her, so she turned round to say something but nobody was there.

In the summer of 1994 we had a large conference in the Gueston Hall. It was crammed with people and I was sitting in a corner of the stage. Halfway through the proceedings, something brushed my right shoulder blade. I put my left hand up to my shoulder and turned round, but nothing was there. I didn't think anything about it, but a few seconds later I felt a tremendous thud on the back of my shoulder. It took me completely by surprise. It did frighten me but I couldn't register any emotion as so many people were there. I had to behave as if nothing had happened.

Just before Christmas 1994/5 I was working with my daughter, Stephanie, in the Gueston Hall. I nipped out for a ciggie and when I went back Stephanie was in the kitchen bending down by the crockery cupboard. She was there for a few minutes and when she turned round, I noticed that she looked really weird. I said to her, 'What's wrong?', she replied, 'Nothing'. I said again, 'What's wrong?'. Then she told me. Apparently, she was working in the kitchen and had walked to the kitchen door, then she happened to look up at the balcony. There she saw what she described as a large, almost-transparent silk-like mist. She rubbed her eyes thinking, 'Silly me' but when she opened her eyes the shape started moving towards her. That freaked her out. She rushed back into the kitchen and shut the door. It really frightened her. She didn't scream or shout but she behaved quite strangely for some hours after that. I know my daughter and I can tell you that she isn't the type to make things up and tell lies.

Last week, a lady came into the hall and said, 'You have a tortured soul in here!'. That sounded just like Thomas Morris.

Grandy's grave

Near Avoncroft is a large house built about half a century ago. One of its past occupants was very glad to put it on the market:

> We lived there for twenty years. My parents-in-law lived in it from new, then when they retired we eventually bought the house. My mother-in-law always said it was an unlucky house. She had a most miserable life, she was always unhappy. The only time we felt genuinely happy was out in the garden. The house wasn't peaceful at all.
>
> I can't think how it started. We would lose things and find them in strange places. You could hear footsteps going up and down the stairs at night. Stupid little things happened - there was an incident with the hairdryer. It was one of those hairdryers with an attachment. I dried my hair, then I put the hairdryer down but when I went back to it later the attachment was off and lying on the floor next to the hairdryer. I thought that perhaps I hadn't put it on firmly enough, so I put it back on and this time I really pushed it. When I went back again it had come off and was on the floor. This happened three or four times.
>
> Early one Sunday morning we woke up to music. I thought one of the kids must have got up early and put a tape on. We lay there, thinking 'What's going on?'. It got louder and louder. In the end, I had to get up and turn it off. All the children had been asleep but it woke them up. It was Oasis, one of Jack's* tapes. Jack was my eldest son and a very lively child. One Christmas, when he was five years old, my husband brought a wreath home from work. Now, I don't like wreaths in the house so said, 'I'll take it up to the cemetery in the morning'. Bromsgrove cemetery is a huge place but as soon as we walked in through the cemetery gates John ran straight up to his grandfather's grave. He said, 'Here's grandy's grave'. He had never been there before. That was incredible.

The white lady walks again (Tardebigge)

Saint Bartholomew's church on top of Tardebigge hill is a landmark for miles around, especially at night. The ground drops away from t he church to a canal, a tunnel and 58 locks, one of them the deepest lock in, perhaps, England. A famous meeting occurred at the Tardebigge canal in August 1945 between Robert Aickman and Tom Rolt which led to the formation of the Inland Waterways Association, responsible for saving many of our canals and waterways.

Although the public house only goes back to 1911 it has an unusual history as it was built by the Earl of Plymouth for the residents as a village hall, but when two Earls of Plymouth died in rapid succession, the death duties meant that a lot of their property had to be sold. The deeds to the village hall had been lost so the residents could not prove that the building belonged to them, consequently, it was taken from them.

Nearby is Hewell Grange, for nearly 500 years occupied by Lord Windsor and his descendents, the Earls of Plymouth, but now converted into a remand home. Two prisons have been built in the gardens. Hewell Grange has a traditional White Lady and perhaps the best account of a sighting came from Arthur Bunegar who used to play in the ruins in the 1940s:

> One November evening, when we were about ten or eleven years old, we went chestnutting there. The evening was cold but a bright moon made everything clear as day. Suddenly, only a few yards away, we saw this lady rise slowly from the lake. She was wearing a huge voluminous dress like a ballroom gown and was all white from head to toe. I had the impression tht she was covered by a cloak, the hood of which hid her hair and most of her face but I caught a glimpse of her profile (we saw her from the side) and would guess that she was in her early twenties. She was walking towards the derelict ballroom and her dress flowed and fluttered as she moved. She looked quite solid - as real as you or me. We were terrified. She disappeared and we did too, we just ran for home.

Almost every book of local ghost stories contains a sighting of some apparition or other at Tardebigge. David Shephard lives on the edge of Hewell Grange and in 2002 remarked, 'The whole area is brimming with ghosts'. On 13 June 2005 a young lady was so intrigued by the sight of an unusual figure that her sister made an appeal as follows:

> I am writing on my sister's behalf. Having spoken to her today - she claims to have seen a ghost of a young dark-haired girl last night (13 June 2005) at the side of the road near the Tardebigge Pub, Bromsgrove, by the Tardebigge Court Barns and the Tower.
>
> Apparently the young girl (aged early to mid 20s) was standing at the side of the road in a long white 'nighty'-type robe to the ground, the collar having three buttons right up to her neck with long sleeves gathered at the cuffs. My sister said that the young woman held both her hands clenched up to her chest, looking extremely startled and almost petrified. She actually looked at my sister.
>
> My sister was in a taxi with her friends. None of her friends or the taxi driver saw anything, yet my sister worried the driver when she said, 'Did you see that woman? What is she doing out at this time of night?'. She was so convinced that she saw the woman just standing there by the gates that the taxi driver actually turned round to go and see if she was still there. She had gone when they returned a few seconds later.
>
> Does anyone know who she was, why she was standing there and why indeed she looked so frightened?

I see dead people

On the western suburbs of Bromsgrove lives a young man with a strange aptitude:

I'm always seeing things. It used to worry me a lot. I used to have doubts and think, have I seen it or haven't I? I couldn't cope with it but recently I've been seeing a psychiatrist [a live one, presumably? - ed] and he told me to have confidence in myself. I hadn't used to want to talk about it but I feel that I can talk about it now.

To take one example: I'm a light sleeper and when I was a teenager I was woken up by a scratching at the bedroom door. I looked over the bed-clothes and there, standing in front of the bedroom door, was an old man. He was skinny in the face with a pointed nose, there was a pipe in his mouth and he had a white and brown Jack Russell in his arms. My mother knew immediately that it was my granded from the way I described him, especially with the dog, as he had a dog just like that who was devoted to him. I never saw my grandad, he died when I was about five.

My mother is the one you should talk to, she's always seeing things. She has seen her grandmother and her mother. She saw her mother, who had died some time previously, when she was pregnant. Her mother said to her, 'You are going to have a healthy little boy'. That was me.

Mum was in bed the one night when she woke to find her mother-in-law by her side. She was surprised that she should pay her a visit because they didn't get on. The mother-in-law said that her mother was going to fall ill. The next day she had a telephone call to say that her mother had been rushed into hospital and was in intensive care. Last week she saw my grandad's brother. He told my mum that my grandad's sister was going into hospital, and she did. My mum has all these things happening to her but she won't talk about it.

The vision

The following is a very sad story but the narrator asked for it to be published in the hope that it would help someone in the same situation:

My wife, Mary*, passed away just over a year ago. I was absolutely heartbroken. We had made all kinds of plans for our retirement but she fell ill soon after I retired and became progressively worse over the next eight years. She went into a nursing home for the last few months before she died as I was unable to cope but I visited her every day.

Suddenly, one night about eight weeks after she had passed away, a vision appeared on my bed. It was Mary, wearing a long white dress and smiling, and she looked as she did when she was about thirty. I couldn't believe it. I'm a realist and I was an agnostic, I thought it was a dream. I moved towards her and she vanished. I was disappointed and upset.

A few weeks went by and she appeared again. This time, I didn't move, I just sat and watched her. Then a shaft of light from a parking light came in through the bedroom window. It fell upon her and she disappeared.

Just a few weeks after that, I woke up one morning at about ten to two. First I saw the back of a tall man, level with my head. Next to him, lower down, was my wife. On the other side was another tall man but not as tall as the first. The first man had his arm round my wife. At first I felt a pang of jealousy but then I realised that he was protecting her. I don't know anything about angels but I assumed he was angel. I was overwhelmed. I said, 'Please don't go, I want you to stay'. He looked down at me, without smiling, stayed there for a few minutes, then vanished. It was about three weeks before they came again, the next time they stood by my bed.

I said to a friend of mine, 'Why am I so privileged to see her?'. He thought it might be because I had nursed her with such devotion for the years that she had been ill.

The 'angels' visited me with my wife about ten or twelve times. I could make out their silhouettes. I put chairs in the bedroom for them and they sat on them. It was incredible.

I began to learn when they were coming. The window of the bedroom is quite large and the curtains are drawn but there seems to be a light behind it, then a silhouette walks across the window, the light goes out and I know that they will be here soon.

On two occasions Mary began to say something. She hadn't' spoken for five years because of her illness. I said to her, 'Oh you can talk' but she said, 'Oh, I mustn't speak', put her hand over her mouth and vanished.

Once, I spoke to the 'angel'. My wife had written on her cuff that she hadn't washed since she had been in heaven and she was getting smelly. That worried me, I didn't know how to deal with it in a sensible way. I said to the angel that she was bothered about her hygiene, bearing in mind it may not be feasible for her to get washed, if there was anything he could do, I would be grateful. I asked if it would be possible for her to acknowledge that she had received my message in some way, even if it was only three rings on the telephone? That night, at three o'clock in the morning, a male voice spoke my name loudly and clearly three times. I suddenly thought, 'That's it, they can't ring but they have spoken my name loudly three times instead'.

On another occasion I heard, in my head, a direct spoken voice. The voice said that Mary was worried about me and what I was doing in the garden. I had been moving paving stones.

When I had lost something, I got in touch with the 'angels' and within half-an-hour I had found that which I had lost.

I felt that I would like to see my wife on her own without her 'angels', and so I said to them, 'To be honest, I feel it's a shame that you are spending time here, as just seeing my wife is more than enough for me. Although I'm still broken-hearted I now know that I haven't lost her. That keeps me going'. The two angels stopped coming then. My wife appears at odd times and doesn't stay for long, she just pops in and out. Her visits have become less frequent of late.

I know that these experiences must sound strange to some people, I'm only telling them because I think they may help someone.

5. CLENT AND THE LICKEYS

n the time of the Domesday Book Clent was in Worcestershire, then in Staffordshire until 1832, then, bit by bit, between 1832 and 1844 it became part of Worcestershire again. In the time of Henry VIII, this too-ing and fro-ing between counties led to a happy accident. Historians read that 'Clenet' in Staffordshire had belonged to the king in 1086 and was therefore eligible for a variety of privileges; it was exempt from tolls and other taxes, it did not have to send knights to Parliament and so on. Henry VIII confirmed these privileges. It was not until centuries later that it was discovered that, in 1086, Clent had been in Worcestershire and so 'Clenet' did not refer to them but to another town.

Clent stretches for five miles from Wychbury Hill to Waseley Hill, with its highest peaks a thousand feet up. Tradition states that it was on Wychbury Hill that the Romans encamped before their great battle with the Britons. The latter could have been on the Walton and Clent Hills, and the struggle is said to have taken place south of West Hagley, between Thicknall farm and Churchill.

Surprisingly, the traditional ghosts of Clent Hills are not the ancient Brits but a variety of horsemen. We have already met Sir Ryalas, the jovial hunter of Bromsgrove. The Devil and his chief huntsman, Harry-ca-Nab, mounted on white bulls, are said to hunt wild boars by night on the Clent and Lickey Hills, with a pack of hounds that the devil kept at Halesowen.

Another old tale features Peter Corbett, who, it is said, lived in a large house in the centre of Chaddesley Corbett. Passages went from this house, under what is now the A448, to the house across the road. In an annexe to one of these passages, so the story goes, Sir Corbett kept a vicious pack of hounds behind bars. Peter Corbett had a beautiful daughter, who fell in love with one of the local youths - a most unsuitable match. The kennelman heard the couple planning to meet in the passage under the house at a certain hour. When the time came, Sir Peter locked his daughter in her bedroom and the kennelman unleashed the hounds, who had not been fed for a couple of days, so that the suitor was torn to death. The daughter went mad with grief. Overcome with remorse, father drowned all his hounds in the local pool. Now, for his sins, he rides at night with his pack of hounds across the nearby hills.

There may be a grain of truth in this story. The manor of Chaddesley Corbett came into the hands of the Corbett family in 1199. A member of this family by the name of Peter was in existence in the late 1200s. They seem to have been quite brutal family, and in 1340 William Corbett's conduct to his wife even came to the attention of the Bishop of Worcester. Furthermore, there are people alive today who say that they have walked through the tunnel beneath the road.

A king's murder

No mention of Clent would be complete without referring to the legend of Saint Kenelm, which was appearing in manuscripts by the eleventh century. According to tradition, the Kings of Mercia once had a residence in Clent. On the death in 789 of Kenulf, King of Mercia, his son Kenelm, then a child of eight, became king. Kenelm was described as 'endowed with every grace of body and mind'. Kenelm had a dream, which he described to his nurse. He said that he saw a beautiful tree that reached to the stars standing by his bed and he stood on top of it, and could see all things. But as he wondered at the sight, some of his people cut down the tree and it fell 'with a great crash'.

The nurse guessed that his sister, Quendrada, wanted to be queen and was planning Kenelm's murder but, despite her warnings, Kenelm went off hunting with the queen's lover, Ascobert. The latter took Kenelm into the Clent woods, killed him and buried him under a thorn tree. Legend states that the spot was marked by a shaft of sunlight and a milk white cow who refused to leave the spot (in some versions said to be the Dun cow).

The Pope was officiating in Rome when a white dove appeared, and tied to its leg was a message which said:

> In Clentho vaccae valli Kelemus regius natus,
> Jacet sub spino, capite truncatus'.

Roughly translated, it reads:

> In Clent, in Cowbach, Kenelm King born,
> Lyeth under a thorn, his head off-shorn.

The Pope sent an embassy to recover the body and bury Kenelm in Winchcombe beside his father. The body was gently lifted up and a sacred spring burst from the spot.

When Quendrada saw that the body of the king had been found, she began to sing the 108th psalm backwards but when she reached the end of the verse, her eyes dropped out on to the psalter she was reading. Quenrada died soon afterwards and her body was thrown into a ditch. A psalter with blood stains trickling down the page, was the prized possession of Winchcombe Abbey until it was stolen in the 20th century. The water from the sacred spring brought good health to all who drank it and the tomb of St Kenelm became famous for the many miracles performed there.

The church of St Kenelm was built near to the spring on the parish boundary between Clent and Romsley. The spring has been renovated and is open to visitors, although drinking its waters is not recommended. Historians say that there was a King Kenelm but unfortunately he died before his father, possibly in a battle with the Welsh, and his sister, Kenrada, was the abbess of a Minster in Kent.

Revenge is sweet

By the 1700s the Amphlett family were the chief landowners in Clent, but in 1868 the head of the family died after an accident involving a frisky horse, his older grandson was killed at Gallipoli and the younger grandson died in 1949. The great grandson was killed in 1942 while serving with the RAF, so the male line died out.

John Amphlett (1845-1918) of Clent House devoted his life to the well-being of the locality, he was county councillor, deputy county court judge, chairman of the Board of Guardians to the workhouse, he sat on Clent Parish Council and was a manager of the local school. He was therefore very annoyed when the villagers took him to court, accusing him of enclosing more land than that to which he was entitled, and even more annoyed when he lost the case. To get his own back, he ordered all his staff and anyone associated with Clent House to attend the local church of St Leonard's every Sunday morning and sit in the choir stalls, so that the choir had nowhere to go. As he owned the chancel, he had every right to do this. Time went by, John Amphlett moved away from Clent House and the staff gradually stopped filling the choir stalls so that the choir returned. Then one Sunday morning, church members arrived and discovered that all the choir seats had been chopped into pieces. Only the ends of the pews remained. In 1956 the heirs to the estate made amends by donating the deeds of the chancel to the church, on condition that the Amphlett memorials remained untouched.

The haunted architect

A middle-aged lady who lives in Clent says that in the village is a lovely Georgian house, a listed building. She continues:

A few years ago a very, very with-it lady lived in it, she was an architect and not at all fanciful. The house was three or four stories tall and it had attics on the top which were never used, nobody ever went up there.

I was quite friendly with her, and we were just having a normal conversation when she began telling me about the strange events in her house. One night she heard the window bang in the attic. She felt that she should do something about it or the window would fall out. She went up there but it was obvious that the window hadn't been opened for years. It was covered in cobwebs and you couldn't reach it, the attic was solidly packed with bric-a-brac.

Her husband slept in a dressing room which only had one door into a larger room. One night, he went to sleep then he felt something heavy getting on his feet. He thought it was the cat so he kicked it off and it went bump on the floor. Then it got on again. Again, he kicked it off. He suddenly remembered that they hadn't got a cat so he put the light on but there was nothing in the room.

Am I dead?

Patricia* has had two strange experiences. The first occurred in the mid 1950s when she had been married for a year and was living in Clent.

One of the elderly members of the family had died and we were living in her house. It was a bright, sunny morning, when the light comes through the curtains. I know I was awake but when I decided to get up, I couldn't move. I was paralysed from head to feet. I couldn't move my toes, my fingers or my eyelids. I could feel that there was someone by the side of me but I couldn't turn to look at them. All sorts of things went through my mind. Was it the person in the family who had died? Had I had a stroke? Was I paralysed? I even thought I might be dead.

I tried very hard to move but I was kept frozen for a few minutes. When I got up I was shaking with fright. I told my husband what had happened, I know I wasn't dreaming.

Then we went to live with one of the in-laws in a modern bungalow. There was a large hall in the middle of the bungalow with nine doors going off it. The in-law was very elderly and in a lot of pain. She got up very late in the morning and went to bed very late at night. She was in the habit of doing little jobs late at night, she would dust the cobwebs away and that sort of thing. That was fine, but of course, we both had demanding jobs and needed our rest. We would lie in bed and hear her bumping about as she dusted.

Now, I'm a very careless untidy person and I leave windows and doors open. She would go round and close the doors which was very sensible because they were a fire hazard, but she would do this very noisily and it echoed a lot. You would go to sleep and then a door would bang and then another door. We would think, 'I wish she would stop it, I want to go to sleep, I have got to get up in the morning'.

She died suddenly somewhere else, not in the house, and for the next two or three weeks afterwards I always left the doors open and in the morning they were always closed. It just happened for two or three weeks then it stopped.

It's her again (Frankley Green)

Frankley Parish is on the eastern side of the Clent Hills. Before the 1640's, the village of Frankley was the home of the Lyttleton's, who later settled at Hagley Hall. Frankley Green, now covered in housing, was originally common land running along each side of the roadway that bears its name. Frankley was heavily involved in the Civil War of 1642-6. The Manor House, to the west of the church, was occupied by the Royalist leader Prince Rupert, who burned it to the ground so that it would not fall into the hands of the Parliamentarians.

Perhaps past occupants of the old cottage in the next story were involved in the upheaval and tragedies of the civil war. The story was told with some reluctance (and persuasion by a friend) at the Worcestershire Skills Show of 2001:

We used to live in a thatched cottage in Frankley Green. There was a presence, not an unpleasant one. You could feel someone was there and sometimes you could hear a high singing voice in the distance, definitely a lady's voice. We had no neighbours so it wasn't them. One of my sons felt the presence so strongly that he wouldn't stay in the house.

My husband used to think it was me that was calling him. He used to come in and ask, 'What?' and I would say, 'It's her again'. One night everybody thought that somebody had called them and we all went into the hall saying, 'What is it'.

We used to hear things fall but we never found anything. There would be the noise of a picture falling off the wall or a glass knocked over.

We had this very long room (26 feet long) with a new three-piece suite in it. It was all wooden, made of Canadian oak. The one armchair was situated in the middle of the room. We used to hear something like the tinkling of a piece of broken glass, it always came from the direction of the chair.

My husband said there was no such thing as a ghost. One evening he was downstairs reading a book when he heard footsteps overhead going from one end of the bedroom to the other, sounding as if they were on wooden floors whereas upstairs was carpeted. This changed his way of thinking.

The strange visitor (Belbroughton)

On the lower slopes of Clent Hills, and about a mile south of Clent village, is Belbroughton, only a small village but carrying the status of having been mentioned in the 1086 Domesday book. It even had a vicar at that time. A Saxon church was replaced by a Norman one which was renewed by the Victorians.

Belbroughton was famous for its scythes, hooks and hay-knives. The industry was established there by the mid 1600s. The well-known factory of Isaac Nash began with two men in 1835 but by 1881 he employed 105 men and two boys and owned all the forges and mills along the stream. It only closed in 1968.

Hannah says that, in 1965, she moved into a Victorian Georgian gentleman's residence in the middle of Belbroughton.

It was a lovely house, large with a cellar and a walled garden. My eldest son was away at boarding school and my youngest was with me at home in the kitchen and we were just standing in the kitchen talking when we became aware that, although neither of us heard the door opening, a little old man had walked into the kitchen. He was wearing striped trousers and a grandfather shirt without the collar but with gold studs. He had a round ruddy face and was balding with dark hair either side of his head but none on top. He walked straight through into the hall.

My son saw him too. He said, 'Mum, where's that man going?'. I said, 'I don't know, I'll ask him'. We had business premises next door and I thought someone had lost their way. I said, 'Just a minute'. He walked up a step and into a door which led into a cupboard - and he had gone. I said, 'Where's he gone?' I couldn't believe what I had seen. I ran outside to my husband and I said, 'A man has come into the house and he's disappeared into a cupboard'. My husband thought that we were both hallucinating.

Shortly afterwards we started renovating the house and found that this cupboard was, in fact, a door which led into a back staircase to the servants quarters. When we pulled down the hardboard we found all the postcards that the servants had sent to each other over the years when they were on holiday. We think he must have lived there.

We often talk about it. He was a lovely man, he looked so kind. Afterwards, if there was a bang or a knock we would say, 'That's him!'.

Neither my son nor I have seen anything before or anything afterwards. However, both my sons have said that when they were going off to sleep they have felt that someone was brushing their cheeks. One of the lads said that he woke up one night and he was sure that there was somebody looking down at him, but we dismissed it and said that he was dreaming.

The hound of Cofton lane (The Lickey Hills)

A century or two ago the Lickey Hills were, to Birmingham folk, what Majorca is to them today. You could catch a tram in the centre of Birmingham and you could sit upstairs or downstairs, inside or outside, all the way to the Lickey roundabout, of which the decorative wrought-iron work only disappeared about 20 years ago.

On the western side of the Lickey Hills is the village of Cofton Hackett, surrounded on three sides by hills or reservoirs. In the old manuscripts, the 'f's' and 's's' are difficult to tell apart and, according to the Victoria County History, the name should really 'Coston Hackett'. It was in existence in 780, when King Offa give it to the monastery church of St Peter, at Bredon. By 849 it had become the property of the Bishop of Worcester, who leased it to the King of Mercia for five lives. That is, the King would have chosen five healthy-looking people and Coston was his for as long as at least one of these people lived. When the last of the five died, it went back to the Bishop.

In 1633 Coston (or Cofton) Hall came into the possession of Thomas Joliffe who was a great friend of Charles I. The king stayed with Joliffe at least twice during the Civil War of 1642-1646. He was there on 14th May, 1645 and returned a day or two later to hold a council of War with the governors of the garrisons. After Charles was defeated, Joliffe was given a key to the King's prison, so that he could visit whenever he pleased. Joliffe also looked after the king on the scaffold, before his execution. To commemorate such an important situation, Joliffe had his portrait painted wearing a solemn expression and holding a key in his hand. Cofton Hall has now been rebuilt but parts of the old hall, such as the 14th century hammer beam roof, are still there.

Tina is now 53 years old but she remembers clearly a curious incident that occurred when she was 15 years old and living in Cofton Church Lane:

I went to see Dracula at the cinema with my friend, Pauline. We had put on lipstick and high-heeled shoes and were pretending to be older so that we could get into the cinema.

We came home late at night on the tram. It was a pitch black night, with only a few street lamps. The Lickey Hills were on one side of the road and I had to take a turning on the left. Cofton Church lane is a long, dark lane and I lived near the end.

On the other side of the road from the hills was a gate and in the gateway was a lovely dog, a cross between an Alsatian and a Collie. I said to Pauline, 'Oh look at that dog' but she couldn't see it. She said, 'What dog?' and walked on.

After a few minutes Pauline left me to go to her home and I was on my own. I found that the dog was keeping me company, trotting along with me.

When I got to my gate, it seemed to vanish. I told my father about this lovely dog and he came out to see it but it had disappeared.

I can remember it after all these years. I saw it as plain as plain.

The following day when my father went to work he heard there had been a group of undesirable people in the area, with burglaries and break-ins roundabout. I think the dog came home with me to protect me.

I have never seen it before or after that one night.

6. DROITWICH

 roitwich is the great salt town of England, for it has been built above a huge lake of rock salt, formed millions of years ago. Until the last half century, salt was one of the most important commodities in the home. As well as flavouring food it was used as a preservative, in dyeing, in health treatments, as an antiseptic and so on. When the Romans arrived somewhere between the years AD 47 and 70, they appropriated this town of white gold, and built a fort on Dodderhill, overlooking the town, where the church of St Augustines now stands. Two Roman villas were erected in Bays Meadow. Their burial ground stretched for several hundred yards between Roman Way and Salwarpe Road. A skeleton was also discovered in Hampton Road, and the wooden coffin crumbled when an attempt was made to lift it. Within the skull were shrunken pieces of preserved brain.

The town was known as 'Salinae' and soldiers were paid in salt as well as coins. It is said that this was the origin of the word 'salary'. Saltways from Droitwich spread out across England. When William the Conqueror ordered his 1086 inventory of England, Droitwich was mentioned 25 times compared to Worcester's 11. So much salt water was drained from beneath the town that the middle of the High Street gradually sank and had to be rebuilt. Even now, the houses lean slightly towards one another.

The strip of land running alongside The Saltway, on the opposite side to the car parks, is now a pleasant stretch of green, watered by the river Salwarpe and the Droitwich canal. However, for centuries it was a hive of activity, a bustling industrial area, where makeshift sheds stood side by side, where men sweated and heaved, and steam rose from vats of boiling water. This is where many of the salt springs were situated, bubbling up with salt water ten times stronger than ocean water. One plank-lined salt pit has been preserved, opposite The Saltway car parks. The brine was collected from the springs, stored in long pits, heated in hearths to produce the salt, then transported in ceramic pots.

The wells or 'pits' were owned by the King, the Bishop and other such eminent persons and were heavily regulated. Salt could only be mined for six months of the year and the boring of other pits was not allowed. In Henry VII's time there were five wells in the town with a great number of furnaces around the wells. Then in 1670 a wealthy gentlemen, Robert Steynor, created a scandal by sinking two salt pits on his own land. The case went to the courts and he won although it cost him a fortune. From then on, everyone was hoping to find salt on their land and many pits were sunk, the supply of salt increased and the price dropped. Two hundred people were made bankrupt and schools and hospitals which had invested in salt were ruined.

Wells were only sunk to a depth of about 35 feet when a soft stone was reached, but in 1725 it was learned that better salt lay at a depth of about 150 feet, beyond the soft stone. The first two men to bore a hole this deep were killed by the brine that rushed up with tremendous violence.

The heroes of Droitwich are those who revived its salt revenue. There was Saint Richard, who was born, it is said, in 1197 on the site of the Raven Hotel and rose to become Bishop of Chichester. He visited the town when the springs had refused to flow and found the superstitious towns folk using heathen dances of the Wiccans to try and revive the wells. He gave the wells a Christian blessing and the springs flowed again. The Senior Bailiff cried 'My Lord, you have saved the town, let this day never be forgotten!'.

Then, more recently, there was John Corbett. By the 1850s the salt trade had begun to decline because of contamination with fresh water and competition from other companies. In 1854 John Corbett bought 6 acres of land at Stoke Prior and, using the latest methods, built the largest salt works in Europe. He was a great philanthropist and provided better working conditions, a school, a dispensary and a working man's club. The fortunes of Droitwich were also in decline, so John Corbett launched it as a great spa health centre, with treatments for afflictions from rheumatism to eczema. He rebuilt the Old Manor House of Wyche as the Raven Hotel and provided other hotels. There was already one brine bath but he built a second in 1888 with a swimming pool and nine private bathrooms, each with their own bath. It was so popular that he extended it to two baths and 48 private bathrooms. These were only closed in 1975. In 1995 new baths were opened on the site of the old.

John Corbett set his sights on becoming an MP. He stood against John Pakington who lived in the magnificent Westwood Park, and so it was necessary for him to have an equally sumptuous home to impress the voters. He purchased a manor at Impney and hired a French architect, August Tronquois, to design the building now known as 'The Chateau Impney'. Rumour has it that he also hoped the design would please his wife, who, although Irish, had attended a French finishing school. Corbett died suddenly in 1901.

Near to the corner of Victoria Square and Saint Andrew's Road is the Tourist Information Centre, with a charming and informative little museum.

Monks and friars

Friary Street gets its name from the Augustinian Friars who at settled in Droitwich in 1331. They were given a plot of land, 300 feet square, on which to build an oratory and a dwelling. Twenty years later the plot was extended to five acres. Apparently, by 1388 Thomas Beauchamp, Earl of Warwick provided a small cell so that a monk, Henry de Stokebrugge, could spend his life praying for 'the founder and his kin'.

Two hundred years later, in 1531, The Bishop of Dover visited the house and reported that it was in great poverty. Everything had been sold: 'in the house is not left one bed, one sheet, one platter nor dish'. The building was eventually divided into apartments and eleven years later, in 1542, it was bought by a couple of speculators in monastic lands.

The property fell into the hands of the Norbury family who were distant relatives of the Beauchamps. John Norbury was already wealthy in 1473 when his grandmother's brother died 'without issue' and he inherited half of his estates. In St Andrews Church is an elaborate monument of 1734 to the memory of Coningesby Norbury, 'Captain of one of his Majesties Ships of War / and Envoy from King George the first to the Court of Morocco / to redeem the British Slaves. Norbury House was built on the site of the old friary. It became a hotel in 1936 then, in the early 1960s, part was demolished and rebuilt as flats while a section was converted into Norbury theatre.

Many a ghostly monk has been seen in the theatre, for example, Peter Mellors was alone painting scenery one cold night in November when the howling of the dog made him look up and he saw a white face at the window. He rushed to the window just in time to see a dark monk gliding through the bushes.

Ghostly monks have also been seen in the attractive half-timbered house, as the end of Friar Street, known as Priory House. Parts are said to go back to 1500 so it must have been there at the same time as the Friary - was it, as its name suggests, the home of the Prior? One recorded incident was in 1875 when a terrified guest, Miss Porter, woke to find a monk in her bedroom. Gladys Bourne's grand-daughter also has the story of a sighting in about 1938:

> My aunty would have been 86 by now. When she was about 18 or 20 she worked as a maid at Priory House. She was sleeping in a room there with her sister, Iris, when she woke up and saw a monk sitting on the edge of their bed.
>
> My aunty blinked, and when she opened her eyes again the monk had gone.

Priory House was restored by the Droitwich Preservation Trust in 1970 and is now privately owned.

A town of troublemakers
(information supplied by Bill Thomas)

Droitwich once had the reputation of being such a town of troublemakers that officials organising a train journey for Queen Victoria refused to allow the train to stop at Droitwich railway station. On the night of the local elections in Saturday, January 29th 1910, the Riot Act had to be read in Droitwich.

The elections were between Hon John Lyttleton (Unionist) and Mr Cecil Harmsworth (Radical). The salt industry was running down, many were unemployed and it was believed, quite erroneously, that Harmsworth could revive the salt industry. There was no difficulty in spotting who belonged to which side. The Lyttleton Unionists were quiet and dignified while the Harmsworth Radicals shouted and banged kettle drums. After the polls had closed on the Friday, despite the cold and the rain, about a thousand people crowded into the narrow St Andrew's Street. A shop belonging to a local Unionist supporter was wrecked. The local leader of the Radical party was sent for and it took him three hours to quieten things down.

The police were therefore expecting trouble again on the Saturday, after the results were announced, so they brought in reinforcements of 100 police from the rest of the county. During the afternoon there was a hint of the trouble to follow. A car, bedecked with Unionist red ribbons, was driving past the Raven Hotel when its windows were smashed. A young gentleman and two ladies wearing Unionist colours were surrounded by a howling mob and the young man had flour thrown in his face. Counting took place in the old workhouse and the crowd waited patiently outside until, at one o'clock, the results were announced. Unfortunately, Hon John Lyttleton was unable to attend. He had been unwell and, furthermore, his car had broken down.

About eight o'clock, Frank Kench, licence holder of the Wagon and Horses and a staunch Unionist, had a stone thrown through his window from a growing crowd. Mr Lyttleton's committee room in Friar Street was treated it in a similar manner. All hell was let loose. The report in Berrow's Worcester Journal states that 'Now and then a dull thud, followed by a crash of glass, told that another window pane had gone'.

The crowd lifted one of the ringleaders, John Sankey, shoulder high and asked him to make a speech. He was later accused of inciting the crowd. The Chief Constable, the Superintendent Sheriff and the local Inspector tried to persuade the crowd to disperse but without success. The Mayor, Mr Jackson Gabb, a very tall gentleman, had been anxiously watching the proceedings all evening. Eventually, it was decided that he should read the Riot Act. Deputy Chief Constable Wesley held a candle to enable him to see it.

This was a very serious matter. It gave magistrates the power to arrest 12 people or more who refused to disperse within one hour of the reading of the Act, and it gave them the power to call in the army or, in this case, the mounted police.

Up until that time, the police 'behaved with coolness and restraint' some waiting quietly in a thick line, others mingling with the crowd in an attempt to calm them down. However, the mounted police charged into the crowd, swinging their batons freely. One of the troublemakers, James Sparkes, said in court that the police were after him 'like greyhounds and he 'ran away for his life'. Elizabeth Sparkes was standing outside her house, the police rushed at her and pushed her indoors, saying 'Get in you dirty cat'. George Evans, another troublemaker declared that he only went to look for his son but he got caught in a rush of police and although he ran, he was not quick enough. One officer struck with him with a baton across the shoulders and arms, then he was kicked four or five yards. He remarked, 'The police were hitting everybody they came across'. The streets were soon cleared.

The leaders of the riot were taken before the magistrate and put on remand to appear before the Assizes. They were then acquitted on a technicality - it was said that they hadn't heard the reading of the Riot Act.

Surprisingly, nobody appears to have been badly hurt, whereas at a peaceful political rally earlier that month, 24-year old Mrs Watton, the wife of the lock-keeper, was seriously injured. The balcony at Salter's Hall had been reserved for ladies, it had been boarded round to avoid accidents but there was a gap in the boards. Hon John Lyttleton had just finished addressing the meeting when Mrs Watton, forgetting about the gap, took a step backward and fell fifteen feet onto the back of her head.

The hasty exit

The old workhouse was opposite what is now the library, near the corner of Victoria Square and St Andrews Street. Lloyds Bank now stands on the site. A retired lady says that, before the workhouse was demolished, her husband had a small manufacturing business there with an office on the first floor:

My husband spent a lot of time there in the evenings trying to get the paper work done. Our home was at Inkberrow, so he used to give three rings on the telephone when he was about to leave work to give me time to prepare the evening meal.

One evening, he came home in such a state and he hadn't given me the three rings. His office was a very long room and at the far end the door was locked. He saw somebody standing there. He was so terrified that he rushed out, leaving everything unlocked. He never worked late at the office again.

The missing customer

Roy Williams now lives in Halesowen and says:

My story comes from a few years back. My sister and her husband were running the West Croft pub as tenants in Droitwich and when they were on holiday, my wife and I would relieve them. One day, we opened up at eleven o'clock and as we opened my wife went over to a shop which is directly opposite. I was putting some bottles away under the counter and as I popped my head up I saw a real old-fashioned kind of lady standing there, all dressed in black. My comment was, 'I won't be a minute, love'. Five seconds later my sister who lives in Bromsgrove, called in to see me and a few seconds after that my wife came back from the shop. I said, 'Where's that old dear gone - the elderly lady?' and they both said, 'What old dear?'. They both looked at me as if I had gone mad. She couldn't have gone anywhere. Now, I'm very cynical by nature but if you know where the pub is on the Droitwich ring road you will know that there is nowhere that anyone could walk to in five seconds.

The nursing spirit

The twelve-year old in the next story lives in Stratford:

I slept at my friend's house in Droitwich a few weeks ago and while I was there I saw a ghost. Four of us were sleeping in one large bedroom - we virtually had the floor to ourselves. One of my friends got out of bed in the night and went to the loo. He left the bedroom door open and that's when I saw her. There were two steps up to our bedroom and a parallel landing and a lady was just standing on the landing. She was quite thin and had a thin face. She seemed to be wearing 1950's type clothes, with a knee-length skirt. I couldn't see her that clearly, the edges were blurred. She was mostly greyish but I could see hints of colour and I could see that she had red curly hair.

A friend of mine who stayed at the house says that he felt someone sitting on his lap. He waved his arms to get them to go away but nobody was there. It was a very old house and our bedroom used to be a children's nursery. I am told that the lady who worked there had red curly hair. We think she probably came back to see if the children were alright.

Brief encounter

The following is the unusual tale of a poltergeist who existed for two days only:

There's not a lot to tell. In the 1970s we were living in a house in Droitwich. There was me, my husband and two teenagers, one boy and one girl who were in their mid-teens. On two consecutive days we had strange things happen. I know our teenagers were not playing tricks as they were staying with friends and were not in the house.

We had a lot of ornaments over our fireplace. They were just little ani-mals, like the Wade ones. When I came downstairs one morning they were all in the middle of the floor, on the carpet, in a circle. When I saw them I thought, 'How did they get from the fireplace to there?'.

The only other thing was that just about the same time, I don't think it was the same day. I went into the linen cupboard - I'm not a tidy person but I know that the towels had been in a neat pile and they were completely rumpled up. Also, the valences of the beds had been folded nicely and they were all rumpled up. Nobody else had been in the cupboard.

When the children came home I said, 'We've got a poltergeist' and everybody laughed. I called it 'Fred'.

We were in the house for 20 years or so and nothing else happened. However, the family that lived in the house before us suffered a lot of tragedies - a divorce and a nasty accident. I don't know if that was anything to do with it.

The shadow

Ann had not long moved into her house when she began to notice strange dark shapes and shadows:

This is the story of two ghosts, each from different houses. The first ghost lived in our house near Roman Way. When I was reading a newspaper, a shadow would go across the paper as if someone was walking past. I would look up, but nobody was there and the shadow would still be there. Something black in the shape of a man would walk through the house. It never bothered me. One day, I was upstairs drying my hair when a figure came from behind me and walked out through the panelled wall between the windows. When he had gone I noticed that the light was swaying. I went into my son's room and asked him, 'Did you come into my room just then?' which was a silly question because he couldn't have walked out through the panelling.

I wasn't the only one who saw it. My eldest son said he had seen a dark shape several times but it didn't seem to faze him. My parents came to stay and my dad said to me, 'Have you got a ghost in this house?'. When I said that I thought we had, he said, 'Don't tell your mum or she'll never come and visit you again'.

I know the identity of the second ghost. I was friendly with a woman that I worked with for several years. Some afternoons, after work, she would come round to my house and we would have a cup of tea together. Within five minutes her sixteen-year old son would be banging on the front door. We would shout 'Go away' and he would come in with a big grin. Then he died, very tragically.

At that time I was having a terrible problem with the front door. You couldn't open it and then once you got it open, you couldn't shut it. You really had to pull it to open and you had to throw yourself at it to close it again. Soon after her son died, my friend came round to my house and there we were, both pushing and pulling at the front door. To our surprise, we were sitting down having a cup of tea and a natter and suddenly, the front door flew open. We both looked at each other.

After that, I never saw the first ghost again. My friend thought that perhaps her son had taken it with him.

Cowled and cold (Fernhill Heath)

Halfway between Droitwich and Worcester is the hamlet of Fernhill Heath. In medieval times it was surrounded by religious establishments, with an early church at Claines another at Martin Hussingtree, plus all the religious activity in Worcester. The following story in which a monk seems to have strayed from one of these institutions, was told at the Worcestershire Skills Show:

We lived in a little house in Fernhill Heath. We were miles away from anywhere, there were no houses near us. We could only see the chimneys of the next house. There was a lane running past our house but nobody ever walked down it because it didn't go anywhere.

My husband was alone in the house one night when he happened to look through the bow window. It was a winter's night with a white frost. In the front garden was a holly tree and he saw a figure emerge from the tree. He could just make out a cowled figure bent over. There was no light on the figure but a light seemed to be shining from the cowl on to whatever he was holding. The figure was gliding, not walking. He watched it the whole length of the garden until it disappeared on the far side. He went out but nothing was there.

White and shaking (A38)

The Copcut Elm is just outside Droitwich on the A38, where the road follows the line of the old Roman road. The inn was built in about 1806 as a coaching inn. The owner was the local landowner, John Amphlett - a descendent of his quarrelled with the villagers of Clent (see chapter on Clent). In 1992 the Copcut Elm was taken over by the Mad O'Rourke chain and renamed Trotter Hall. In *Haunted Pubs and Hotels of Worcestershire and its Borders,* Trotter Hall was one of the most haunted inns. Doors opened and closed of their own accord, the electrics went haywire, coins shot out of cigarette machines, various characters suddenly appeared and walked through walls, and cookers ignited of their own accord. One last incident comes from a young man who told this story at the Worcestershire Skills Show of 2004:

There was no light on the figure but a light seemed to be shining from the cowl on to whatever he was holding. (Fernhill Heath).

In the one room was a very long bar, with an ornamental cupboard that came from a church, it was part of the decor. One morning, I was doing some cleaning at the back of the bar with a colleague, then I had to go into the kitchen.

She said that she was working one end of the bar when she saw, standing behind the far end of the bar by the ornamental cupboard, the figure of a man. At first she could only see his top half because he was behind the bar, but she could see that he was short in stature and elderly, with grey hair. This figure went from behind the bar, and walked down to the other end of the room, then he went through the open doorway and walked the whole length of the pub. She cautiously followed him, keeping her distance, but he seemed to disappear. She searched the far end of the pub but nobody was there. She even went into the men's toilets. She thought perhaps somebody had opened the front door and he had come in that way, but it was locked.

All kinds of strange things happened there. Often, the electricity would suddenly be shut off at the mains for no reason.

The Mad O'Rourke chain has now sold Trotter Hall which has reverted to is original name.

Coaches and horses! (Martin Hussingtree)

After the Copcut Elm, the A38 runs straight through the scattered houses of Martin Hussingtree which was originally two separate villages, the manor of Martin and the manor of Hussingtree. In about 1280 they began to be listed as one place. These were two of the villages give to Pershore Abbey, then appropriated by Edward the Confessor and handed over to Westminster Abbey. One of the villagers says:

By Martin Hussingtree, is a big sweeping bend that's known as Sandy Way corner. It's a notorious corner, a number of vehicles have had accidents on that spot with some fatalities. We wondered if they had swerved to avoid the coach and horses that have been seen there several times. On the apex of the bend is a bridleway that leads to Martin Hussingtree church, and the coach of horses are said to come out of there. A lot of people have seen them, especially on New Year's Eve and Christmas Day. It's been a couple of years since the last accident.

The author would be glad to hear from anyone who has seen the coach and horses.

7. Evesham

vesham was once a place of great importance geographically, for it was in a loop of the river Avon and on the main road from Wales to London. It is famous for a great battle that took place there in 1265. Simon de Montfort believed that the king was too powerful and some of his authority should be passed to the barons. He raised an army of 5,000 and was on his way to London to fight the king's army when he decided to set up camp at Evesham. De Montfort was waiting for his son, also named Simon to join him.

Old records state that a barber (in those days barbers were often dentists and surgeons as well as hairdressers) was keeping watch from Evesham tower. Suddenly, he shouted that he could see the flags and banners of Simon's army, but as the army drew nearer de Montfort realised that they were mistaken, for his son had been defeated at Kenilworth and the approaching soldiers were using his insignia to trick de Montfort into a false security.

De Montfort's army was surrounded on three sides by the loop of the river Avon. The only bridge across the river was at Bengeworth but news came that this was blocked by the Earl of Mortimer. Their only escape was to the north, but the Earl of Gloucester's men held the ridge to the left and Prince Edward's troops were in front and to the right. De Montfort saw that the situation was hopeless and cried out 'God have mercy on our souls, for our bodies are theirs'. It was a dark morning and pouring with rain. His army charged up the hill to try to break through the ranks of the King's army, but it was no use and both he and his son, together with most of the army, were slaughtered. De Montfort's body was cut into pieces and his head sent to the Countess of Mortimer. Some of his remaining parts found a final resting place in the park behind the abbey. He did not die in vain, for he struck a blow for democracy which resulted in the founding of parliament.

The name of the hill was Greenhill, and 749 years later, a young lady by the name of Stella moved into a flat on that very hill:

In 1998 I moved into an early Victorian house on Greenhill that had been made into two flats. The first day that I moved in I thought I saw my flatmate's granddad. He was sitting in our rocking chair in a blue army uniform. I said, 'Hullo, how are you?' but he ignored me. I thought, 'Miserable old man'. My flat mate was in the kitchen, I went in and said, 'I have just seen your granddad'. She said, 'My granddad's not here'. I told her there was an old man in the lounge. She remarked, 'It must be the ghost'. She had seen him fairly often.

I saw him a lot. If you were in the lounge downstairs, watching telly, the couch would go down and you could feel him sitting next to you. He was always around and we named him George.

Our flat was upstairs and across the landing. One night, when I came back from the cinema, I was lifted a few centimetres into the air, and carried up the stairs! I felt quite safe at the time, it was only when I got in the flat and shut the door that I freaked out. I thought, 'What was that?!'. It only happened once.

The upstairs flat was haunted by a lady and a load of girls. My flat mate could see lots of little girls running round her bed at night, I didn't see them but I used to hear them rustling. One night, when I was in the flat on my own I heard them laughing. Our socks would be floating round the room. We would leave our shoes in a neat row but during the night they would be all rumpled. Every morning your name would be called to wake you up.

My flatmate and I had a room each, but during the first two weeks I was there I had to share a room with another girl. The door creaked at night so we would put a chair against it. We slept in a big double bed. I got in late one night, saw a lump in the bed, and I thought it was my flatmate, so I tiptoed round and got into bed very carefully so that I didn't disturb her. About two o'clock in the morning there was a knocking in the door, and my friend was shouting 'Let me in, what are you doing?'. When I looked at the other side of the bed, the lump had gone.

I asked my uncle, who is a clairvoyant, if he could do something and he said, 'If you're not scared, don't bother, just leave them'. To be quite honest, I wasn't really scared, more fascinated. It wasn't a nasty feeling and I didn't mind being in the flat on my own.

I was there for about a year. In the end I bought myself a flat, not because of the ghosts.

The Holy Prince

The various myths and legends regarding the founding of Evesham are well-known. Saint Egwin was Prince of the kingdom of Mercia but he set aside his princely titles and privileges to become a Christian evangelist. He ignored the dangers of the vast forests and swamps which then covered most of England, and walked the Cotswolds, Malverns and Welsh foothills to preach the gospel. Eventually, he became Bishop of Worcester. He especially condemned adultery and working on a Sunday which did not make him popular with the locals, and so he was accused of fraud and deceit. In an attempt to clear his name, he announced to his friends that he would go to Rome and see the Pope, 'not as a Bishop but as our Lord Jesus went before Pilate'. He insisted that heavy fetters were put on his feet, then he led his supporters to the banks of the Avon, to a place called Hurdingpool, and threw the key of his shackles into the middle of the river.

The story goes that after a long and difficult journey, the little party reached the river Tiber. Egwin went off to pray while his supporters decided to do

Whenever I go there it evokes in me the vison of two people ... They're quite clearly defined. (Near the Bell Tower, page 76).

some fishing. They caught a salmon, and when they cut it ready to be eaten, they found the key to St Egwin's fetters inside. Another version of the tale is that Egwin was invited to a meal with the Pope, a salmon was cut open on the table and there was the key. Egwin's shackles were unlocked and the Pope blessed Egwin who returned in triumph to Evesham.

However, this isn't the end of the story. Egwin vowed to found a monastery and was looking for a suitable place when he was approached by the swine-herd, Eof (or Eoves). One autumn morning, Eof had been sitting, watching his pigs and hogs at Hurdingpool when he had a vision. Again, the stories vary, some say it was a vision of the Virgin Mary, others that he saw three angels. Eof felt compelled to tell Egwin about his vision. There was already an ancient church there, where Egwin prayed. Again versions vary, perhaps he, too, saw the vision. Anyway, Egwin decided that this was where his monastery should be, which was founded in 701. Some versions say that the place was called Eof's ham(let) in honour of Eof, others that it was already known as Hethoome which became corrupted to Evesham.

How the two figures in the following story, from a young man by the name of Lawrence, come to be associated with Eoves, is anyone's guess:

I have been all over England, North America and Europe, working with photography and music and the only place where I have seen a distinct manifestation is in the churchyard at Evesham, between All Saints Church, St Lawrence's Church and the Bell Tower.

I feel that it's something to do with the story of Evesham, perhaps that of Eoves, the swineherd. Whenever I go there it evokes in me a vision of two people. I can see the coloured shapes of two figures, a man and a woman. They're quite clearly defined, the man is hunched and old, at least seventy. He has a walking stick and a large nose and he's in a green haze. The woman is also very old, she has a hood and is encased in a red haze.

They're walking together, quite normally. I don't speak to them, I just look at them in amazement. It's as though they abide within that area and some-thing incredible happened there with the result that their being is still around.

I have never felt like this before, ever.

Riots in the Market Place

Evesham Abbey became enormously rich and powerful, owning almost twice as much land and property as the ordinary people. In 1086 there were 67 monks. Despite being cut off from the houses and the surrounding countryside by strong walls, the Abbey ruled the town. In the 1300s the townsmen had to grind their corn in the Abbot's mills and bake their bread in his ovens; a pri-vate oven and several handmills were destroyed. The monks had special privileges so that they were outside the arm of the law. The all-important officers in the town were the bailiffs, and even here, the abbots tried to get their own men appointed. In the early 1500s Abbot Litchfield, the last Abbot, asked if John Matthews, his head chef, could be chosen as bailiff, but the citizens did not want their bailiff in the Abbot's kitchen. So the Abbot appointed another head chef so that John could take up the post of bailiff.

As a general rule, however, the citizens seemed to have been quite happy to be ruled by the Abbot and his successors. Evesham Abbey was appropriated by Henry VIII in 1540 when the monastery was demolished and the rights were handed over to Sir Philip Holby. Forty years later, in 1583, Queen Elizabeth questioned Sir Philip's rights to control the courts of the town. She appointed her own Royal Steward to oversee the courts. When the Queen's Steward wanted to enter a court in New Hall in 1585 he was kept out by great poles with iron spikes at the end. He decided to hold court in the market place, next to the New Hall. Egged on by their elders, small boys dragged a cart through the makeshift court, with a boy sitting on it, yelling, 'He preacheth, he preacheth'. Other boys were shouting, 'a steward' 'a court' 'a jury!'. A crowd of women surrounded the court, armed with stones. The court was hastily abandoned.

Although the poor of Evesham were not able to vote until about 1918, they were able to make their feelings known. Lord Coventry left a charity which distributed money to the poor of Evesham and in 1754, the distribution was delayed. There was rumour that the mayor was using the money to bribe voters so that he would be re-elected to Parliament. A mob was raised, they lit bonfires on the Market Place and the High Street and burned effigies of Sir John Rushout Bart, one of the two representatives on the parish responsible for distributing the money. They also stated that if he ever set foot in Evesham, they would throw him out of his coach.

Friends and Fiends

People often ask why two churches stand side by side in the centre of Evesham. A charter of 1604 and 1605 shows that the town had two parishes, that of All Saints and that of St Lawrence. There is, on Cowl Street, another church which, although not as old as the parish churches, has an even more eventful history of violence and murder. A Quaker Meeting House was on the site as long ago as 1655. It was rebuilt in brick in 1698, and inside are names scratched in the wood from between 1698 and 1712. The old burial ground has been converted into a garden but some of the old grave slabs remain, the earliest dating back to 1799.

The Quakers' correct name is the Society of Friends, but they were christened 'Quakers' because they trembled with emotion when they spoke. They were founded in about 1650, whipped up by the enthusiasm of George Fox. During the first few years they often resorted to outrageous methods to try to persuade people to convert. William Simpson ran naked through Evesham town centre although what this achieved is not recorded. At Claines, Susan Pearson dug up, from his grave, a man who had committed suicide and commanded him to live. She was surprised when there was no response. It is said that William Penn, the founder of Pennsylvania, encouraged the sect to become more reasonable.

The Friends believe that every man has, or may have, some direct experience of God in his soul. They had no desire to found a new sect, but the consequence of their beliefs is that vicars and ministers are redundant, an idea which was not very popular with the clergy. In 1655 George Hopkins, vicar of Evesham, preached such a tirade against them that an angry mob marched to Bengeworth and surrounded the meeting house.

How the Friends came to be treated in each town was up to the magistrate, and in Evesham they were treated very badly. They were fined, whipped and beaten. Their goods were confiscated and the men were put into a dark hole of a prison, beneath what was until recently, 'Priceless Shoes', for weeks on end. They had no light, fresh air or sanitation. The hole leading down to the dungeon from the street stank so much that people could not bear to be near it. Two women asked if they could visit and for this, they were placed in the stocks for 15 hours on a freezing cold night. One of them died soon afterwards. A sixty-year old Quaker was tied to the back of a horse and dragged along until he was near to death. George Fox visited Evesham several times. On his first visit, the magistrate heard that Fox was coming and made a pair of high stocks especially for him, but Fox managed to slip away.

The lady who told the following story lives at Naunton Beauchamp, but she belongs to the Society of Friends and attends the Cowl Street church:

I went into the room where a meeting was being held and definitely behind my chair were two women all in grey. They were having a conversation, one woman said she had not been feeling too well. Then they disappeared. I told one of the other Quakers what I had seen, and she had seen them too.

Lightning in the Lenches

Rous Lench, Church Lench, Lenchwick and Atch Lench, Ab Lench and Sheriffs Lench, are spread across the greenest of Worcestershire countryside between Evesham and Inkberrow. Church Lench is mentioned in the Domesday Book of 1086. Rous Lench takes its name from the Rous family who held the village and lived at the Court from 1382 to 1721, the present Court was rebuilt in 1840. Rous Lench has a spectacular church which is basically Norman. It has Romanesque zig-zag work, carved shafts, intricate capitals and the well-preserved carvings include a rare sculpture of Christ in Majesty. It also has carved Saxon stones, and monuments going back to 1611.

Margaret took her mother to visit Rous Lench church in the late 1960s, then:

> I took mother for a drive round the Lenches, where we both saw a phantom blue car. One minute I was driving behind it and the next minute it had gone. I drove up and down the lane twice, but was unable to see where it could have disappeared. My local historian friend said we had experienced a 'time slip'. As I owned a blue car I wondered if it was some kind of warning but as nothing happened to me and my blue car and I forgot all about it.

Stella and her husband were driving through the Lenches one summer evening at about nine o'clock.

> It was just getting dark. My husband was behind the wheel. There was a light travelling behind us and getting closer and closer, it looked like the light of a motorbike until the light came through the back window, through the car and disappeared. My husband said, 'What was that?' He was really shaken. He had to stop the car and walk up and down for a bit. I inspected the car but it hadn't done any damage.

In *Midland Spirits and Spectres*, Barrie Roberts writes about various mysterious lights and the following is one quotation from three pages of descriptions and possible explanations:

> The movement of underground rock formations creates electromagnetic 'blobs' that discharge into the atmosphere above ground. They appear only when the right kind of rocks are moving, they glow in the dark, they hover and dart about and they shine in daylight.

Odious odours (Aldington)

Just to the east of Evesham is the little village of Aldington. The Manor (ie not only a house but all the rights) of Aldington was granted to the abbey of Evesham in 709 by the King of the Mercians and the King of the Angles. The Benedictine monks built a great farmhouse there. In about 1539 it was appropriated by Henry VIII and afterwards was either rented to, or sold by, a series of eminent gentleman. One of them was William Courteen, a prominent merchant trader and an honourable and saintly man. He acquired Barbados and spent a great deal of money trying to colonise it, but his settlers were thrown out in 1629 and it was a financial disaster. William also lent money to James I and Charles I who never repaid him, with the result that he went bankrupt.

When Maureen was about fifteen she was baby-minding in Aldington Manor with a girl friend.

I can remember it quite clearly. We had probably been frightening ourselves with ghost stories as girls of that age do. The first thing was that a load of soot came down the fireplace. It was loads, it simply poured down. The little boy who had been asleep upstairs woke up and ran out of the room. We put him back to bed, but when we sat down again a plate jumped off the dresser. My friend went upstairs to check on the little boy but he had fallen asleep. She came back in and suddenly, the whole room was full of this terrible smell. It was absolutely awful. We did everything we could to try and get rid of it, we opened the windows but it wouldn't go. We had arranged for our boyfriends to come and they arrived at that moment. When they came in, the one said he felt really sick from the smell and they wouldn't stay. It lasted for about fifteen minutes and disappeared just as quickly as it had arrived. It didn't suddenly fade away, it just went.

I always felt the manor had a strange atmosphere. I didn't baby sit any more, I was too nervous. Although I'm interested in that sort of thing, when you come face to face with it, it does put you off.

Aldington Park is said to be haunted. A man who lives nearby was walking through the park at night when he heard a strange ticking noise behind him. He turned round and saw that the noise appeared to be coming from a small circular light. The light followed him through the park.

A house near to Aldington Park and was built just over 20 years ago on the site of some old pigsties belonging to Aldington Priory. Both the mother and daughter have had inexplicable experiences there, the mother says:

The house had just been built when my husband and I came in late one Saturday night. I went into the bedroom and I said, 'One of the cats had done something in here'. I spent ten minutes moving furniture looking to see what the cat had done. I went downstairs and said to my husband, 'Can you come in this bedroom, there's a horrible smell. It was quite overpowering. When I went back into the room the smell had gone!

The daughter adds:

My dad must have been away because, when I was about twelve, I remember sleeping with my mother. I always had a strange feeling in my mum's bedroom. I woke up in the middle of the night and I saw an elderly man at the end of the bed looking at me intently. I thought, 'Oh God', then 'I'm imagining this' so I put my head under the bedclothes for a few minutes but when I looked out again he was still there. He was tall, thin and quite wrinkled, he had grey hair and strong, angular features with dark eyes. I could only see him to halfway down but he appeared to be all in black with long black clothes. He looked a bit like a monk except that his head was exposed. It wasn't a fuzzy vision at all, the man was quite clear. After that, I went under the bedclothes and didn't come up again.

Hide and seek and a surprise find (The Littletons)

On the north-east borders of Evesham are the three Littleton villages, North, Middle and South All three villages passed into the hands of Evesham monastery early in the eighth century. Abbot John Ombersley, in 1376, built the huge, 140-feet long tithe barn, now owned by the National Trust.

The well-known Lyttleton family (Viscount Cobham at Hagley Hall is a descendent) at one time held property in the Littletons and it is said that they decided to adopt the name. Sir Thomas Littleton (1410-81) was born at Frankley, then in Worcestershire, and became a lawyer in London. In 1481 he published a study on property laws which became the basis for a whole branch of the legal system on property. He was so important that he is buried in Worcester Cathedral. Stephen Lyttleton also has a claim to fame as one of the conspirators in the gunpowder plot. He founded a tradition in dubious activities which has been continued by the siting of Long Lartin maximum security prison in South Littleton.

Both Middle and South Littleton have 12th century churches, but very few remnants of these early churches remain and both have been modernised down the centuries. The Littleton's were once famous for their flagstone quarries and in the churchyards are many ornate headstones sculpted by the expert craftsmen.

Unfortunately, Julie cannot remember whether the following story comes from South or Middle Littleton:

It was about 16 years ago, I was about nine years old and I was with my family in the Social Club one evening. From what I can remember, this was in the recreational ground, next to the Church. I was playing hide and seek outside with my two cousins. My older cousin went off to hide and after several minutes my other cousin and I went to look for him. We ran down a footpath which led to a small lane down the outside of the churchyard.

As we ran around a bend in the path, we both stopped in our tracks, screamed and ran back to the club. Once there, out of breath, we described what we had both seen - which was the same thing. There were about ten girls, all with long hair and they seemed to be dressed in night clothes. They were very grey in appearance and were looking straight towards us. About five girls were standing up, and the others were kneeling on the floor in front of them.

We told our parents what we had seen but they dismissed it and told us to go back out and play. After several minutes we decided to go back down the path - my older cousin was still hiding and we wanted to know if he'd seen anything. When we turned the bend where we'd previously seen the girls, all we saw was a puddle.

After finding my cousin, we asked if he'd seen anything and he said that although he hadn't seen anything, about five minutes beforehand he had heard a man's voice shouting from the path several times. He described the man as being angry and his tones echoed.

My cousin and I still talk about this experience and often wonder what history lay behind what we had seen.

It seems as if they encountered some kind of timeslip and came across a group of Victorian girls having their photograph taken. Many of the old photographs show girls standing at the back and others kneeling in front. Until the last few decades it was necessary to keep perfectly still while having your photograph taken, which could explain the annoyance in the man's voice. If anyone has a photograph which answers the description, both the author and Julie would be interested to see it.

Tracking the ghost (North Littleton)

The narrator of the following story moved into 'a lovely old house in North Littleton' in the late 1950s:

When you stripped the walls down it was all wattle and daub. There wasn't a straight wall in the house. We never altered anything, we kept it the old way, even the bread oven.

There was a benevolent presence. The latch of the door used to go up and sometimes the door would open slowly. Both my husband and I saw it at different times. Now, how does a latched door open unless someone lifts the latch? We had a dog and before the latch would lift, the dogs hackles would rise. When we moved in, we had a baby sitter as my youngest was a month old and his brother was two. The baby sitter saw the latch of the door lift up and when he opened it, no-one was there. He was quite frightened and glad to see us when we got home!

We were only in the house for a month or so when there was a movement upstairs, as if someone was walking about. I went up to investigate but both the boys were fast asleep. I know that children can feign sleep but they really were asleep.

Objects used to move round. We used to put something on the telly, an ornament or something, and the next day it would disappear. My husband would think that I had moved it and I would think that he had moved it.

Because it was an old house, the bathroom was downstairs so if, during the night, one of the boys wanted to go to the loo, he had to go out of his bedroom and down the stairs. My youngest son saw someone standing in the door of the bathroom. The ghost wouldn't let him past. My husband decided enough was enough so he stood in the bathroom and said in a loud voice,

'You can haunt this house if you want to but if you frighten my children I will burn this house down and then you'll have nowhere to haunt'. After that, things calmed down a bit.

As the boys grew older they wanted a train track down so we boarded in the beams, put a carpet down and laid the track in the loft. From that moment on the ghost disappeared. We wondered if we had boarded it in.

It was a very happy house and we loved living there. We moved away, but my son was so fond of the house that many years later, he decided to get engaged outside the house and so he took his girlfriend there and went down on one knee to propose. Then he knocked on the door and the present occupiers very kindly gave him a guided tour. The house had changed quite a bit.

The good life! (Offenham)

About a mile west of South Middleton is the curious village of Offenham. The Main Street is full of black and white thatched cottages. Seven of them, named appropriately 'Long Thatch', are under one thatch and date from about 1643. Main Street is a cul-de-sac ending in an 80 foot high Maypole, the tallest in England! Young ladies still dance around the Maypole, as they have done for hundreds of years. Mayday festivities were banned by Oliver Cromwell but restored by Charles II. In gratitude, for the past 300 years or so, Offenham ladies have been dancing round on May 29th, instead of May I, Charles II's birthday. The mayday celebrations now last for a week.

The visitor to this tiny, sleepy village may be surprised to know that one of the main roads to London once passed through it, and that it was the administration centre for the surrounding villages. Offenham was given to Evesham Abbey in about 703 or 709 but seized by the wicked Duke Alfere in 976. However, it seems to have been returned to the Abbey, as it became a favourite place of residence for the abbots. In the twelfth century a large residence was built on the site of Court Farm, and a deer park provided so that the abbots could enjoy venison for their dinner. Most of the Abbey's properties were rented out, but not those at Offenham, as the abbots themselves liked to stay here.

Offenham is said to be the cradle of market gardening. In 1852, James Myatt arrived from Camberwell. He took 70 acres of agricultural land and opened the first market garden. Before James arrived, farmers would grow twenty acres or so of one staple crop. James shocked the local farmers by introducing new produce, for example strawberries, cabbage, and rhubarb; and growing them in patches as small as a quarter of an acre. The strawberry fields across the Evesham plain are probably the result of Myatt's enterprise.

Venison, strawberries and Maypole dancing! We can sympathise with the monk who seems to be reluctant to leave! We have to thank a young man, Marcus, for the following story. He went to a party at one of Offenham's ancient dwellings and wrote down the following ghost story that he heard. The owners of the property have asked to remain nameless:

Over the years, there has been a lot of unusual activity in our home. It's not unknown to be alone in the house and hear creaks and bangs. It's due to the age, I suppose, - but footsteps and muffled talking is another thing! A few years ago we had friends round for a meal and some drinks - you know the sort of thing - well, we were all sitting, eating, when suddenly one of my guests dropped her knife and fork. She looked pale and cold, she just stared at the opposite wall. When I asked her what was wrong she said that a figure almost like a shadow, had walked from behind her, passed across the room and through the wall opposite. It reminded her of a monk. Well, straight away I fetched her a glass of water.

During the evening we would notice that whoever stood next to the fireplace kept fidgeting and asking if there was a draft anywhere, (which there wasn't).

After the party, nothing was mentioned again until a few weeks later, when all of us began to feel a cold spot by the fire. It unnerved me a little so I asked the same lady round who had seen the mystery figure vanish through the wall.

When the conversation came round to the mysterious happenings, I asked her about the night at the party and said that we had since felt a cold spot by the fire. She asked, 'Do you mean, where the little boy was sitting?'. Well, this shocked me because there had not been any boy in the house that night. We talked about him a bit more and she said she thought it was a shame for him because of his deformity on his face and the tatty clothes he wore.

Perhaps it was the little boy who was making the footsteps and other noises that we heard.

We still hear the footsteps and feel cold spots, also things get moved around, but it's our home and we have learned to live with it. It's part of us now and we want to keep it that way.

8. KIDDERMINSTER

idderminster was in existence when William the Conqueror compiled his Domesday Book in 1086. It stands on the river Stour, the waters of which have special properties and contain fuller's earth and iron. The dyes created using these waters were said to be especially long-lasting, consequently Kidderminster became famous for its carpets. The industry was founded in about 1730 but there are now, sadly, only a few carpet manufacturers left in the town.

The great church of St Mary's is separated from the town by the Kidderminster by-pass.

Tradition says that the church was not originally intended to be on the present site, but on high ground on the opposite side of the river Stour. However, each night the stones laid during the preceding day were carried by angels to the rock on which the church now stands, so that the builders eventually changed their plans (the same legend is associated with many religious buildings in Britain, including Lincoln Cathedral). The original site is known as 'Cussfield', said to be a corruption of 'cursed field'. In the old church was the carving of an angel holding a fragment of an arch, said to depict the old tradition. Although the original carving has disappeared, there is a stone copy on the restored tower.

The vicars or ministers of most churches pray for a religious revival, but when one comes along it often destroys the fabric of the church. This has happened twice in St Mary's lifetime, once when the puritan Richard Baxter ripped out all the church icons and decorations (fortunately leaving some fine monuments and brasses), and again in the Victorian era when the zealous Victorians 'modernised' the building. However, it has managed to keep the fifteenth century tower and a fourteenth century chancel.

Scandals at St Mary's

St Mary's is best known as the home of Richard Baxter.

On the western side of the Kidderminster Bypass stands a life-sized white marble statue of a man with long hair and flowing robes, one arm raised as if to hail the traffic. This can give the motorist quite a shock and may account for the ghost reported by a number of casual visitors. The statue (by Sir Thomas Brock) is of Richard Baxter who was minister at St Mary's for 25 years with a few breaks. He was born in Shropshire in 1625 and educated at Worcester. Always a serious, dedicated young man, he chose to enter the ministry.

In 1641, a year before the outbreak of Civil War, the parishioners of Kidderminster were having problems with their vicar, George Dance. They described him as 'an ignorant, weak man, a frequenter of alehouses and at times, drunk'. Worse, he kept a curate who was a 'common tippler, drunkard, railer and trader in unlawful marriages'. The parishioners wanted to get rid of Dance, but he was keen to keep his job. A compromise was arranged. Dance said that if he could stay, he would get rid of the curate and pay £60 a year out of the church profits to support a lecturer. This was agreed, the curate went and Baxter arrived as lecturer. He came to a hotbed of superstition and ignorance, for example, many believed that God was the sun and the Holy Ghost was the moon.

The following year the conflict between the Royalists and the Puritans began. Baxter sympathised with many policies of the Parliamentarians, and was one of a growing army of preachers who felt they had been especially sent by Providence to overthrow spiritual wickedness in high places. His beliefs brought him into conflict with the authorities and the townsfolk. First, he was censored by the Royalists for preaching against them. Secondly, he agreed with the Parliamentarians that churches should have no pictures and no statues, nothing to distract the congregation from their worship. However, the parishioners of Kidderminster were not happy about having their beautiful religious icons destroyed and when Baxter tried to demolish the carved crucifixion on top of the cross in the churchyard, he was attacked by an angry mob, shouting 'Down with the Roundhead'. He escaped to Coventry and remained there during the Civil War.

The Parliamentarians were the victors and Baxter was able to return to his parish in 1647, remarking that 'the rabble' had all gone into the King's army and been slain'. Baxter should have lived in the splendid vicarage but it was occupied by George Dance and Baxter refused to turn him out. He lived instead in the humble attic of another house on the north side of the High Street. He threw himself, body and soul, into the task of evangelising the town. He was eloquent and caring, he visited the sick and, as there was no doctor in the town, he acquired a great skill in medicine. Typical of Baxter is a remark that he made when he saw someone being led away to prison: 'There, but for the grace of God goes Richard Baxter'. His congregation was so large that galleries had to be built in the church. He converted the inhabitants of Kidderminster from a lawless and amoral community into 'as godly a people as any in the kingdom'.

Baxter was not only a great preacher, he was also an influential writer. He invented popular Christian literature, in fact his most famous work, The Saints Everlasting Rest is still read today.

Unfortunately for Baxter, Cromwell died, Charles II came to the throne and Baxter was in disgrace for his Protestant views. However, knowing how powerful Baxter had become, the King and the Archbishop offered him a post as

Bishop of Hereford. Baxter believed that all ministers were equal, and a Bishop was no higher in God's eyes than a curate. He therefore turned down the offer, saying that he wanted to continue his work in Kidderminster. He asked if he could be given a licence to preach but the authorities refused. Instead, the licence was given to the old incompetent minister, George Dance, who had always held Royalist views. Dance owed Baxter a favour, as the latter had refused to turn him out of the vicarage when first appointed, but Dance actually blocked his reinstatement. Baxter was banned and went into retirement. Charged with preaching against the Church of England, he came before 'Bloody' Judge Jeffreys in 1684, who wished to have him whipped through London 'at the cart's tail'. Instead, Baxter was sentenced to 18 months in prison. He died in 1691.

The Baxter Congregational Church has been built in his memory. The site in Bull Ring Street was purchased in 1694 and the church was rebuilt in 1753 and again in about 1824. A larger church with a steeple was built in front of the old one in 1884.

Julie suspects that the kindly old Rev Baxter pays a visit there from time to time and says:

> One evening last year (2004) a friend of mine went with his wife to a musical evening at the Baxter Church. Normally, they sat downstairs, but they were late arriving and church was full so they had to go upstairs into the balcony. He sat there, listening to the music, when all of a sudden it went very cold up there. He felt so cold that a ring that never comes off his finger, fell to the floor. He bent down to look for it but couldn't find it anywhere. He whispered to his wife that his ring had fallen off and he couldn't find it. She said, 'Never mind, we'll wait until after the show, then we'll look for it'. They waited until people started to leave then he looked down and there, between his feet, was the ring. He knew it wasn't there before.

Just the trousers

The Severn Stars Inn is one of the most haunted public houses in England and the licensee will only be too happy to regale you with a story or two. It has such a macabre reputation that Kidderminster Ghost Walks meet there and while they were waiting for latecomers a couple of years ago the bell summoning the licensee rang all by itself.

Many of the sales assistants in the town centre report inexplicable bumps and groans. Near the Baxter Congregational Church is a well-known store and a retired sales assistant says:

> I worked there in the early 1970s and we had all kinds of weird things happening. When we went into the stock room we could hear bumping

and rustling in one of the corners as if someone was there. A manager was working overtime one evening when he saw a pair of trousers walking up the stairs — there was no top half, just the trousers. One of the sales assistants, Janet, regularly saw a ghostly lady there.

Creeping doors

The following story is told by Joyce, a long-term resident of the town:

Opposite the main police station in Habberley Road was a lovely house, The Elms. It had once been a gentlemen's' residence and it had cellars and dressing rooms. There was a handicapped school in Stourport-on-Severn and they were moving into a new school being built in the grounds of the Elms. It was decided that they should stay in the old house while their new school was being built.

The old caretaker came with them and early every morning she went to the Elms to clean for them. In the Elms was a long corridor with a lot of doors and several landings with large cupboards. As she finished cleaning each room she would close the door and move on to the next but when she looked back, the door would always be open. This also happened to the cupboard doors when she cleaned on the landing. In the end it got on her nerves. She wouldn't go in on her own, her husband had to go with her every time.

After the new school had been built The Elms was used for storage. Some of the younger ladies were sent over to fetch a few items and they saw something that frightened them so much that afterwards they would never go in the house in their own. They would never tell anyone what they saw.

Apparitions in Mill Street

Near the town centre and running alongside the river Stour is the ancient Mill Street, well known by Kidderminster folk because of the hospital at its northern end, between the road and the Stour. Liz was a nurse there:

Mill Street Hospital was built as general hospital in the 1850s. The place had the reputation of being haunted, as most hospitals do, particularly by the ghost of one surgeon, John Stretton, who actually died on duty in the hospital. He was reputed to visit the wards at two in the morning. You always expected to see him in the early hours.

We used to keep the curtains round the beds closed at nights so that the lights didn't shine on the patients. I was on duty one night in one of the wards and I saw all the curtains drawn aside one by one as if someone was walking through the ward. I thought it must be a draught. I got up and checked the windows but they were all closed, and the door wasn't open.

Graham used to run the Flamingo Pub in Mill Street during the 1970s:

Further along the road was the Coach and Horses pub. Do you know, we heard the coach and horses going up our road several times. This would happen about midnight or in the early hours of the morning. They used to wake me up in the night. You could hear the horses hooves galloping and the wheels rumbling.

The ghost in the cellar

Kidderminster's spacious Methodist Church was built in 1911 on the Birmingham Road, next to the ringway. Marjorie told the following story at a meeting there:

My house was built in about 1850. When you are going out of the kitchen into the dining room you have the cellar door on your left. About nine months after I had moved in, I was standing in the kitchen when I saw a man in front of the cellar door, all in black. He had a tall black hat, and a long jacket. He was so real. His eyes seemed to be moving and looking round. It so happened that the little boy from next door was with me. He kept asking me if I had talked to the man in the cellar, his cellar is next door to mine.

Although I had a strange man in my house, I wasn't in the least bit scared. I took my eyes away from him for a second to push a chair under the table and when I looked again, he had gone. I have now lived in the house for 20 years and have never seen him since. That was my one and only paranormal experience.

Franchester walks again (Paddington House, New Road)

Young Craig Shell is sensitive to these kinds of things. If there is a ghost about, Craig will find it. He can also sense people's thoughts and feelings and his aim in life is to become a parapsychologist.

A few years ago I had an office at Paddington House, New Road in Kidderminster. I was working late one night and I knew no-one else was in the building because all doors were locked. At about midnight, I needed the toilet, I came out from my office on the first floor, and walked on to the landing towards the toilet. Suddenly, the figure of a lady, dressed in a worn red and white dress, appeared about 3 metres away on the stairs. I would say she was aged about 20 or 22 years old, and I must say she was pretty. I can remember clearly that in one hand she was holding some books while with the other she kept pointing towards my office and she was crying. I was not scared but interested and was about to speak to her when she walked down the stairs and disappeared through the wall.

I told the owner of the complex who wasn't that surprised. He said "Franchester" has been seen before. The last tenants of my office were so intrigued that they did some research and found out that Paddington House was an old carpet factory. My office used to be the night watchman's room.

The story is that the night watchman supposedly raped "Fran", a young carpet weaver. She fell pregnant and decided to commit suicide by jumping off the stairs on the third floor, landing to her death. The watchman disposed of the body by cutting it up and placing it in the factory waste.

Every time I went to my office I always felt a warm presence which must have been "Fran". I'm glad to say that I haven't picked up on the night watchman, he was middle-aged and must have been an evil and twisted man.

So, if ever you go to Paddington House, just remember you are not alone, the presence of Fran will always be there.

Strange events in Summer Place

As the A456 Kidderminster to Bewdley Road leaves the bypass. it becomes Bewdley Hill. Where Blakebrook and Sutton Road cross the hill is a line of houses known as Summer Place. A past occupant says:

These houses have quite an interesting history. My house was built in the mid 1700s, when a group of businessmen got together and pooled their money in order to build houses. As each house was finished, they pulled a name out of a hat and that person had the house. This went on until everyone in the group had a house.

I only lived there for 18 months. My eldest daughter was two and she slept in an attic bedroom at the top of the house. We used to hear her chattering away but we took no notice until she started telling us that a lady came into her room at night and woke her up.

While I was in that house, I often had the feeling that I was being watched. We kept hearing a baby crying but there was no baby in any of the neighbouring houses. Sometimes, my husband said that he could hear a rustling noise like that of a long dress.

When we did some redecorating we uncovered an early wallpaper and after that, these strange events began to get worse.

The dogs used to act strangely. Their eyes used to move in unison and they used to watch something high up on the wall. During the redecorating we uncovered an old door there, it had once been the top of the staircase but the staircase had been turned round.

My husband is convinced that someone tried to push him down the stairs twice. The one time he was decorating the stairs and balancing on a ladder and he swears that someone tried to push him over the banisters. Another time he was in the loft, seeing to some bats that had got in, and he says that someone tried to push him down the stairs.

A lady lived next door for six months and she said that the ghost used to visit her and she used to talk to it. The ghost wore a long black dress and had a scarf over her head. Her name was Elizabeth and she had died in childbirth, she had waited many years for the baby and it was a great tragedy.

A friend of a friend lived in the house on the other side, and I heard that she moved out because of the strange goings-on. She heard weird noises and had the feeling that she was being watched, but worst of all was the sensation that she wasn't welcome there, whatever was in the house wanted her to get out. We reckon that the ghost had come from the house on their other side, two doors away from me, because they were doing a lot of renovating and we reckoned they had disturbed the ghost and it had gone next door for a bit of peace and quiet.

Tragedies at Harvington Hall

Behind the large grim, red-bricked facade of Harvington Hall is one of the most exciting histories in Worcestershire. If some of the folk who lived there during the late 1500s and 1600s had been caught by the authorities, they would have been arrested, hung, and while they were still alive, they would have been cut down, their torsoes cut open and their insides ripped out. Their crime? - they were Roman Catholic priests. Their persecution began in the time of Henry VIII and reached fever pitch in the 1670s, whipped up by Titus Oates. He was one of life's failures but managed to be ordained as a priest in Spain, came back to England and announced that the Catholics were planning to kill the popular Charles II and put his Roman Catholic brother, James, on the throne. Thousands of Roman Catholics fled from London in fear of their lives.

Harvington Hall was one of the Roman Catholic homes of Worcestershire. The road from the Hall ran straight into the centre of Chaddesley Corbett so that the staff were able to see who was coming. The approach of the bailiff and his men resulted in any priest or priests in the house being rushed into their hiding places. Harvington Hall is honeycombed with priests hiding places, stairs lift up, fireplaces open, a book cupboard has a false wall, even the altar has a concealed trap door nearby. It is said that Harvington Hall has more priests' hiding places than any other building in England.

One of the priests who once lived here was Father Kemble, famous for taking a last pipe with his gaoler before his execution. Another was Father Wall who was discovered at nearby Rushock Court and hanged, drawn and quartered on Red Hill in Worcester. He was the last English martyr. The persecutions abated in 1685 when James sued Titus Oates for £100,000 in damages and had him whipped through the streets of London with 3,000 lashes.

There are many ghost stories about Harvington Hall. Father Kemble's ghost has been seen in the cafeteria. A dark shape walks through the rooms at night. School children see faces at the windows of locked rooms. The daughter of Jessie Love heard an unusual story from her mother:

Jessie Love lived in Stratford and there are still members of the Love family living around there. In 1914 she was a young girl working in a team of ladies going round stately homes doing repairs. They would spend several days in each house.

The team went to Harvington Hall where she was working on the draperies and curtains. In the house is a long staircase and a balcony, the girls were working in a room on the left. After a few days they got to know all the staff except one, a lady in a long black dress who, early every morning, walked along the balcony and into the mistresses' room. They didn't see her during the rest of the day. They mentioned this to the woman who looked after the house and she said, 'Oh, you have seen our resident ghost!'.

At the back of Harvington Hall is a separate building, in Victorian times it was used as a schoolroom. The ghost of a female schoolteacher has been seen there several times. In 1823 the building comprised two cottages and an upstairs chapel.

The altar was hollow and the priest kept several odds and ends inside it, round the back, out of sight. There were priest's vestments, books and a brass box. In 1884 Mrs Anne Parkes was doing a spot of spring cleaning round the back of the altar and she saw something glittering through the chinks in the panelling,. She told the priest but he was just off to Grafton and he said he would look into it when he came back. When he returned, he was too tired. That night, the cottages and the chapel burned down. Among the wreckage was a bundle of smouldering metal, hastily thrown into the moat.

Years later, when the moat was cleaned, a bundle was found containing bits of charred gold lace and half-melted decorative pieces of metal. It seems that the Harvington treasure, carefully hidden by the old priests, had come to a sad end.

9. THE MALVERNS AND THE SUCKLEY HILLS

he dramatic range of the Malvern Hills has been the inspiration for innumerable mysteries and legends. For example, there's the ancient story of the giant who lived with his wife in a cave on the Malverns. One day, he looked down at the village of Colwall and saw his wife talking to a man whom he presumed to be her lover. In a rage, he threw a huge boulder at her. To this day, the stone is said to cover her body.

Some of the legends may contain a grain of truth. The famous Witch of Endor is alleged to have lived in its forests, though seems extremely unlikely. There are tales of terrible battles - the British Camp is said to have been, in 50 AD, the site of the last battle of Caractacus against the Romans. The Victorian historian, Rev W S Symonds, wrote that Druids and Bards assembled on the hills to worship the sacred mistletoe, they lit bonfires and sacrificed snow-white bulls. There are stories of saints, Malvern Priory Church has a series of pictures in glass showing Saint Werstan who founded an oratory there in the third century.

Many of the springs and wells of Malvern were reputed to have magical properties, in fact Great Malvern may have been founded to serve the visitors to St Ann's well. Its waters healed skin and eye diseases and the name may come from Anu, a Celtic water goddess. The well is still in existence. The Devil's Well lies in the Tumuli Valley, in Puck's Wood. Puck was a mischievous spirit and one of his tricks was to entice people off the beaten track into bogs and wild heathland. His usual method was to light a fire in a remote place which travellers would mistake for the lights of house. The modern explanation is that these were self-igniting combustible gases escaping from damp places. In Chase Road is Pits Spring or Moorall's Well, which was said to be, in the 1600s, ' like the Pool of Bethsada by reason of the number of sick people brought to lie on its margin'. The booklet,Springs, Spouts, Fountains and Holy Wells of the Malvern Hills identifies more than 80 of these sources of water, and many of them are associated with saints and magical cures.

A woman scorned

In medieval times, most of the Malvern Hills were covered in trees, described as 'so much overrun with wood as to be called ... a wilderness'. Before William the Conqueror arrived in 1066, it is believed to have been owned by a Saxon, Brictric Maewe, son of Algar, a great English lord. Like other Saxon nobles, he lost his estates to the Norman conquerors of 1066 but, according to legend, in Brictric's case, there was a little more to it than that.

Brictric was young, charming, intelligent and handsome, and whenever Edward the Confessor (1042-1066) needed to send someone to do a spot of delicate negotiating, it was Brictric that he chose. Brictric was therefore sent over to France, to the court of Baldwin, Count of Flanders.

Now, the Count had a daughter named Matilda or Maud. Although she was less than five feet tall, what she lacked in height she made up for in temperament. Matilda fell madly in love with Brictric, but he would have nothing to do with her and returned to England. However, the Duke of Normandy took a liking to Matilda and asked for her hand in marriage but Matilda turned him down. The Duke was not accustomed to rejection, he was furious, and the next Sunday he waited for her outside Church and when she emerged, he gave her a smack. The Count was outraged and started gathering an army together but Matilda told him not to bother, she had decided to marry the Duke of Normandy after all.

Unfortunately, for Brictric, the Duke of Normandy became William the Conqueror and Matilda was crowned Queen of England in 1068. Legend says that on the very day of the coronation, Brictric was attending the consecration of a chapel by Bishop Wulstan, when Matilda's soldiers arrived and arrested him. His estates became the property of the queen and Brictric was thrown into Winchester prison, where he remained until he died.

The cursed shadow

In the late 1800s, Rev Symonds of Malvern wrote that a friend had showed him a bundle of old papers in his attic, and on examination he discovered the following story:

During the 1400s a young monk from Malvern Priory blotted his copybook by marrying a girl to save her from an unwelcome marriage, and, even worse, he was involved in a family feud and murdered the villain. As a punishment, he was ordered by the Prior of Malvern to climb up Raggedstone Hill every day on his hands and knees.

Before the year was out, he stood on top of the hill, stretched out his arms and cried: 'My curse be on thee, thou Heaven-blasting hill, and on those which laid this burden on me and on all that be like as they are ... May thy shadow and my shadow never cease to fall upon them ...'. After uttering the curse, he died.

The curse is thought to refer to those upon whom the shadow of Raggedstone Hill falls. Examples are said to be the Prior of Malvern, who died soon afterwards, Sir John Oldcastle, a Roman Catholic priest who was burned at Smithfield, and Cardinal Wolsey, who failed to persuade the Pope to annul Henry VIIs marriage to Catherine of Aragon.

These were the days before copyright, and, scandalously, Grinrod, a well-known Victorian author, rewrote the story which became a best-seller and he received all the credit for it.

The tale is so well known that any apparition tends to be labelled as the tragic monk. This story comes from Hollybush, on the lower eastern slopes of Raggedstone Hill.

We had been living here for only a short time when I thought I saw some-one go past the window. He had grey hair and he was about the same height as my husband - five feet eight inches. I opened the front door but no-one was there. I thought, 'They haven't gone into the garden, surely' and so I went to have a look out the back but nobody was about.

Some time later my husband was in the sitting room and he said, 'I'm sure I saw someone go past the window just then'. I mentioned to him that I had had a similar experience.

Later still my son was sitting at the table in front of the window and he remarked that he had seen someone go past.

I happened to mention this to a lady who has lived in the area for many years. She said, 'Oh, that's the monk from Little Malvern Priory going up the hill on his hands and knees'. It didn't look like a monk to me and he certainly wasn't down on his hands and knees!

The scandalous Prior

The oldest building in Great Malvern is the magnificent Priory Church, bought by the townsfolk for £20 when Henry VIII dissolved the monasteries. It's one of the grandest parish churches in England today.

The Priory was founded in 1085 by the hermit, Alwy. He hid himself in the Malvern hills to be alone, but, unfortunately, he was joined by about 300 people who also wanted to be alone, resulting in the Priory. Eight centuries ago it was at the heart of a scandal that rocked Europe. Alwy put his Priory in the care of Westminster Abbey, but the Bishop of Worcester considered the Priory to be his property. The Bishop of Worcester discovered, in 1282, that the prior, William de Ledbury, was keeping 22 women at various houses and farms round about, consequently the Bishop deposed him and excommunicated his supporters. The monks elected another Prior and sent him to the Abbot of Westminster to be blessed.

However, instead of blessing the new Prior, the Abbot clapped him into prison together with all his supporters, saying that the monks did not have the authority to depose one Prior and elect another. The Bishop of Worcester issued excommunication after excommunication and he appealed both to the king and the Pope. The king took the part of the Abbot. Eventually, William de

Ledbury was reinstated (no-one knows what happened to his women) even though he was totally unsuited to be Prior, simply because the Abbot wanted to assert his authority. The supporters of de Ledbury were released from prison and the excommunications were all withdrawn. It was decided that Malvern Priory came under Westminster Abbey, but the Bishop of Worcester was given the manor of Knightwick as compensation.

An ice cream van creates a museum

The second oldest building in Great Malvern is the old gateway to the Priory of 1480, commonly known as Abbey Gateway although properly it should be called 'the Priory Gateway'. Tradition says that Henry VII with his queen and two little boys visited the Priory and the king lodged in the rooms over the Priory gateway. The older of those little boys was to die from TB when a teenager, while the younger became Henry VIII and many years later he acquired all the treasures of the Priory. The north window of the north transept in the Church was made at his request. In *The Priory Gatehouse of Great Malvern,* Cora Weaver writes:

> When the Priory was built, a wall encircled all the monastic buildings and lands - which included fishponds, and well-stocked vegetable gardens - and the Gatehouse was the only way in or out of the Priory. The black-robed, cowled Benedictine monks were not allowed to receive letters or parcels even from close relatives and were unable to go anywhere without the consent of the Prior; also they took a vow of silence shutting themselves off from the world, so the wall may have helped reduce any inclinations they may have had to change their minds'.

Of the monastic buildings, only the Gueston Hall and the Gatehouse have survived. The Gatehouse became a museum of local history in 1980 and was founded because of a shocking incident with an ice cream van. Cora Weaver explains:

> A Walls icecream van had just deposited its load at the Abbey Hotel and was proceeding in a northerly direction through the archway when it be-came inextricably jammed. At 10' 6" (just over 3m) in height it shouldn't have been there at all! The force of the impact was so great that later in the day, when the hotel staff went to collect their belongings from upstairs, they could see daylight through the floorboards. At the time of the impact, a local man was decorating upstairs. He reported that he noticed 'an almighty bang' and said, 'All the filler I put in the walls came out'.
>
> The Divisional Surveyor reported that the building had been shifted one and a half inches towards Church Street. The cost of the repairs was over

£10,000, the old Gatehouse had become a liability. In March 1980 the arch-way was closed to vehicles and later that year the Gatehouse was officially handed over to Malvern Museum.

The grey lady of Malvern

In the centre of Malvern is an old hotel with a resident ghost. Janice was work-ing there in the late 1990s and tells the story:

It's quite well-known that this hotel has a grey lady that lives in the Board Room. I saw her once when I was helping out for a few weeks. I was doing some serving and I was going from the reception area towards the Board Room when I saw there was someone in front of me. I stopped because I was carrying a large tray and the door had to be opened. It was quite a trial getting the door open with a large tray. I walked on and came up close behind her because I was in a hurry and to my surprise, I walked straight through her! Then she was gone.

She didn't look like a ghost at all, she was quite solid. She was wearing a puffy white hat and a formal grey dress with black stockings. I think she wore an apron but I couldn't be sure.

There's a story about this hotel. Sometime in the 1950s the licensee was a retired soldier. The locals say that he shot his wife then returned to the bar and calmly carried on serving.

More ghosts of Warwick House

In *Worcestershire Ghosts and Hauntings* are several tales about the ghost of War-wick House in Malvern Link, once a high class departmental store but now converted into flats. The ghost used to take a particular interest in new girls. The new arrival would hang her coat up, turn round and there would be the ghost of a middle-aged lady peering at her. She would usually let out shriek and make a hasty exit.

Janet Wheeler had a bridal and hat showroom on the top floor. Unfortu-nately, she died recently but her friends report:

She used to tell us about the ghost and she mentioned a strange smell of lavender when it was about. She said that she had seen an elderly lady walking as if she going down a staircase but no staircase was there She was so intrigued that she did some research and discovered that that there was an old staircase once in that very place.

Zeppelins and Body Works

On the Wells Road in Malvern is a church that has now been turned into a beauty parlour, called 'Body Works'. the narrator's grandfather was the minister of that church some time just before or just after the first World War:

> In those days the Manse was underneath the house. My mother tells the story that when she and my father first got together, she lived there during the winter. It was bitterly cold and there was snow on the ground. She heard a whirring noise and went to the front door to see what it was. A Zeppelin was coming over. When she looked down at the snow she saw that there were footprints in the snow going towards the house but none going away. My parents couldn't make this out. There was a story going round that it was the ghost of the Zeppelin pilot.

The ghost comes to lunch

In Malvern there's a house called 'Woodgate' which, in the 1940s, was the sanatorium of Malvern Girl's College. It has now been made into bedsits for elderly people. My husband was an electrician working in this house for a firm in Malvern.

> It was the school holidays so the house was empty and my husband and his mates were alone in the house, all sensible young men.
>
> The carpets had been pulled up throughout the house. They were sitting on the floorboards of a bare room, eating their sandwiches, when they all heard footsteps coming up the stairs, ringing out clearly on the bare floorboards. They rushed out to the landing to see who was coming but nobody was there.
>
> Later, they mentioned the incident to someone who had been connected with the building for a long time. She knew straight away what it was. She said, 'It's an old housemaid'. It was well known, one of those traditional ghosts.

Faggots and phantom footsteps

Norma lived in Upton-on-Severn in the late 1940s:

> At the end of the Second World War everyone was trying to get some semblance of normal life going.
>
> I was about 14, and in the Girl Guides. One summer I went camping just south of the Malvern Hills. Everyone was given a duty to perform and this one particular day another guide and I were supposed to get firewood. We

walked off and eventually we came across an old, derelict cottage. In the garden were some plum trees. Everything were on rations then and so something like plums were a real treat. After we had eaten as many as we could manage we said to each other, 'Let's go and have a look round the cottage'. We put down our faggots and went in. It was very decrepit, the windows were broken and the doors were hanging off. I said to my friend, 'Mind where you put your feet, the floors are very dodgy'.

Suddenly, we heard footsteps upstairs. We looked at each other. Then we heard heavy footsteps walking down the staircase. The only problem was that there were no stairs, they had completely crumbled away. We did no more than rush out, pick up our faggots and run back to camp. We told our Guide Leader and she told us off, she said we had no right to go trespassing.

Newland revisited

Where the A449 from Worcester reaches Great Malvern is Newland, a small village which probably began in the 1100s as a clearing in the forest. Until recent times Newland was famous for its perry, made from a bitter pear known as Barland.

Parts of the fourteenth century chapel still exist in St Leonard's church which was mostly rebuilt in 1864. Over the next 40 years a collection of charitable buildings were added - almshouses for poor men and women and houses for retired clergy. Jim's* mother was particularly fond of the old church:

We were having mum for Christmas lunch but she said that, before she came to us, she wanted to go to morning service on Christmas day at Newland so I had arranged to meet her at Church.

In the 1970's my mother's brother lived in Buckinghamshire and had been very ill for some time. We knew that he had gone into hospital, but it was just before Christmas and we said that we would visit him after Christmas. We were a very close family. However, at about 6.30 on the Christmas morning the phone rang. It was my cousin to tell me that Uncle Jack had died.

I said to my wife that I had better go to see mum before she goes to church and tell her the bad news. I went up in plenty of time, I went through the back door and into the hall. A year before, on the previous Christmas, my father, Jim, had died and yet there he was, now standing at the foot of the stairs. He was turning just as if he was going to go up the stairs. That gave me a bit of a shock.

Mum was sitting in the kitchen having a few tears. I said to her, 'Have you heard the news then mum?'. She said, 'Jack's died', I asked, 'How do you know?' and she answered, 'Jim came to tell me'.

Kempsey - Children beware!

Kempsey is one of the oldest villages in Worcestershire, named after Kemeys, a Saxon chieftain of AD 799. There is evidence of Iron Age occupation, a Celtic fortification, Roman villas, an early monastery of 799 and, most important of all, a Bishop's Palace. It lay in the fields to the west of the church. Bishops and their noble guests were rowed down the river to be fed and entertained in splendid style. The Palace was in ruins by the end of the 1400s and has now disappeared altogether. Such a historic village will lay claim to an old legend or two. Glenn James was born in Kempsey:

My mother befriended an elderly gentleman in the village. He must have been in his sixties or even older because he had a long white beard. Along the front of his garden was a high privet hedge and, when I was about seven, I can remember walking past with my mother. He was cutting the hedge and as it was a very hot day, he stopped working and told us the following story:

In the 1700s there were two children of a local farmer who were real nuisances. They wouldn't keep away from the river where they would damage the boats, let the geese out and get into all kinds of mischief. One day, they were told to stay indoors because there was storm brewing but as soon as their parents' back was turned they went out. The heavy rain caused the river to flash flood and they were swept away.

Now, on foggy nights, if you go along the road that goes over the ford by the Church of St Mary's known as Squires Walk, you can sometimes hear them playing and laughing and calling to each other. They try to lure other children to their deaths.

The grey lady of Madresfield

West of Kempsey and southeast of Newland is Madresfield village. Half a century ago or more, a conundrum was going the rounds of Worcestershire as follows: where is a grave that holds no man, a monument that bears no name and the site of a church with no foundations? The answer is in Madresfield Court and church. The grave is that of a horse, Sharach, who survived the Charge of the Light Brigade but died in a hunting accident. The monument with no name is a Celtic cross marking the grave of 6th Earls Beauchamp who died in 1891 and left instructions that no memorial should be erected giving his name. The site of an Anglo-Saxon church is surrounded by railings in the churchyard - this was replaced in 1852 but was on the verge of collapse after only twelve years as it had been built without foundations.

*... you can sometimes hear them playing and laughing and calling to each other.
They try to lure other children to their deaths. (Kempsey).*

The site of Madresfield Court has been occupied by the Beauchamp/Lygon family, since about 1160. It has now achieved national fame as it was featured by Evelyn Waugh in *Brideshead Revisited*.

It comes as no surprise that strange entities have been seen wandering round the Court, as many of its characters have been involved in exciting political upheavals. Over the years at least three members of the family were sheriffs of Worcestershire and responsible for law and order. During the civil war of 1642-6, Captain Lygon was a Parliamentarian but the family were turned out of their splendid house and the Royalist Governor of Worcester, Captain Aston, took up residence. The house was placed under siege and could have held out for three months, but Captain Aston was offered £200 plus payments to all his men if he surrendered. He lost no time in handing over the house which was returned to the Lygon's.

There are not many houses in Madresfield, the parish is chiefly occupied by the Court, but Dorothy* knows one of the few parishioners:

> Some friends of mine were driving into Worcester from Madresfield towards Callow End. Just before you get to a sharp bend in the road, and near to where the road leads off to Madresfield, there's a high stone wall. On the left hand side of the road is a footpath, and near to the footpath they both saw a youngish lady walking along dressed in a loose grey coat with a hat or a hood. Most noticeable was the greyness of the whole outfit. Just as they got round the bend the woman stopped. My friend's daughter looked in her rear view mirror and, to her surprise, saw her starting to cross the road. There was nowhere she could go to on the other side of the road because there was a high stone wall.
>
> The woman looked so strange and they were so intrigued that they went a little bit further down the road towards Powick, turned the car round and drove back. There was no sign of the woman anywhere and there was no indication of a door or gateway in the stone wall. My friend said it made her feel quite queer.

The haunted cow (Madresfield)

We have come cross a variety of ghostly animals but this is our first haunted cow:

> In our courting days, in the 1970's, my husband and I were walking down the long stretch of road from Newland to Madresfield. We had just turned into the main part of village when we noticed that a large shape without any form, about the size of a cow, had joined us on the other side of the hedge. We saw it as plain as anything. As we walked, it kept pace with us, all the way down that field. We took a look but couldn't see anything solid. The strange thing was, it was absolutely silent, then it simply disappeared.

My husband is a country person and used to walking about in the country in the evening and he was terrified.

We wondered if it had been an optical illusion or something so the next day we checked with the farmer to see if there had been any livestock in that field, and he was certain that the field was clear.

THE SUCKLEY HILLS

On its north-western side the Malverns comes to an end with a series of gentle hills, known as the Suckley Hills. Old Storridge Hill, with its common, is 600 feet above sea level and a favourite for walkers as it has wonderful views across both Worcestershire and Herefordshire.

Rock-a-by baby

The lady who tells the next story lived in a bungalow in Storridge that was built on the site of an old house:

Several strange things happened there. We had a sort of chalet attached to the end of the house and when my daughter came to stay, we put her in there. She said that in the middle of the night, her bed starting rocking violently for no reason so she asked if she could sleep in the house the next night.

We lived there for ten years, then we decided to move and put the house up for auction. Just before we moved, I woke up at four o'clock in the morning and decided to open the window. I got out of bed, but when I went to go towards the window there was a sort of ice block there. Something solid was stopping me. I couldn't reach the window.

The next morning I said to my husband, 'Did anything strange happen to you in the night?'. He said that he had been woken up at about four o'clock in the morning by the tree tapping against his window. As soon as he got out of bed, the tapping stopped. He had gone to the window, but no tree was there. He got back into bed and the tapping started again. This happened three times.

I mentioned this to a friend who is into these kind of things, and she said, 'It seems to me, that something in your house likes you living there, and doesn't want you to go. It didn't want your daughter there, either'.

Between the crosses (Ankardine Hill)

About five miles north of the Malverns and on the furthermost edge of Worcestershire is Ankerdine Hill.

A friend of mine used to collect an elderly gentleman from time to time who lived on Ankerdine Hill, and take him for a run in his car. When he noticed a lot of poppies in bloom, he thought the old man would like to see them so he went and knocked on his door. There was no reply so he looked through the window, saw the old man asleep in the chair and decided not to disturb him. Later that day he happened to bump into the old man's son, and he told him that he had tried to collect his father but he had been asleep. The son said, 'He died a few weeks ago'.

10. PERSHORE

isitors come from all over England and Wales to look at the beautiful remains of Pershore Abbey. Although only part of the Abbey exists, it is still one of the best examples of Norman and medieval architecture in Worcestershire. The nave was so long that it reached the present entrance gate. The Abbey is said to have been founded as long ago as 681 when King Ethelred gave Pershore to Oswald, his nephew (not the saint). The abbey was re-established by King Edgar in 972 when Saint Oswald brought in the Benedictine monks. The first abbot was named Foldbriht or Fulbert who was famous for his saintly self-denial. The story goes that when he died, Saint Oswald brought him back to life. Fulbert described the wonderful visions he had seen before he expired again.

The monks were given a quarter of (what is now) the county of Worcestershire, however, the abbey did not enjoy its vast wealth for many years. In 976 the abbey fell into the hands of the Duke Alfere, who is described in the old chronicles as leading 'a life of crime and plunder'. It is said that he appropriated three-quarters of the abbey's properties and these were never returned. Divine retribution brought him a terrible end being 'eaten by vermin'. His grandson, Earl Odda, vowed never to marry in case he had a son like his grandfather.

In about 1041, Edward the Confessor became king, but instead of returning the property of Pershore Abbey to its monks, he founded Westminster Abbey and in the 1060s, he transferred most of the property plundered by Alfere to his new Abbey. Consequently, over the centuries there were frequent squabbles between authorities at Westminster and Pershore about who was responsible for what. For example, the bridge over the Avon (in Bridge St) seems to have been in a bad state of repair for more than 20 years when, in 1346, the men of Pershore decided that it was necessary for someone to pay for the repairs. The matter went to Court, and although the Abbot of Westminster owned land on either side, the courts decided that Pershore Abbey and the citizens of Pershore should foot the bill. Incidentally, the bridge was blown up 300 years later, in 1644, by King Charles' army, when forty men were drowned.

The monks at Pershore seem to have had more than their fair share of misfortunes. In 958 the Abbey was laid waste by the Danes. It was burned down in the early 1000s and rebuilt by 1020. In 1102 there was a massive fire and in 1223 the eastern part of the Abbey and the greater part of the town were burned to cinders. In 1288 the church burned again.

The Abbey is now known as the Abbey Church of the Holy Cross, but originally it was dedicated to Saint Mary and Saint Eadburgha. The latter was the grand-daughter of Alfred the Great and born with such a saintly disposition that at the age of three she refused jewellery and opted instead for a prayer book and holy chalice. The story of Saint Eadburgha's bones has been told many times. Saint Eadburgha was abbess at Pershore but she was also an abbess at Winchester, and when she died she was buried at Winchester. Miracles occurred at her tomb which brought in the crowds and a very healthy revenue, and so the wealthy Earl Odda asked if he could purchase some of the Saint's bones for Pershore. Three bones were despatched but unfortunately, the miracles stopped at Winchester and started happening at Pershore. The monks at Winchester said that these were evidently the three vital bones and please could they have them back. Earl Odda at Pershore refused. The wrangling went on for many years. The time came when the bones were of no value, and so the authorities at Winchester magnanimously gave all the bones to the priests of Pershore Abbey who buried them under the floor of the chancel of St Eadburgha's Church at Yardley.

The Abbey was at its height about the 1300s when it had about 30 monks. However, it was not always a life of piety that attracted the brethren. The behaviour of the monks was already causing concern when, in 1320, a murder took place in the churchyard so that it had to be blessed by the Bishop. Twenty years later, the Abbott was recalled because of the scandalous behaviour of the monks. A century later, in 1536, came the famous letter by a monk of Pershore, Richard Beerley, to Cromwell, saying, 'the monks drink and brawl after collacyon until ten or twelve of the clock and come to matins as drunck (drunk) as myss (mice), and some at cards and some at dice and at tables.' The Abbey was dissolved in 1542 and given to Westminster Abbey.

Bob Davis, who lives in the town and supplies us more stories later, says that his mother used to walk her little dog in the Abbey grounds each evening:

> One night she heard singing. There's a rather large keyhole in the main door so that you can look straight into the abbey. When she peered in the abbey was in total darkness.

The Plough and its strange inhabitants

Folks complain about current legal restrictions but these are nothing compared to the bye-laws that began to appear in the late 1300s. Citizens were not allowed to play tennis, football or 'the dice'. All tenants were to be home by nine o'clock. Streets were to be thoroughly cleansed once a month. Citizens were not allowed to have any 'inmates' or sub-tenants in their houses. Bakers could only buy grain at the Tuesday market. All dogs called Mastiffs were to be kept indoors at night. If you owned pigs or cows these were to be put with the common herd. Pubs could only sell their liquors at one designated house in the town.

The name of the 'designated house' is not on record, but knowing the priests' liking for alcohol, it is reasonable to suppose that it could have been the inn which is opposite the end of Priest Lane, known as 'The Plough'. It is thought to be the oldest inn at Pershore. Parts go back to 1645 but there could have been an earlier inn on the site as it was situated on the main road from Worcester to London. Originally a black and white building, The Plough was 'modernised' in the 1700s by having a false front fitted. A room upstairs is thought to have been used as a court room.

The Plough was a common name for Inns and was named after Plough Monday, the first Monday after Twelfth Day of Christmas. This was officially the end of the Christmas holidays when the farmhands had to go back to work. In some parts of England the ploughmen decorated themselves with ribbons and dragged a plough from door to door, asking for money.

Ken and Terri are now the licensees and Ken (aided by Terri) says:

When we first moved in, we didn't use the top floor at all and we kept hearing footsteps overhead all the time. This was very unsettling for new people and it took us some time to get used to them. We heard them again only the day before yesterday.

We had a lot of building work done in the August and September of 2004. We were ripping toilets out and putting a brand new boiler in. The whole building was in total chaos. There seem to be several ghosts here and they didn't like being disturbed. You could feel the tension getting worse. The footsteps became louder and more frequent, things would move of their own accord and glasses fell off the shelves for no reason and smashed. I remember when four or five one pint tankards leaped off shelves under the counter and smashed into tiny pieces on the floor. I heard the barmaid saying 'Oh my goodness!'.

The traditional ghost is a lady by the name of Mary who lived here in 1745. She allowed a house of questionable repute. The regulars talk about her and she has been featured in several books. A previous licensee saw her and he says she wears a striped dress. She never left, she lives in the old part of the building and you can hear her footsteps.

Another ghost, Tom, inhabits the bedroom and hallway area. We hear him going up the stairs, it's a man's footsteps. He sits in the wicker chairs - you can hear them creak for no reason and you can feel that somebody is there. Sometimes, in the night, our continental quilt will move and shake. At first, I thought it was Terri and she thought it was me but it turned out that the quilt was going up and down all by itself. That bedroom is always cold even with the radiator on.

The third day after I took this pub on I thought I saw an old man sitting in the chair next to the fire. He was a guy of about 60 plus, in a hand-knitted Fair Isle cardigan. The pub was closed at the time, we kept very traditional hours at first until we found our feet. When I let the public in I said, 'Who's the old man?' and the regulars said, 'Which old man?'. I said, 'He was sitting in that chair only 20 minutes ago'. He had disappeared. The regulars told me that it was a previous licensee by the name of John Hemming. He was also a currier, that is, someone who provides uniforms for servants. He died when he was 72 in unusual circumstances and the inquest took place in this pub on 27th March, 1951. I've seen him a couple of times since then, he just seems very interested in the newcomers and stands there for a couple of minutes watching us. He's here on a regular basis. At about 12.30 to 3 am we can hear his footsteps. Sometimes he walks through the place and opens all the doors. At night I shut the gate to the old part of the building which is now the entrance to the flats, and when I next look, the gate has been opened.

Where the kitchen is used to be a thoroughfare to all the buildings. When I'm cooking, all the staff swear blind that they heard their name called to say that a meal is ready. They come into the kitchen and say, 'Oh, isn't it ready?'. I tell them it wasn't me who called. At around six o'clock in the evening I stand at the little hatchway near to the kitchen and that area goes ice cold. Sometimes, the cold spot follows me around all night. You can walk in and out of the pillar of cold air behind me.

We shouldn't talk about the ghosts. The more you talk about them the more prolific they become, they like to hear what you are saying about them. These ghosts are just part of the building, they're not harmful. The pub has a nice, comfortable atmosphere.

Hair-raising happenings

A little further towards the centre of the town, on the opposite side, is a row of Victorian houses and one of these has been converted into 'Hair Elite'. On the ground floor is an up-to-date hairdressing salon while the first floor has become an office and a beauty salon. One of the hairdressers, Chris, says:

Upstairs is absolutely freezing and heat rises, so it should be warm. All kinds of strange things happen up there. You open a door and it closes very slowly after you all by itself. We had three huge 3-litre empty drinking water bottles. One evening, we put them neatly in a row and when we went upstairs the next morning they had been turned over and were lying on their sides. One of the hairdressers was doing a tan and using a new product. Suddenly, the top came off the bottle and flew across the room.

Wendy has been working at the hairdressers for eight months:

The owner's son has an office upstairs. Late one afternoon, I heard someone walking about upstairs and I thought, 'That's funny, I thought he had gone home'. About half-an-hour later his mother arrived. I said to her that I had heard noises upstairs but I thought her son had gone home, and she said, 'Oh yes, he has'. We went upstairs and had a look round but no-one was up there.

That happened when everyone was on holiday and I was here on my own, but it doesn't bother me. You don't feel anything bad up there. Ghosts can't hurt you unless they throw things at you!'

We have put a load of crystals round. They should have a calming effect and bring a balance to the environment.

Blood on the stairs

From a house nearby comes another strange story:

When I was a child I had a dream. I dreamed that a ghost met me downstairs and pushed a long nail through my chest, it went in at the front and out the other side. When the last part of the nail had gone through, I ran back upstairs. The next morning when I woke up I assumed I had had a bad dream.

However, there was blood all up the stairs. There was no sign of anything else, nobody else had blood on them. It was very frightening. Nothing else curious ever happened.

The affectionate ghost

Bob Davis says that the High Street is the least prominent of the three main Pershore streets, having a much lower historical social standing than Bridge Street and Broad Street which were, respectively, the focus for woolstaplers and markets. However, the ghosts seem to prefer the High Street. One of the old houses was a bakehouse for the town and the occupant has seen the baker several times. Another occupant has had to move out of her bedroom and into another room because of the presence of a young girl. Bob's own house had an affectionate ghost:

Number 102, High Street is the family home, I lived there until I went to National Service and University at eighteen, then fifty years later I returned when my mother died. Our house is listed and presumed to be Elizabethan. The first of our deeds goes back to 1704, this is for the whole house. When an archaeologist paid us a visit he reckoned that there were probably three cottages here originally and it was around that time that they were turned into one building or possibly two. The owner in 1704 was an upholsterer, when he died he only left a shilling to each of his sons and everything went to his wife - she must have been a strong person, she lived for a good many years after. About that time the house became a smithy. We still have a workshop but it was rebuilt about a hundred years ago.

We have got an old brewhouse at the back with a cellar, a ground floor and a first floor. In Pershore we had special days which were called 'Bush Days'. If a bush was hung on your door you were allowed to sell beer. No doubt number 102 acquired a bush but there is no record of it ever having been a pub.

My mother felt there was a presence here, she sensed that it was female. In the evening this particular person would put her arms round my mother's shoulders. This happened a number of times, but only ever upstairs. My mother was a restless sleeper so she slept in a separate room to my father. I remember her saying to him one morning, 'Did you come and put your arm round me in the night?'. His response was, 'No thank you, not in the cold'. The ghost was a very pleasant person, there was no fear element. My mother said it was a lovely experience. We wondered if it was anything to do with the upholsterer's wife of the 1700s. Of course, in the 1700s it was all open, there no rooms up there. The main room opened on to the stairs and it was a substantial place.

The only sense I got, was that there was a place upstairs where I couldn't sleep at night. Whether or not this was in the path of the ghost, I don't know.

We had a neighbour who thought he knew something about ghosts. He went upstairs and came down again and said, 'Yes, I think there is definitely a presence up there'. My mother's response was, 'So what?'. The person said, 'I will exorcise it for you'. My mother said, 'OK, it's up to you'. Two days later the person came back. He said, 'Not only have I removed your ghost, but I have taken it home with me'.

To my knowledge nobody has seen this particular ghost. My mother was sensitive to these sorts of things.

The secret chapel: Arcade Bookshop

In 1999 Mrs Payne's family had all grown up and left home and she found herself with time on her hands. Her husband said, 'What would you most like to do?' and she replied, 'Start a bookshop'. Her first bookshop was in the Arcade, hence the name. She was there for three years before she heard of interesting premises becoming vacant in the High Street, and so she moved into number 21. This is on the same side as the Angel Hotel but further from the bridge.

When you go into the bookshop, you must find an excuse to buy a children's toy or book, for the children's department downstairs, is a medieval chapel. It's divided into two by a cross wall with a four-centred arch and on the left hand side, as you enter, is a well-preserved piscina. The architectural historian, Pevsner, dates it as 12th century. From the Victoria County History we learn that in 1302, Adam, the Chaplain, was summoned to the local court because he secretly performed a marriage ceremony in there.

Mrs Payne says:

I have never seen anything, but I have often felt something, and other people have, too. Before we took over this shop it was a hairdressers, and a young man helped me to strip down mirrors, move sinks and footrests, and that sort of thing. He's a very straightforward young man, I would think he doesn't have a fanciful bone in his body. He was sometimes working here alone, late at night and he has definitely felt a very strong presence. He also sensed that it was a woman, he doesn't know why.

However, I do know when 'it' doesn't like somebody. Occasionally, I have taken people downstairs and it has gone icy cold. There's a really strong temperature change. Once it was somebody I didn't like myself but on a couple of occasions it has been somebody I either didn't know or somebody that I did like, and it's still gone icy cold.

Several customers and one of my staff have smelt a very strong smell of old-fashioned roses down there on a few occasions although I would say that I have never smelt them myself.

When we first opened, I was showing my brother-in-law's girlfriend round the whole building when she suddenly said, 'Did you see that man?'. We were on the middle floor. She said that she saw a man in modern clothes gradually disappear through the floor. Apparently, where she saw him going down was where the stairs used to be. I didn't know that stairs had once been there until afterwards. I must admit I haven't seen or felt anybody up there. I feel very comfortable in this building. It's just very welcoming to me.

A chap came into the shop and he told me that two teenage boys lived here in the 1940s and he used to come and visit them. In those days a doctor lived here and they were his sons. They were the ones who started to clear the tunnel. There's tunnel vaulting going from here under three buildings, then evidently it's angled off towards the abbey but there had been a fall and it was blocked with rubble. The boys started clearing it in the hope of finding further tunnels but their father stopped them as he thought the tunnel might collapse. When I told the visitor about the woman who had seen the man disappearing, he reckoned 'it' was one of the boys who had died about three weeks beforehand.

Another chap came in who knew the premises in the 1930s or earlier and he said the road was a lot lower then, you could walk down steps at the front into the basement. Coal and other commodities were delivered there for storage. When we first moved here the basement was only a coal cellar. None of the architectural features, including the piscina, were obvious.

The building has gone through quite a few changes. My brother in law is an architect and he says there have been three changes from the doorway to the end of the steps. I did notice we had a Tudor lintel. As for the rest of the building, if you look at the back of the house you can see that it's timber-framed. We were up in the attic last weekend where there are ancient timbers used in a very old way, infilled with wattle and daub. The young man who came to help me with the renovations told me that, in the time of Henry VIII and previously, a lot of wood was taken from this part of the world to built ships, and the shipbuilders had to promise that if the ships were ever dismantled they would return the wood to this area. I would think that some of the timbers in the attics are from those ships. They have obviously been reused and they have the kind of holes in them that you would expect from a sea voyage.

A few weeks ago two Catholic priests came into the shop and they measured the distance from the piscina to the floor. Evidently, there's a standard distance and this measurement was too short, and so it looks as if the floor level has been raised. They told me that it means that the basement could have been used as a crypt and there could be bodies buried down there, under the floor

.

Although Mrs Payne has never seen an apparition on these premises, her mother told her that she used to talk to a ghost when she was about three years old.

I don't remember it, but I do remember that, although I was an only child, I never felt lonely.

My mother used to come up to my bedroom in the late evening and I would still be awake. Mother would ask why I wasn't asleep and I would say, 'How can I go to sleep when that lady keeps talking to me?'. Apparently I described the lady very precisely. I said that she wore a mobbed cap and that she had on a large white apron tucked up at one side.

My mother never saw her but both my grandmothers saw her when they came to babysit. The one grandmother saw her going up the stairs and the other saw her sitting on my bed.

Another old building in the High Street well worth a visit is the Heritage Centre. There is so much information about old Pershore that you wished your ancestors lived there, so that you could look them up.

Tragedy at the Brandy Cask

Traditionally, ghosts are supposed to appear on sites where there has been a great tragedy, but in actual fact, most of the time they are seen in places with an uneventful history. There's a place in Pershore which should be haunted with the ghosts of five airmen but despite being visited by a series of mediums and other sensitive folk, nothing seems to have materialised. In 1943 or 1944 a Wellington bomber was flying low over Pershore Abbey. No-one knows why it was down to 50 or 60 feet. Engine failure has been suggested, also it was carnival day and perhaps the pilot wanted to get a better look at the carnival, or perhaps he attempted a 'fly past'. Anyhow, the plane clipped the trees round the Abbey and crashed into the garden of the Brandy Cask, taking off the roof and killing all five airmen on board. A large portion of one of the plane's 3-bladed propellers was preserved in the rear yard of the (rebuilt) Brandy Cask as a memorial.

The dead were five Canadians from RAF Tilesford at Pershore, a bomber crew training station. Technically, they were only trainees but during the war a shortage of airmen meant that most airmen flew before they had completed their training. The ground staff from the Tilesford station had to march with the funeral cortege from the airfield to the Pershore cemetery on the Pershore to Upton Road, a distance of about two miles. Many Canadians are buried there, their graves are at the back of the cemetery.

The psychic mum (Cherry Orchard)

Before fridges and freezers became commonplace, cherries were very popular as they were the first fruit of the season. Cherry orchards were common and a housing estate at Pershore was evidently built on one from which it takes its name.

The next story shows how a psychic mum can sometimes be very useful:

I'm sensitive to these things, it runs in the family, my mother is sensitive too, even more than I am. I often sense illnesses before they have happened and my mother knows when accidents are about to happen.

One day, she said to her husband, 'Be careful and don't park by a white wall and trees'. He did and a lorry went straight into his car. Fortunately, he wasn't in it at the time. On another occasion, they were going along and her husband was driving when she said, 'Pull over to the left, a motorbike will be coming round that corner in a minute and he'll go straight into you'. Her husband did pull over and, sure enough, a motorbike appeared and just clipped his car. If he had been in the correct position on the road the bike would have gone straight through his windscreen.

I can think about my mother and she will ring me. I've been sensitive since I was a little girl. I remember my mother taking me to church one day. I got there, sat down and I just felt that I had to get out. The church felt so evil.

My parents used to live in the centre of Pershore but then they moved to a new house in the Cherry Orchard. I never liked the house and neither did my mother.

When I was about fifteen or sixteen my friend and I had been walking round graveyards in the school holidays, seeing who had died in the most popular year. I don't know whether it was anything to do with it, but about two nights later I was fast asleep in my bedroom when something woke me up. I got out of bed and opened my bedroom door. A Victorian-looking gentleman in a tall hat stood facing my sister's door (which was opposite) with his left hand on the handle, as if he was going to go into her room. He turned to look at me and said, 'I'll return'. I went back to bed and in the morning, when I woke up, I found my bedroom light was on and the door open. That's most unlike me, I'm always careful to switch the light off and close the door. I assumed it was a dream but when I got to the bedroom door I went really cold.

A few weeks later I was sitting in the living room, watching TV and waiting for Blue Peter to start, when I happened to look at the China cabinet. The cabinet seemed to change to sooty bricks and I saw the face of the Victorian-looking gentleman laughing at me. His head was thrown back so that his chin was upwards. As I watched the head grew bigger and bigger. I rushed out into the kitchen and my mum said, 'What's the matter with you?' I told her and she said that when she went upstairs, something had brushed past her on the landing. I would never stay in the house alone. If my parents were not at home when I arrived back from school I would sit on the doorstep and wait for them to come home, even though I had the key.

A friend of my parents was a businessman who owned quite a large company. He came to the house a few years later and said, 'I'm just going upstairs to the bathroom'. He came rushing down the stairs and out into the car. A few days later my mother said to him, 'What on earth was the matter?' and he said, 'I saw your ghost on the landing'.

Then my parents started knocking the house about and the man was never seen or felt again.

Odours of cooking (Tilesford House)

Will Dallimore has provided us with many a good ghost story and the following is no exception:

Tilesford House, a large 16th century black and white farmhouse near Pershore, had lain derelict for many years before being sympathetically restored to its former glory.

The building work had been going on and off for several years but its completion was hastened when the owner decided that he would like to move out of his nearby farm cottage and into Tilesford House before his wife, who was expecting their second child, gave birth in early September.

The rambling old building retained many of its old features including its stone-floored kitchen, however it would never be used as such, as a new kitchen had been sited at the other end of the house.

I, and my brother John, were working on the house as decorators towards the end of its restoration.

One morning we turned up for work at about a quarter to eight and were walking through the old kitchen to get to our tins of paint, which were kept in an adjoining room when we both noticed a strong smell of what could be best described as 'cooked breakfast', fried bacon etc. We never thought a lot about it until about an hour later when I returned to the same location and was met by a carpenter called Pete who remarked, "Someone's having a good fry-up". The smell that I had noticed earlier had returned.

We could not put our fingers on where the smell had come from. None of the handful of building workers in the house were doing any cooking (they never usually ate till one o'clock and then it was nothing more exotic than a cheese sandwich), the nearest house was over a hundred metres away, and it was improbable for an odour so strong to travel such a distance without dispersing, especially as no-one outside the building, or in any other part of the house, smelled anything. The new kitchen was also ruled out as it had not yet been equipped with its cooking stove.

Another theory that was put forward was that the previous day, whilst digging out a new driveway, a JCB digger had uncovered a previously unknown opening to the cellar which ran beneath the old kitchen. This let sunlight fall into the cellar for the first time for many years.

Local historian, Michael J Barnard, told me that in the 1930s the house had been home to the Worcestershire Flying Club. Its 120 members would have taken advantage of the many clubhouse facilities there, including a 'cooked breakfast' before they took off from the nearby grass strip, which later came to be incorporated in Throckmorton Airfield at the advent of World War II.

The smell never returned after that initial day and we dismissed it as one of those unsolvable mysteries. However, on our last day at the house the owner's mother-in-law had brought a casserole to christen the new kitchen's farmhouse cooker. We were working upstairs when a young carpenter named Rob, who was new to the house, came into the bedroom and said, "Bacon and eggs". We replied, "No, it's a casserole!" He explained that he had smelled 'bacon and eggs a moment earlier whilst he in the OLD kitchen.

There is a footnote to this tale. Once the house was completed, the owner and his family moved in. We were asked to touch up their previous home, the nearby farm cottage, before it was let out. The day the owner's wife was expecting their baby, we were sitting in our van having our lunch when three magpies landed on the ground in front of us. They stayed there for some time before being disturbed by the owner's cleaning lady who was heading towards us from Tilesford House with some good news. Before she could say anything we said, 'It's a girl' to which she wondered how we knew already that the baby was a girl. We told her of the three magpies:

One for sorrow,
Two for joy,
Three for a girl,
Four for a boy!

Bird of Wonder

Another version of this rhyme is:

One for sorrow, two for mirth,
Three for a wedding, four for a birth.

The actions of birds have always been carefully watched and there are hundreds of ancient superstitions where birds are thought to predict the weather or good news or bad news. For example, two crows seen together mean a wedding, and one a funeral. The flight of a bird over a sick bed, a robin entering a house or a bird fluttering at a window were all portents of death. .

Joy is a great believer in bird lore. She says that a few days before her dad died, a bird came into the kitchen, it flew in and couldn't get out. Budgies have not so far become part of the traditional pattern but times move forward and Joy has a story about her budgie:

He seemed to know how I was feeling. If I was stressed or upset my budgie would come and bomb me across my head as if to say, 'Don't worry, I'm here'. Every day we let him out of his cage and he could fly around quite freely. He didn't make any attempt to fly away. He kept to the one room and only flew out twice. Each of those times it was under strange circumstances.

A few years ago, my sister died. A friend of hers bought flowers every week to put on the grave, but she said that at Christmas she would send them to me, in memory of her friend. Consequently, there was a big bouquet of flowers in memory of my sister on the dining room table. My budgie came into the room and hovered over the flowers. It's very rare for a budgie to hover and that's the only time I have known him go into the dining room.

My whole family were going off to Australia to a family wedding. The day before we were going to Australia he just disappeared. I don't know what happened to him, whether he flew out the window or not. I never saw him again.

The Coach Driver (Drakes Broughton)

If you go past Pershore station on the B4082, just before you join the A44 road to Worcester, is a small road on the left known as Gigbridge Lane. Edward has a large house along there and has researched the local history. He says that Gigbridge Lane was once much more important than it is now, as it led to Drakes Broughton. Drakes Broughton is mentioned in the Domesday Book. For centuries it was just a tiny village, only acquiring a church in 1857 and a school in 1891, but in recent years it has seen large housing developments. A member of the local historical society says:

> Where the houses are now along Gigbridge Lane was the old funeral route, as Drakes Broughton church didn't have a cemetery. One night, the lady in about the third house up, heard a violent knocking at her door and when she went to open it, there stood a lady in a crinoline dress and behind her was a coach and horses. The lady asked for directions.

The Vale reprinted a story from *Haunted Worcestershire,* about Mrs Bryant and her family in Drakes Broughton who were experiencing a ghost named George. Julia also once lived in Drakes Broughton and named her ghost 'the coach driver'. She wonders if she lived in the same house before Mrs Bryant:

> I moved to a brand new council house in Drakes Broughton in December 1962. If you remember, the winter of 1963 was a hard one and the walls of our house had not properly dried out. My husband was poorly, he had bronchitis and all sorts of things. When he was better he wanted to do the garden, so he got out the wheelbarrow, took some clay from the garden into the woods and brought back topsoil. As he dug deeper into the clay he came across a coach wheel. He said, 'come and look at what I have found'. I said, 'I'm sorry, I'm in the middle of cooking tea'. The next thing I knew he was struggling into the house with the wheel. I said, 'What on earth have you brought that old thing into the house for, do get rid of it'. He said, 'No, its an old coach wheel, it might be worth something'. The wheel was then put outside against the wall of the house, but disappeared overnight!'
>
> Everything was alright up until that night. Then from the October to the March, the man that your article called 'George' and I called 'the coach driver' visited me at three o'clock most mornings. He used to stand at the bottom of my bed but as soon as I opened my eyes he would go. I would catch a glimpse of him before he disappeared. He looked to me like an old coach driver. He was very tall, he had a three-cornered hat, a cape-like cloak, a frilled shirt, high boots and moleskin trousers that flopped over the top of his boots. I had rearranged my bedroom with the dressing table one side and the wardrobe the other. One night after that he became agitated and leaned across my bed and the bed shook, but he didn't scare me.

I only once had a nasty experience in that house. My youngest was fast asleep in her cot when the bedroom door opened forcefully and slammed against the edge of the cot. She opened her eyes then went off to sleep again. A few seconds later the bulb over the top of the stairs flew out of the socket. Instead of falling down the stairs it went smack into the airing cupboard about three yards away. My husband picked it up and it was still hot. He put it back in the socket and it worked.

We exchanged houses with another family. They experienced more dreadful things than we ever did, of the sort that were reprinted in *The Vale*. They moved because of this and another family moved in. The husband of this last family came round and said to us, 'Can I ask you something? Did you ever experience anything in the house?'. I said, 'Yes, but it won't hurt you'. He said, 'My wife's really nervous about it'. Apparently, they eventually moved from there because of her nerves.

George must have been something to do with the coach wheel. I often wonder if he was a coach driver who had been involved in a nasty accident nearby as the wheel had been found in our back garden and also because he had a large lump on the left side of his face.

The Poltergeist (Drakes Broughton)

The last story came from the occupier of a new house, the next is from a lady who, a few years ago, lived for several months in an old farmhouse in Drakes Broughton:

When I was going through a divorce I took a room in an old farm in Drakes Broughton. The person who owned it let it out as rooms. I used to come home to find my jewellery thrown across the floor. I would be in the middle of doing something like brushing my hair and my hairbrush would fly over to the other side of the room, or the hangers would fly out of the wardrobe. Sometimes, my friends who lived in the other rooms would come and sit on my bed and we would hear dreadful noises coming from the room above. I asked the young man who lived above, 'What do you do in your bedroom when you come home?' and he would say, 'All I do, is sit on my bed, take off my shoes and put my slippers on'. I happened to be up there one day and I saw him doing this while my friend was sitting in my room below. I saw that he was doing nothing which could make these noises but my friend in the room below said that she still heard them.

All kinds of strange things happened in that house but I was the only person who had things going on in her bedroom. These things happened particularly if I was under stress - if there was a hitch in my divorce or something.

Wheeling and dealing at Wick

Most of Wick was owned by Westminster Abbey as part of the great Manor of Pershore but over the centuries it was divided up and sold. For example, in 1160, 90 acres were given to a certain dignitary who styled himself 'Peter de Wick'.

Bishop Gifford who was Bishop of Worcester in the 1200s, appropriated enough money from the struggling Pershore Abbey to build himself a splendid manor at Wick, suitable for entertaining such eminent people as the Archbishop of Canterbury, in those days as important as the king.

By 1520 part of the Wick estate was in the hands of the Haselwoods whose effigies are at the back of Pershore Abbey. Although Thomas Haselwood, his wife Elizabeth and their son Thomas were branded as rebels in 1622 after a fight with the sergeant-in-arms, their descendants became Sheriffs of Worcestershire. In about 1745 Wick House, probably the building now known as Wick Manor, passed from the Haselwoods to the Hudsons. The story has passed through both the Haselwood and the Hudson families, that it was gambled in a mega game of cards in which the Haselwoods lost. Whether the Haselwoods continued gambling is not known, but in the mid 1700s the rest of the estate was sold to a vicar, the Reverend Wilson, then in 1776 it was bought by Richard Hudson, who was already living in Wick House.

Wick has been described as a peaceful village set in orchards and particularly picturesque is the large black and white house now known as Wick Manor. Although it appears to be Elizabethan, it only goes back to 1923 and was built as a memorial to a member of the family, Lieut Alban John Benedict Hudson MC, who died at the battle of Messines in 1917. However, behind is a much older building, part of which had been converted into stables, but which previously is thought to have been an old chapel dedicated to St Cuthbert.

The young lady in the following story was living in Evesham when she was overcome by a premonition:

> We were walking the dogs, and I saw Wick Manor through the trees. I was fascinated by it. I had never been to Wick before. My husband said, 'It's not very old, it was burned down and it's been rebuilt very authentically with wooden pegs instead of nails'. I was just standing in the archway, staring. I turned to my husband and said, 'I'm going to live here one day'. I just knew it. He said, 'In your dreams'. I've never felt that way about anywhere else.
>
> Anyway, three or four years later, we were thinking of moving to another flat and we were looking through the paper when we saw an estate agent at Leominster advertising a flat. Colonel Hudson had converted the Manor into three flats. I was convinced that I was going to live in one. I said to my husband, 'I'm sure that's Wick Manor'. Anyway, it was, and the

agent said, 'I'll meet you there and show you round'. As soon as I saw it I knew that was the place for me. They were lovely flats, in fact a woman with three children lived below us.

The Colonel came home most weekends. One morning I heard a knock at the door and it was his housekeeper. She used to make sure that the bed was made and the flat was heated for when he came home. She said, 'Have you seen the Colonel this morning? It's strange because he always unlocks the door for me so that I can come in and get his breakfast and he hasn't done that this morning. I haven't bothered to bring my key'. We knocked on the door but there was no reply. She had to go back home for her key. When we eventually got in we found that he had had a heart attack during the night and died in bed.

There's an old saying, 'Wick will have blood on the walls'. One day, I went into my bedroom where there were thick wardrobes set in the wall. We had a cream carpet on the floor and suddenly from under the door came this huge red stain. I thought, 'This is the blood on the walls'. Anyway, it was a bottle of Chianti that someone had brought us back from their holiday and the neck had snapped off.

The bedside visitor

Pat lived in an old cottage in Wick.

One night I saw a gentleman sitting on the side of my bed. He wasn't frightening, he was a very friendly chap. I told my husband and he said that he had felt a presence in he room. Then a neighbour told me that his brother had died in our bedroom. I thought, 'Thank you very much'.

11. REDDITCH

 edditch began in 1138 when eleven white-robed monks came from Leicestershire to found an abbey at Bordesley. Near the entrance, by a ditch filled with brownish-red water (the Red-ditch), a group of stonemasons built a few dwellings for their use while working on the abbey. The town developed from there, later moving up the hill. Although there is now very little left of Bordesley Abbey, it was once the fifth richest in England. Next to the ruins of Bordesley Abbey is a unique and little-known cemetery. Needle Mill Lane leads to Forge Mill and the Bordesley Abbey meadows. Only a few yards past the entrance to the lane, on the left, is a car park. At the far end of that car park is a gate leading to an enchanting tiny graveyard. Here are tiny tombstones dating back to 1635. Some have been reused and are inscribed on both sides. The victims of the 1832 cholera epidemic, many of them children, are also buried here in an unmarked mass grave.

On the far side of the cemetery is the marked outline of the tiny chapel of St Stephen's, built at the entrance for the use of the general public and, except for a small Quaker chapel, the only place of worship for Redditch folk. It was pulled down between 1805 and 1807, and the building material used for a church in Redditch centre, on the site of the present St Stephen's.

Churchyard ghosts

Ben Cooper was a local Councillor and well-known for his work with young people. His widow said:

In the 1960s, he would have been about thirteen, and he was playing with two or three friends in this part of the meadows, when they saw a monk in a brown robe and cowl gliding slowly towards them. Nothing would shake his story and he was a very down-to-earth man.

From her description, he seems to have been in near the site of the old chapel and the monk was gliding across the field towards him. The monks were Cistercians and wore white robes but the lay-brothers, who lived in the monastery and were not as important as the monks, wore brown.

Another strange story comes from Margaret, a Redditch resident nearing retirement:

In April 1994 I set out to take our overweight black spaniel, Patsy, for a walk. We had inherited her from my husband's parents who had died the previous year. I was trying desperately to get Patsy's weight down with a healthy diet and two daily walks but it's very difficult when you're at work all day.

My preferred walk was round the eastern side of the Bordesley Abbey meadows, but the last time I went to park in the Forge Mill car park there must have been a function on at the Mill and the car park was full. So I decided to park near the little graveyard on the crematorium side. Although there are giant pyramids stopping the entrance you can just squeeze between them with a small car.

When I started out at about 6.15 the sun was shining but in the five minutes it took me to drive to the abbey meadows the clouds went over the sun and it was so dark that everyone was switching on their car lights. I parked at the far end of the car park, heaved Patsy out of the back seat and clipped on her lead. It was a windy day and I remember that the narcissi at the foot of the entrance were dancing about as if they were in an earthquake. We only had a few yards to go up a dirt path before we were in the old cemetery. The grass was quite long, Patsy was not very happy and I had to tug her lead to get her going. When I got to a point just beyond the graves I stopped. Above the whine of the traffic I could hear something crying, carried on the wind, faint but as clear as anything. For the first few seconds I thought it was the meowing of a cat and I assumed a kitten had got lost so I gave Patsy another tug and pulled her over to the left, as the noise seemed to come from that direction.

To my horror, I suddenly realised that it was not the meowing of a cat but a baby crying, I would estimate it to be a few months old, and a niggling, tired, end-of-my-tether kind of cry. The nearest house was at least 100 yards away. The thought flashed through my mind that someone had abandoned a baby, then I pulled myself together and decided there must be some other explanation, perhaps someone was taking a baby for a walk nearby. Between the trees on the left is a patch of barren ground from where you can look across a few yards of scrubland to the main road. Nobody was there and it would have been a foolhardy mother to push a pram along a fast road with no pavements. Then I suddenly realised that the crying was coming from the other side of the graveyard. Another tug at the reluctant Patsy and we made our way across the twenty or thirty yards to the right hand side. There's a gap between the hedges where you can look across the meadows. No-one was to be seen. I was about to start searching the undergrowth when I realised that the crying was coming from the left hand side of the churchyard, where I had just been. It was very weird. I felt myself going hot and cold. Then the noise stopped.

There's a little grassy bank at the top of the cemetery then a flat area where the old St Stephen's church is marked out in stones. From here a set of steps leads into the meadows. I looked across and again, no-one was to be seen. I stood there, undecided. Should I make a fuss? Should I phone the police? Had it all been my imagination?

I decided to retreat for home. The wind was sharp, and although I was well wrapped up, it was hurting my ears. Over the next two weeks I felt so guilty for not reporting it and opened the local papers with dread, expecting to find news of a deceased abandoned baby. But there was nothing.

Shivers still go and up and down my spine when I think of that evening and I have never parked there again.

Surprisingly, churchyards are not popular with spirits of the deceased who seem to prefer modern housing developments, but an occasional ghost has been seen in the old cemetery off Plymouth Road. Locals tell of a tall thin man with top hat, bow tie and bloody gash to his chest who stands at the gates. If you try to exit the cemetery by another gate, he moves to that gate and prevents you from leaving.

Schehezeranne's experience was less macabre. She is descended from Clarke's, the Showmen, who owned Clarke's yard where the new market is now situated. This is where they lived and stored their fairs during the winter. The fair folk have proved to be a great asset for the town, giving a large proportion of their takings to local charities.

When I was about sixteen years old I used to have to take a short cut home in the late evening through Redditch churchyard. There was always quite a few of us, and one night there was Juli, Laraine and a few other girls. One of the girls said, 'Look at that man!'. We turned round and there was this strange-looking man, with a very white face and a big hat and a cape. We all saw him. I said, 'What's the time?' but he never answered. Then we just ran.

We went on to the pub, we shouldn't have been in the pub really, we weren't old enough but there weren't so many restrictions in those days. We said, 'We have just been through the cemetery and we have seen a man there with a cape and a hat'. The fellow from the pub said, 'He's always there. He's known for it'. Apparently it was said that somebody had been murdered and he used to stand there to protect them. He only appeared when young girls were there.

It was ever so strange. I wouldn't go there at night now.

The growling ghost

Bordesley Abbey Meadows are steeped in ghosts and legends. The meadows themselves are said to be haunted by a black dog, representing Guy of Warwick, nicknamed the Black Dog of Arden, who was buried at the Abbey. On the surrounding roads, dark monks and brown shapes terrify car drivers and passers-by.

Part of Forge Mill Road runs alongside the Bordesley Abbey meadows. One of the occupants tells how a house in the Road was haunted for nearly thirty years:

I lived in a house in the Bordesley area for thirty years. My husband was away on business a lot of the time. Once, when he came back, I woke up during the night and I saw a man looking out of the window. I thought it was my husband and I said, 'What are you doing?'. Then I moved my foot and touched my husband in bed. I thought, 'If he's in bed with me, who is that looking out of the window?' and I screamed as loud as I could.

That man was around for years. He was solid matter, all in black, every time I saw him I screamed and my husband would end up shaking me. He couldn't see it. Some nights I knew he was there but I wouldn't open my eyes. Lots and lots of things happened in the house.

I was always moving the rooms round, and he hated it if I turned the bedroom round. Then he became aggressive. He floated over the top of me and as he moved along he would make a growling noise.

When the kids got older we had an extension built on the garage and we moved from our bedroom into the extension. One of my sons moved into our old bedroom. I was sitting downstairs, chatting to my husband when we heard such a thud upstairs. We had open plan stairs and my son came down the stairs. His knuckles were bleeding, he said, 'I went to bed and there was this face looking at me and I thought it was my brother. Then I thought, 'If it's not him, who is it? I thumped it and hit the wall'.

When we moved into the extension I wondered if the ghost was coming to follow me. The bed faced the door, and soon after we moved in I saw him there in the doorway, all black but then I was able to see his face which looked so angry. It was as thought he was thinking, 'You have moved again'. He came over towards me.

I thought, 'I will have to do something'. I had been told to tell it to go away. I swore at it and I said, 'Get out of this house'. My husband woke up and said, 'Who are you talking to?'. Then he swore and he said, 'What's that?'. That was the one and only time that he saw it.

After that, it never appeared again. Quite frankly, I don't care who believes me and who doesn't. It happened and that was that. I'm as interested to know what it was all about as anyone.

A telepathic mum

The paranormal covers a huge range of inexplicable events and circumstances. There are ghosts, poltergeists, predictions, premonitions, and so on. One area which has received a lot of attention is telepathy, as in certain cases, it can be tested and measured. Perhaps the investigators should have met the family in the next narrative who seem to have curious telepathic abilities. The daughter says, 'I can make my mother ring me. When I was at college, I used to run out of money and I would think, 'Oh mum, I wish you would ring' and she would ring up.'

The family joked about being telepathic until something happened that made them take it more seriously. The mother says:

About twenty years ago, while we were on holiday, I woke up at two o'clock in the morning. I had had a terrible dream, I kept hearing a voice and it was calling my name urgently. Two days later we came home late in the evening and early the next morning, the doorbell rang. It was the lady next door. She was quite elderly and she had no relatives so we kept on eye on her. While we were away her husband, who suffered from bronchitis, had had a heart attack. There was no-one she could turn to, the neighbours on the other side had only moved in three weeks previously. She didn't have a telephone and she had to run down the road to the telephone box. By the time the doctor arrived, it was too late. She kept thinking, if only I was there. This happened on the same night and at the same time that I had the dream.

Screams in the shop

Redditch was designated a new town in 1963, with a proposed population rise from 32,000 to 70,000. When the new town centre, known as the Kingfisher Centre, was under construction, many strange tales were in circulation. Dark shapes of monks were seen, crying babies were heard, ordinary-looking people walked through metal shutters, and lifts went up and down in the middle of the night. However, after a year or so they petered out. Nowadays, something unusual happens occasionally, but no more than for any collection of shops and stores.

When he told this story, Abdul was working at the Indian Takeaway in Beoley Road West. There's also another story from him later in this chapter:

The toilet area, the Pound Shop, Canon Newton House and part of Allders are on the site of the old Evesham Street Methodist Church. It was demolished when the town was redeveloped in the 1970s and all the bodies were exhumed and reburied in consecrated ground.

I was at Redditch College (now the North East Worcestershire college) in about 1988 and we were told that the security guards at the Kingfisher Centre kept hearing a child or a baby screaming. Some of them wouldn't work there. So it was arranged that about ten of us, all students, would hold a vigil in the upstairs of Sharp's, a store that sold beds and fitted kitchens. The room was quite warm but when we walked towards the one corner it went very, very cold. We all heard the child screaming. It was a sad, miserable cry and it went on for several minutes. It came from the rear of the toilet area, where there is a short hallway to reach an exit, the noise came from the hallway. One girl in the group felt the presence of one of ghosts. She said, there's a girl here, she's not very happy because her body has been disturbed. As for the rest of us, we were more spooked than anything else.

Joyce used to work in one of the card shops:

Every night before we went home we would tidy up and put the cards straight but in the morning, when we came in, all the cards on the bottom shelf of the whole length of the shop would be lying in their backs. They couldn't have fallen over as they were in little pockets but they had been carefully taken out of the pockets. Other strange things happened there, doors would lock and unlock all by themselves. It wasn't scarey, you didn't feel uncomfortable, but it was just strange.

Ghosts and demons of Halloween

The evening of October 31st is Halloween, one of the most important days for the Celts. It was the last day of the old year, for November 1st was the festival of Samain, the new year. It was a time to prepare for winter. The Celts killed off any extra animals so that they didn't have to feed them during the winter, and sheep were mated so that they would have lambs in the spring. They built huge bonfires, probably on top of burial mounds because they believed that times and places where something connected with another | an old year with a new year - were gateway to other worlds through which evil spirits could pass. The Celts believed that at the eve of Samain, all natural laws were suspended and ghosts and demons roamed freely.

The Romans held the festival of Pomain on the same day. Pomona was the Roman goddess of fruit and nuts, that's why a lot of the Halloween festivities involve fruit and nuts.

When Saint Augustine and the Roman missionaries arrived in the 590s they knew that it would be difficult to get rid of these old festivals and so they rededicated them to various saints. The festival of Samain was given to all the saints in heaven, so that November 1st is now 'All Saints Day'. Generally, no more ghosts seem to appear on October 31st than at any other time of the year, however, here is one of them:

I was a training manager for Quantum in 1988 and I was going out with the Placement Officer, to visit a company in Redditch. Quantum was one of those organisations set up by the government to train people so that they could get back into work. We were based in Canon Newton House which was over and above Owen Owens (later Allders).

Our car was parked on one of the upper floors in car park 3. We walked through the open doors into the stacker car park where there are two lift shafts, side by side and were just in time to see the dark shape of a person walking into the far lift. We were talking so we didn't take much notice, afterwards, when we discussed it, all that we could agree on was that he or she had their head down. The doors closed but we hastily pressed the lift button so that the doors opened straight away, before the lift had had a chance to move off.

To our surprise, there was nobody in the lift. There was a cold feeling as we went in. My colleague joked about it and said there was probably a draught from somewhere but the feeling wasn't like that, it came from inside you, just as if there was an ice block inside you.

We didn't go in the lift again, we used the stairs. We didn't realise until later that it was October 31st.

Tales from WH Smith

Rose is the supervisor of the book department in WH Smith. During her lifetime she has had a couple of inexplicable experiences:

When I was about fifteen I was a real so-and-so. I wanted some money from my mother to go out and she wouldn't give it to me. I saw some money on the table and thought, 'She won't miss this' so I took it. Just as I was going out of the front door someone tapped me twice, hard, on the shoulder. I turned round, expecting to see my mother, but no-one was there. It frightened me so much that I put the money back on the table.

These days I keep having this recurring dream. I'm running away and as I do so, I keep looking behind me. I'm terrified of something - it seems to be man. I'm wearing a long skirt, perhaps Victorian, so I'm gathering this up on front of me as I run. Then something hits me in the back between the shoulder blades. My arms fly up, I fall forward and I wake up. I usually find that I'm lying face down on the bed with my arms above my head.

My husband has said more than once after the dream, 'You were having a nightmare, weren't you?' because I was thrashing about in the bed.

When I was on holiday last year my husband was putting the suntan on my back when he suddenly stopped and said, 'What's that scar between your shoulder blades?'. He said it looked like an old knife wound.

Sick at heart

Pauline Thorne has been manager of the British Heart Foundation shop opposite Saint Stephen's in Market Place for four years now and she says that nothing like this has every happened before:

'It started upstairs. Last year, we cleared out upstairs, had some building work done and moved the office up there. Before that, we didn't go upstairs very often. If you sat at the desk upstairs you would find that you would keep looking behind you, thinking somebody was there. You felt that you were being watched.

Things started to move around down here. I put a bible on the corner of the bookshelf and when I came to look for it we couldn't find it anywhere. The next day it was back in the same place. There are loads of things that have gone missing, we have lost them and they have never been found. Early one morning we put some cigarette cards on the middle table, those disappeared and nobody had been in the shop. A Meccano set vanished that we put on one of the units. Nobody has found that. It's mainly old things that disappear. We keep reassuring ourselves that these strange occurrences are just coincidences but too many things have happened for them to be coincidences.

We were hunting high and low for something at the end of one day, the shop floor was completely empty and we had even turned the lights off when, all of a sudden, we heard this great bang upstairs. We said, 'What's happened?'. A stack of four or five jigsaws had come off the shelf and were on the floor. They hadn't tipped over or anything, it looked as if somebody had taken them off the shelf and carefully put them on the floor.

The fluorescent kitchen light keeps flashing. I changed to a tube with a lower wattage yesterday to see if that helps. Then we keep having little power cuts when the electricity goes off for a few seconds. The bulbs blow terribly, we have to replace one a week at least. One bulb goes and you change that, then the next one goes.

Quite a few times the CD has turned itself on. You go to touch it to switch it on and it comes on by itself. A couple of times we've thought, 'We'll turn it off' and its done it by itself.

Another strange thing - a woman was going through the shop with a pushchair and behind her was an elderly man. Somehow or other, the pushchair must have knocked the book shelf and a book about the Falklands War dropped out in front of the man and fell open. On the open page was a photograph of that man. He didn't know he was in the book. He was totally amazed, so was I! Anyhow, he bought the book and we made a sale!

We hear loads of footsteps when no-one is there. It seems as if we can hear someone walking up our stairs but we're so close to the shop next door we assume the noise is coming from there so we don't bother. We've heard those footsteps ever since we've been here.

My colleague and I were working together upstairs and we were both chattering away when, for no reason in particular, we suddenly stopped talking. We both went really cold, looked at each other and ran down the stairs. There was no explanation. It was really strange. I felt ever so cold after that, I had goosebumps. We hadn't been talking about ghosts or anything like that, just general chat.

Two weeks ago I came into the shop to find that the books had been taken off the shelves and the clothes off the coat hangers and they were all on the floor. A mirror shot out of nowhere and bumped me on the head. Fortunately, it wasn't a big mirror, just a little hand one. It didn't hurt but it gave me quite a shock!

A clock actually flew off the wall and hit Janet, one of the volunteers. I saw that happen. It flew across the room for about three metres, over a clothes rail and straight to Janet. It hit her on the head. The pin holding it to the wall hadn't come out or anything, and if the clock had fallen it should have gone down behind the shelves but it hadn't. That really did it for us.

I got the feeling that, when we moved upstairs, we disturbed whatever had been living there, but we may have another explanation for the activity. As you know, we have loads of stuff coming in and we have to sort through it. Stella came across a small, sealed pot. Being Stella, she had to open it. She took all this polyfiller away from the top, and thought at first that someone had been using it as an ashtray. Then she saw that bits of bone were in it and she realised it was somebody's ashes. She was so shocked that her immediate reaction was to drop it in the bin.

Although we don't like being here on our own we're not particularly bothered by the activity as long as it doesn't get any worse. However, we would like to know what we're dealing with.

The lost dog (The Palace Theatre)

In the early 1900s a Mr Ales came to Redditch and persuaded some of the local people to help him build a magnificent theatre. The Palace Theatre opened in 1910 through the hard work of a clockmaker, a builder and the local milkman who was also in the fishing tackle trade. The theatre was later saved from demolition by the Redditch Development Corporation and in 2005 is undergoing an exciting restoration.

Becky is a drama student and on the Redditch ghost walk (performed by the Redditch Amateur Dramatic Society) she remembered that one of her old mates from the School of Dancing had had an unnerving experience at the Palace Theatre. So she very kindly got in touch with her friend who gave the following account:

I don't know how much the Palace Theatre has changed now, but there used to be a stone spiral staircase on the left hand side of the stage which led up to the changing rooms. It was cold there and not very nice and it was where all the dancers had to line up ready to go on stage. At rehearsals, the technical buggers would sometimes turn the lights off so that you were in the dark. The kids would be screaming but on top of all the screaming you would smell an unusual stench. You would think, 'This isn't right' and you would realise that the smell was that of wet dog fur. When the screaming died down, you would hear the clicking of paws, as if a dog was trotting towards you, and then you would feel a wet dog brushing against your legs. You could smell a dog, hear a dog and feel it. Then the lights would go on and no dog would be there.

It seemed to me that this tied in with the rumour that the Palace was haunted by an old caretaker who had lost his dog and came looking for it. This was the dog looking for its master.

The haunted hospital

Smallwood Hospital opened in 1896 and cost £10,000. The money was given by the Smallwood family who made a fortune from golden-eye needles. When Redditch expanded as a new town it was obvious that Smallwood Hospital could not cope with demand and a new hospital was opened in 1986. Now that Smallwood hospital has closed we can reveal that it had a ghost. A retired nurse who was on duty there for ten years says:

I can't tell you my name because I was doing something that you were not supposed to do, I was asleep when I was on night duty. We were allowed a break and I had gone over to the sitting room in the old nurses home which overlooked the church. I sat in an armchair and I must have gone to sleep. The next thing I knew, something gave me an almighty bump. I didn't actually hear a voice but I could feel something saying to me, 'Time to get up dear!'. It was a very warm and pleasant feeling, not at all frightening.

Magic in the Webb

A day out with Judith is fascinating as she seems to have a sixth sense and can see 'dead people'. In 2001 she was working at the Redditch Standard, Webb House, Church Green East, Redditch, as an Administration Assistant for Customer Services, and as the building is at least 200 years old it's not surprising that Judith found herself watched by a mysterious entity.

At about eleven o'clock one Tuesday morning in November, I was using the photocopier which was situated on a small landing at the top of the first flight of stairs. To the left of me was a another flight of stairs going straight up to the second storey, with a wide wooden banister rail. I suddenly became aware that, out of the corner of my eye, I could see an old lady hovering on these stairs. I could only see her from the head down to where her knees would be. She was bent forwards with age and she was looking straight at me. As I placed the copied work on a small table to my left, right next to

I suddenly became aware that, out of the corner of my eye, I could see an old lady hovering on these stairs. (Webb House, Church Green East).

the banister rail, I had a better view. I noticed that she was wearing a black taffeta dress buttoned up to her neck with pintuck detail, and leg-of-mutton type sleeves. She had a walking stick in her right hand and a fan in the other, again these were black. Her hair was pure white and pushed back from her face, she was wearing a black shawl on her head which loosely flowed over her shoulders. She had a hooked nose, pale skin with rosy cheeks and small lips with mid-blue eyes. I remember the stern expression on her face as she stood there watching me. When I turned round completely to have a good look at her she was gone, as suddenly as she came. I think she had been there the whole time that I was photocopying, about 15 minutes.

Before the building was taken over by The Redditch Standard it was owned by Webb's bakery, and one member of the family was a formidable lady by the name of Catherine who lived till her nineties. Did Judith catch a glimpse of Catherine?

One for the chop

Although Redditch was considerably expanded in the 1970s, it remains at heart a Victorian town of needlemakers. Many of the needlemasters built splendid houses, some of which still stand and are used as residential homes or offices.

I work in one of the old Victorian houses on Church Green which has been converted into offices. It's really old and creepy. I have all the blue-bottles collecting my end of the office, I don't know where they come from, I'm always swotting the things even in the middle of winter.

Sometimes I feel as if someone is watching me. The feeling is so strong that I have put a mirror on the right hand side of my desk so that I can see right past my shoulder so that I know if anyone is there.

I was writing in my book one morning recently, adding up some figures when somebody said my name quite clearly and he or she put a hand on my shoulder. I looked in the mirror and nobody was there. It made me jump. I thought somebody was larking about and I went out to see who it was, but everybody else was down the other end of the office and they were all in the middle of telephone conversations. Nobody was up my end at all. I was by myself.

When I told the others they said that it must be the old butcher come back to haunt us. I assume the premises were once occupied by a butcher.

A short walk southwards from the town centre is another Victorian resi-dence, used by a small company as offices. None of the staff will stay in the building on their own. One of them says:

I have never been into this sort of thing and you wouldn't get me watching programmes about hauntings on television, but I feel that there's something not quite right about this place. We often hear footsteps when nobody else is in the building. Sometimes the back door goes and there's nobody there.

Between my office and the front of the kitchen is a passageway where the hall was, leading up to another office on the top. All the light is artificial and sometimes I see a shadow moving there, going into the corridor. I must say that although I have never actually seen a person, I have a feeling that it's a Dick Turpin-like character with a triangular hat. He is really, really tall and he is hunched over.

Our tea and sugar goes missing. My colleague says, 'I only bought 160 tea bags last week, where have they gone? - and the sugar's disappeared'. We're linked to the house next door, at one time you used to go through our office to next door. We thought it was the people next door pinching it and we set traps but we never found anything.

The boss had been working on his own late one night and he said to me the following morning, 'You're right you know, there is something not quite right here'.

I try not to work here after dark but at this time of the year, when it's dark early, I have no choice. I had to be here at eleven o'clock one night and that's when I saw a shadow in the corridor. I'm not frightened of death but I am frightened in this place. When I lock up at night I have two outside doors to lock and my colleague is in fits of laughing because I lock the one door from the outside, then I go all round the building on the outside to reach the other door.

I sometimes wonder if it's something to do with next door because the footsteps that we hear are on wooden stairs - all our stairs are carpeted and next door have wooden stairs. You hear all sorts of stories and rumours about the place next door. It was a bakery in about 1900 and the story goes that the baker heard that his wife was having an affair and so he hanged himself. Years later when it was a house, the owner of the property died on the premises.

I won't go back into the office on my own. I came in with my daughter one Saturday morning to catch up on some work, she's ten but a very grown-up ten. She wanted to have a go on the Internet so I logged in for her. We were sitting there when my daughter said, 'It's a bit spooky in here'. My reply was, 'Don't be so stupid'. With that there was a tremendous crash as if a clothes rail had been knocked over. Then we heard footsteps running away. I often hear footsteps but these were running. I said, 'Oh my God, just let's get out'. We had a good look round outside but nobody was about.

Spooks at the Tandoori (Unicorn Hill)

You can hear the following story first hand if you visit the Dhaka Balti in Beoley Road West and ask for Abdul. A few years ago, in about 1997, he was working at the Redditch Indian Takeaway on Unicorn Hill:

Our Tandoori chef lived in Aston, Birmingham, and I was asked to take him home after we closed at midnight. It must have been about halfpast one in the morning when I was on my way back, and just before I got to the Westmead Hotel, about fifty yards ahead (just under 50 metres), I saw a dark figure floating, or rather gliding, across the road. I couldn't believe it. I thought I was seeing things because I was tired, so I stopped the car, rubbed my eyes and opened them again, and the figure was still there. It was very tall, about seven feet tall (about two metres) and in dark attire with one of those long heavy overcoats that men used to wear and a top hat. I couldn't see any details, it was quite solid. I watched it carry on gliding across the road until I saw it blending into the bushes. I didn't wait any longer, I sped off.

When I got home my parents and brother said to me, 'What's wrong?'. Evidently my hair was standing on end. My brother still jokes about it to this day. I was so shocked that I didn't tell my friends about it for a long time. I knew they would just laugh.

What's that! (Alcester Street)

On the far side of the Palace Theatre was a row of shops and one of them was occupied by Jean's family:

Alcester Street was full of large houses with long gardens, the horses were kept round the back. My brother's bedroom backed on to the stairs and at night he would hear the stairs creak as if somebody was walking up them towards his room but nobody was there. He would wake up in the night and hear mysterious rustling noises as if someone was rustling paper. When I was living in Alcester Street, I heard my name called several times, 'Jean'. I called my mother, but it wasn't her. Once my name was called three times and when I went to see who had called me nobody was outside the door.

You would be in a room and there would be a knock on the door. Then the knob would turn and the door would slowly open but nobody would be there. I remember that on one occasion my sister said, 'Mum, I know that's you' but my mum was downstairs.

When my mother was first married she was in the house with her grandpa and grandma. The door at the back was a heavy door with two panels of glass. A bang came on the door which shuddered the room. My mother said, 'What's that?!' but my grandma and grandpa didn't hear anything!

The sleepwalker

One of the best known people to come from Redditch is the author, Roy Clews. Abandoned at birth, he was adopted by an unstable Redditch family and the unhappy experiences of his childhood inspired his books. His early novels, published in the 1970s and 80s, told the story of a young factory girl by the name of Tildy and featured Redditch in the early 1800s. It has been said that they made Redditch famous. Roy has very kindly sent us details of a Redditch ghost seen by him and his friends. Beaufort Street is still there, at the bottom of Mount Pleasant, and so is part of South Street:

It must have been in late 1946 when the shielded lamp lights had been relit just after the war. There was a lamp on the corner of Beaufort Street and the Driveway ... and another lamp halfway down the top section of South Street. The old Terry House stood in its own shrubbed and treed grounds, and was then occupied as a hostel by girl munitions workers. Anyone coming out from its main double gates and crossing the road would be silhouetted against the lamp light from either the top or bottom lamps.

A group of we children, ranging from 8 to 11 years of age, were clustered around the lamp at the Beaufort/Driveway. I think it would be around halfpast seven in the evening, and it was fully dark. When quite suddenly, the solid silhouette of a woman walking in the classic sleepwalker mode, with arms stretched out before her, came out from the large gates of the Terry House and walked very slowly across the road. The distance between us would be less than twenty yards. The solid black silhouette was so sharply edged and clear that it seemed to me she was wearing a long floor-length full-skirted dress, and that her long hair was hanging loose down her back. She was fairly short. We kids immediately took it to be one of the hostel girls trying to frighten us in revenge for the pranks we played constantly against them, and we reacted by hooting and shouting and throwing volleys of stones at the figure. But then when almost over the road it disappeared!!!

We exploded in all directions, scared half to death, and it took me ages to summon enough courage to run past where she had appeared, in order to reach my house, where I told my foster-parents what had happened. My foster-mother said afterwards that I was as white as a sheet.

The kids I can clearly remember being there, were Billy Danks, aged 11 or 12, Phillip Wall aged 8 or 9, John Danks aged 8 or 9 and myself, aged 8 or 9. There were a couple more who I can't remember clearly.

The local Wise-woman then was a lady named Esther Smith, and she told my foster-mother that the apparition was a death omen. She said that there had been a maid-servant killed by lightning or other Act of God in the old Terry House just after its construction and that it was she who had come back to warn of another death ... Strangely enough, some time after this,

Billy Danks was knocked over and killed by a bus at the bottom of Mount Pleasant, virtually in a straight line of continuation to the line taken by the ghost and perhaps forty yards distant.

I've pondered many times about this ghost, questioning how it could have been created by other means, and seeking explanations. But the memory of it is as visually sharp in my mind now as on the evening it happened, and I personally am utterly convinced that what appeared before us that night was a genuinely paranormal happening - a disembodied spirit from another world or dimension.

Going to the Dogs (Herbert Terry & Sons)

Alcester Street has been changed almost beyond recognition. It was once a straight road from Church Green to the Ipsley Road. At the one end was, and still is, St Stephen's Church but if you stood with your back to St Stephen's and looked straight down the road you could see another church at the far end, a Baptist chapel. Unfortunately, it was in front of, and surrounded by, one of the largest factories in Redditch, Herbert Terry & Sons, a spring-making company. The company survives in the Anglepoise Lamp of which they were the sole manufacturers. In 1898 Terry's wanted to expand and so the company paid for the Baptists to have a new church in Easemore Road which still exists. Terry's used the old chapel for storage but it burned down in 1932. Locals said it was divine retribution for using a consecrated building for a commercial purpose.

Johanna now lives in Solihull but she was born in Redditch and her father worked at Terry's:

My late father came to England from Poland after the Second World War, where he met and later married my late mother, Mavis. My father was best known to all his mates as Johnny or Ken but his real name was Kazimierz, Kaz for short. One of his jobs was as boiler-stoker at Herbert Terry & Sons, sometime, if my memory serves me well, in the late 50s and early 60s. My father had not long been in this job, when arriving at work around 5 am, he noticed a dog walking around in the boiler room on a few occasions. He ignored this, thinking that maybe the dog had just come in from outside to keep warm, and that the dog could belong to someone who worked there. It wasn't until one day his curiosity got the better of him, and he decided he would ask someone whose dog it was. One morning, he arrived at work early and assumed a gentleman he saw was a work colleague. He asked him if he knew who the dog belonged to, but to my father's surprise, the gentleman never answered. By the time my father had put down his shovel and turned round to speak again, the gentleman and the dog had disappeared. My father naturally assumed that the man had gone off to do another job, and that the dog had followed him out of the boiler-room. When another work-mate (whom my father knew) came into the boiler room, my father asked him about the strange man and this dog, only to be told that the man and the dog were, in fact, both ghosts. They visited regularly and no-one had any idea who they were or what their history had been. My father was not one to be scared easily but it made the hair at the back of his neck stick up.

My father then took up another job within Terry's as an Electrician's Mate, so he never encountered these sightings again. In fact he worked at this factory for many years after (as did my mother) and never thought to ask anyone else about these sightings.

Celestial vibrations (Other Road)

Of all the old Victorian roads in Redditch, residents of Other Road seem to experience the most ghosts. An apparition from this road seems to have featured in every book. Perhaps past inhabitants return to object to the way that the road has had an enormous traffic island plonked right in the middle so that it has now been cut into two pieces. One part goes up the hill to Trafford Park and the other, longer, piece runs past the eastern side of the college. Sylvia's house was once used by the Salvation Army:

They were known as the 'Loafers'. One day recently, my husband was doing the vacuuming, he unplugged the Hoover but it went on vibrating. My grand-daughter had a little plastic toy that you stick on the window and only last night, when we were in the middle of a meal, it removed itself from the window and flew over to the other side of the room. We have net curtains but it still managed to fly right through them. There's one particular bedroom that gives us a lot of problems and the cat won't go in it.

We had so many problems we called a lady in to sort things out. She said that there are two little children in the attic, Elizabeth and John. Elizabeth died when she was small. We don't mind them being there so long as they're not a nuisance.

Goings-on at the Big House (Mount Pleasant)

Mount Pleasant, with its ornate Victorian houses, was once one of the most desirable places to live in Redditch, and there are still many large houses in existence. The house in this story has now been made into flats and so, to avoid frightening the residents, it has not been named:

My grandmother and my mother both lived within four doors of each other on Mount Pleasant. I was a quiet and serious child and my grandmother used to talk to me and tell me all the latest gossip. She said that one of the Mount Pleasant children had a birthday party and they were all playing in the garden when a white lady drifted through the fence and came towards them. They all fled. Aunty would never go down the garden at night.

There was a wall in our garden which was a boundary between us and a large house. My grandmother said that the people there had had an only daughter. She fell in love with the groom and her parents thought it was unsuitable match. They took her abroad and that sort of thing but she never got over it. In the end she starved herself to death. In the cemetery there's an angel which was put up by her parents.

After the war the Bartleets (needle factory owners) came to live there, I can remember them coming down the drive in this great big car.

I had quite a weird experience when I was a child. I had gone to bed early with a headache, consequently I woke up early in the morning before everyone else. I heard some peculiar noises, like a pipe and drum band. At the same time, the clouds in the sky seemed strange, they were an unusual pink and I just knew that they were going in the wrong direction. I was terribly puzzled. Anyway, I fell asleep. Next morning I told my grandmother and she said to me, 'You are not to say anything about this to anyone' but I heard her talking to my mother about the strange goings-on. I gathered that there were ghosts at the big house.

The years went by and I became a school secretary. One of the young teachers came to the school. By that time, the big house had been divided into flats and he lived in one of the flats. He subsequently became deputy head. I said to him, jokingly, one day, 'You haven't seen the ghost have you?' He said, 'What do you know about ghosts at there?'. I told him that I used to live on the other side of the wall and I used to hear things from the grown-ups. You know what Redditch people were like in those days, it was only a small community and people used to gossip. He said, ,'You are right about a ghost or ghosts'. I asked him, 'Have you seen it?'. He told me, 'No but things disappear, and doors bang and open for no reason'. He added that he couldn't stand it any longer and he was going to buy his own property. And he did, he bought a flat in Studley.

Just checking progress (Enfield Industrial Estate)

Royal Enfield moved to the Redditch site in 1906. At first they bought only a few acres but by the time the Redditch Development Corporation acquired the site Royal Enfield had expanded to 30 acres. Norita worked on the Enfield Estate:

When I started work, my first job was on the Enfield Industrial Estate, at the Royal Enfield factory before it closed down. I worked in the Export Department which was downstairs in one of the old parts of the factory.

In those days, on Fridays, anybody connected with the Works Offices or the Works could leave at 5.00 or 5.30. I had to stay until 6 o'clock, so I was often alone in the office at that time. My boss travelled and was away a great deal. There was another secretary but she came under Works so she could leave early, so could the four Progress Chasers in the office.

This particular Friday evening I was in the office on my own, sitting at my desk finishing off my post. The door that led out to the corridor was partly glazed, I was on the opposite side of the office to the door and at right angles to it. Out of the corner of my eye I saw a white coat approach the glazed door and I saw someone come in. The Progress Chasers wore white coats, not the brown ones like the men in the factory. There was no sound, 'I thought it's Geoff and he's going to leap out and make me jump'. The Progress Chasers were all young and there were a lot of practical jokes about. I looked up and there, standing in front of me and looking straight at me, was a figure. He faded quickly. So did I!

I can't describe him very clearly as I was looking at the white coat. I know that he was youngish, tall and slim - he had the dimensions of a young person. I can remember looking at the same spot and just seeing the other side of the office. I told myself, I did see it, I did see it! Afterwards I realised that I hadn't heard the door creak. I didn't feel that there was any danger from him. I don't know who was the most scared, him or me!

I was surprised. It was so sudden, so real and so unexpected. I would have felt better if he had stayed! I went home and I said to my mother, 'I have seen a ghost at work today!'. She said, 'Oh did you?' and that was that.

Afterwards, people at work said to me, 'Oh, you have seen it?' so other people must have had the same experience. Presumably he was a person who used to work there who had come back.

Fire burn and cauldron bubble!

Ghosts seem to prefer fire stations to churchyards. Strange incidents at both Smethwick and Perry Common Fire Stations are described in *Midland Ghosts and Hauntings*. The ghost at Pershore fire station was well-known and from the Redditch station came tales of ghostly monks and inexplicable breezes. Both fire stations have been featured in *Unquiet Spirits of Worcestershire*. The fireman's wife in the following story has lived in two stations, they were both haunted and one of them was, again, Redditch. The latter lies on the old road into Birmingham and is only half-a-mile from the site of Bordesley Abbey:

We used to live in a flat on the second floor of New Cross Fire Station in London. It was well-known that something was lurking there. We used to have lots of inexplicable incidents. Our curtains used to open and close - if we left them open we would find them closed and if we left them closed we would find them open. Then there would be scented smells that would be nothing to do with what we had in the house. We had a flat roof that came out at an angle. The footsteps would go along the flat roof to the end but would never come back. Things were always being turned off. If I put the kettle on it would be turned off, I would be ironing and my iron would be turned off. Things would go missing. We always seemed to lose potato peelers. I thought perhaps I had thrown them away with the peelings so I tied one on to the taps with string and it still went missing. We never found any of them. It was always said that a fireman from New Cross had died in a fire and it was his ghost that walked the station.

The next story is about Redditch Fire Station. The Council decided to widen the road junction outside the fire station when building the new estate at Brockhill. The fire station was too close to the corner of the road, so they had to lose a corner of their forecourt which is next to their dormitory. Because of the disruption the firemen were temporarily moved upstairs.

Just before all the firemen actually moved up one of the firemen went to sleep up there and woke up feeling that he was being held down by someone, although he couldn't see anything. Because of the notorious tradition of practical jokes, he searched every nook and cranny determined to get his revenge but no-one was about. The next morning he was relating his experience to the rest of the watch when one of the firemen said that something strange had happened to him. During one night he had seen a woman walk through the doorway, through the bed and through the glass doors without opening them. It had spooked him so much that he had got out of bed and had sat in a chair for the rest of the night.

Subsequently all the firemen moved into the upstairs dormitory. One night, one of the firemen was woken up by a sudden cold draft. He sat up, wide awake, to find another person sitting up in bed, also looking puzzled, having been woken up by the same draft. They checked all the windows and doors and nothing had been disturbed. When talking to other firemen on other watches several of them mentioned that they had felt someone sitting on them during the night but they hadn't seen anything.

All this happened during the few months that the work on the road was being done. When the work finished the strange incidents stopped.

We looked into the history of the site of the fire station. It lay on the route along which the monks of Bordesley Abbey had walked to their grange at Tardebigge.

The night-time visitor (Abbeydale)

As the wife of a local councillor and magistrate, and mayoress in 1998/9, Monica Fry is well-known in Redditch. She came over from Jamaica in the 1970s and has a firm belief in the paranormal, especially after the following experience:

When my son was born in 1984 I was living in Huband Close. I found it very difficult to sleep as I was in a lot of pain, especially in my back from an epidural, so I woke up in the middle of the night. The bedroom door was very difficult to shut but I had pushed it hard and it was closed. Suddenly, I saw my mother-in-law coming in through the door. She had died a few months previously. I shook my husband to wake him up but he only twitched. His mother glided across the room towards the window and bent over the pram, evidently hoping to see the baby but he wasn't there, he was in the cot next to the bed.

Just before she died, my mother-in-law went very fat but now she was very slim, she looked a lot younger and she wasn't wheezing and coughing. She was wearing a dress with a red motif all over it, rather like tulips, it was one that my husband and I had chucked out when we were clearing her flat. Then she disappeared. Later, I said to my husband, 'I'm sure that if you had woken up you would have seen her'. I couldn't get over it. How had she managed to get hold of the dress that we had thrown out?

A few days later I was feeding the baby in the living room when I felt as if someone was there, watching me. I knew it wasn't my husband because he was at college. A friend of mine came to the house and said, 'Have you had a guest?'. I told her that I hadn't. She said, 'Somebody was definitely here because I can smell their perfume'. I hadn't had time to bother with perfume.

A few days later I was in the kitchen, making up the baby's bottle when I smelt the perfume myself.

Lonely as a cloud (Easemore Road)

We have been asked not to reveal the identity of those involved in the next story:

In the 1980's I lived not far from the bottom end of Easemore road and I walked up and down the road each day to get to work. One of my co-workers was a young man by the name of George*. He was in his early twenties and was planning to get married the following year.

There's a dip in the road, by the bridge, and when I walked past one morning I noticed that men were laying huge pipes there. At the end of the day they had been left at the side of the road and I thought how dangerous they looked. I said to myself, 'I hope nobody goes into those pipes'.

A few months later, I was going home one winter evening and when I got to the bridge I noticed this oval-shaped cloud behind me. When I stopped, the cloud stopped. When I walked quickly, the cloud walked quickly. I thought, 'This is weird'. I was quite scared, I didn't know whether to go back or to go on. I just stood there and watched it. The cloud came towards me, then it opened out, the mist seemed to take shape and there was George. He was wearing an outfit rather like a tennis player, with a white tennis shirt, white shorts, white socks and white tennis shoes. He was all in white except that the socks had coloured rings round the top. He bowed courteously and I bowed back. Then I watched him as he drifted away off the bridge.

I knew that I hadn't seen him at work for some time. I thought he had gone in the army or something. The next day at work I asked where he had gone. They told me he had been killed in a motor bike accident. He had been riding his bike home late one night and he had gone into some pipes left at the side of the road by the bridge.

The mysterious kleptomaniac (Headless Cross)

The old folks can remember a time when Headless Cross and Crabbs Cross were country villages with lines of Victorian houses occupied chiefly by needle and fish-hook makers. Now there is very little left of the needle industry and the two villages have become part of Redditch.

Julie's* house was built in 1938 but it replaced another on the site.

I lived in a haunted house for 27 years. My family moved there during the mid 1970's, when I was sixteen. The first thing that happened was my mum kept asking me every morning why I kept getting up in the middle of the night. It was something I hadn't done before. She would say, 'I heard you getting up again last night'. I kept telling her that I hadn't got up. She thought I was sleepwalking. She said she could hear me walking across the landing, going into the bathroom, pulling the light cord and washing my hands. The light switch would go off and she would hear me walk across the landing, presumably to go back to bed. This went on for weeks and weeks.

My father thought he would try and see what I was up to. When he heard the noises he got up and stood on the landing. He heard the footsteps, the light, the taps, the swishing, the light go off - the lot, but there was nothing to be seen. I was fast asleep. This happened two or three times.

Strange incidents went on and off for months. On one occasion, my mum came charging upstairs, saying 'I have just cleaned this house and just look at the mess!'. Wet muddy footsteps went all the way through the house and the kitchen. I told her that I had been upstairs all the time. I pointed out that the footsteps didn't come from or go anywhere. They started in the middle of the lounge and went into the middle of the kitchen, where they stopped. They were the footsteps of a slender-footed woman.

When I married, my husband and I bought the house from my parents, we moved in and they bought a house elsewhere. While I was living away from home I had bought a little dog and so she moved in with us. She would follow me around but she would never sit on the landing in the house. She hated going upstairs, she was frightened. If she thought you had left her upstairs on her own she would cry.

A lady moved into a house that overlooked the back of our house. She came round one day, she was very pleasant but she said, 'Could you ask the person standing in the back bedroom window every day watching me - could you ask her to stop it?'. She said that she saw somebody there. I didn't tell her that the house was empty all day, we were both out at work. I just closed the curtains in the back bedroom.

We would sit up, waiting for the footsteps and the noise, they were always in the middle of the night. Once, the bedroom door refused to open while the noises were being heard. It had stuck. When the noises stopped the bedroom door flew open.

Then things started going missing - hairbrushes, toothbrushes. You would go into the bathroom where there should be two toothbrushes and two flannels, there would be one toothbrush and no flannels. The hairbrush would be in the bedroom. They were silly little things. You would put a pen down while you were working at the table, go away for a minute and when you returned it would be gone. We never got anything back. I kept thinking that one day we would go into the loft and we would find a pile of flannels and toothbrushes but there never was. Something usually happened every month but you could go two or three weeks without anything happening at all. We once went for a year without any curious incidents.

We started having curtains opening and closing. You would close all the curtains at night but when you went back into the room a few minutes later they would be wide open. We had a house full of people one night. Everybody was in the lounge, the curtains were closed, then everybody went into the dining room. When I went back into the lounge the curtains were open and they had been pulled so hard that they were off the runners. I said to everybody, 'I would like you to see this'.

You often got the feeling that someone was watching you. Once, I was standing at the bottom of the stairs, when I had this feeling of being watched, so I turned round and there was a lady standing on the landing, just looking down. I saw her for a split second. She was tall and very slim and not at all frightening. She seemed to be watching, almost as if she was keeping an eye on things. From below, looking up, the first thing I noticed was that she was wearing little ankle boots and her feet were very slim and slender. She was young and dressed very simply, with a blouse and a long skirt nearly down to the ankles. Her hair was fair but was scraped back. It all happened very quickly.

She didn't like you to change anything. Decorating was pandemonium. All the things you really needed kept going missing - paint brushes, tape measures, pencils - they all kept disappearing. Things would be moved, the lid off the top of the paint would go. It must have been about eight years ago that I was trying to decorate the dining room. Every time I put a piece of paper on the wall she pulled my hair. It was very trying. It went on for two or three days. I can honestly say I was never frightened but it just got a bit wearing. I did actually turn round at one point, I was desperately trying to get this job done and my hair was being pulled so hard it was pulling my head right back. I said to her, 'Will you pack it in!'. This was the only time I have spoken out loud to her. It stopped. A lot of people said the dining room was never a warm room. We hadn't noticed it until people started mentioning it.

In the early eighties it went fairly quiet. A few things happened - things disappeared or my husband would come home and the house would be like a beacon with every light on. We would get up some mornings and all the taps would be running in the kitchen, or at night the taps would be running in the bathroom.

Then we had my son. I always had the impression that she was keeping an eye on him. Regularly his toys were tidied into a pile and sometimes put behind the door. You would try to open the door and all his things would be behind it. Sometimes the books were off the shelf and stacked neatly in a pile on his little desk. When he was a little bit older he would say, 'There's somebody in my room' but we always dismissed it. We didn't want to frighten him.

Then we had our daughter. Her shoes were put in a line in the middle of the bed and her books were stacked. If she left things on the floor they would be piled on her bed. Again, things were stacked behind the door. One day, there was a pile which must have been about four feet high. All the prams and buggies were put on top of each other. They were placed ever so carefully with the dolls' clothes on the top. It would have taken someone with a lot of strength and time to do that. We couldn't open the door, we had to put a hand round, and as soon as we moved the pile half of it fell down.

We had a business acquaintance come to the house and as I hadn't quite finished the outwork I was doing for her, I showed her in. She stood watching me while I was finishing. All of a sudden she said, 'Do you know you have got a lady watching you while you are working? She is just standing there, watching you'. I said, 'Oh, alright' and she remarked, 'You don't seem very concerned'. I told her that I was quite used to her. This business acquaintance told me that the lady was surrounded by dogs. I said to her, 'Do you do this sort of thing often?' She told me that she had done it ever since she was a child. I asked if she wanted to have a walk round the house. When she went into the back room she felt a cold spot. I said that it had never bothered me or frightened me. She said that the lady was not there to do us any harm, she was just keeping an eye on us. I told her that we'd always had that impression.

When my parents first bought the house, the lady living here used the front room as a lounge and the back room as a dogs' room. She had a number of chairs in the dogs' room, one for each dog. The day that we moved in, I said to her, 'You can come back whenever you like to see what we are doing to the house'. Because she was so upset at having to leave the house she died two weeks later.

We recently moved out of the house. We didn't move everything all at once and for a few days we left a lot of the children's belongings behind. We were going back to fetch my daughter's things, but my husband, who was in the house, telephoned to say, 'Keep her away!'. He said that the whole room had been turned upside down. Boots and shoes were flung on her bed, together with her books. They are now teenagers, and so we decided that they were old enough to know what had been going on. My son said, 'I always told you I could hear things and you always said that it was only you or daddy coming into my room in the middle of the night'. My daughter was quite interested.

Before this started, my husband was one of the most sceptical people you could ever wish to meet, up until the point where the bedroom door wouldn't open. A lot of people have heard noises and seen strange things, especially friends who popped in, for example, they saw the curtains pulled back. It never bothered us and nothing ever happened to anybody else who lived there.

The 'Woodend' scandal

A retired gentleman tells the tale:

In Birchfield Road was a large house called 'Woodend'. By the side of the house was a field and in this field was a barn with a pair of double doors going up to the roof. You opened one of the doors to find a hay loft. There was a lot of talk about a scandal that occurred in the 1920s. A local girl was having an affair with a married man. She was pregnant or something and he jilted her, so she hung herself from the beam going across the hay loft. The story has been in my family for some time.

The barn was pulled down and houses were built on the site. I lived in one of them and my great-aunt lived next door. After my great-aunt had passed away, a young couple from Birmingham bought the house.

They came to me one day and said, 'Did your great-aunt used to lived here?' They kept seeing a woman walking across the landing. They said that she was wearing old-fashioned clothes.

I told them that the ghost was probably not my great-aunt but the young girl who committed suicide. I said that it would not be malevolent to them, only to the bloke who jilted her.

Bewitched (Lodge Park)

The new housing estate of Lodge Park is build round an old pool, known in years gone by as 'The Dark Waters'. A few years ago, Rose moved to the estate:

It's not so much ghost story but an evil presence in the house. I was married in those days and we were looking for a house. We found a semi-detached in Lodge Park which had been built in about the 1960s. When we first went to the house I didn't feel 100% good about it. Before we went in I sat in the car outside for some time with my husband. It was a modern well-kept house and the right price but I said, 'I don't know how I can buy it. I feel there's something wrong about it'. Then I thought, 'I'm being silly' so we went in. I said the same to the woman in the house and she said, 'Once you have your things in everything will be fine'.

I seemed to have no interest in the house. I love gardening, but I didn't do any gardening. I'm always decorating, but I didn't do any. Once I heard banging upstairs when I was the only one in the house, I don't know what that was.

Not long after we moved in I started having nightmares. Every time it was exactly the same. In the back of the house there was a double bedroom and in the dream I slept in this room. In the garden below was a man in evening dress, late Victorian or early 1900s but without hat or gloves. He was a dark-haired man, good-looking with broad shoulders and tall, about 38/40 years of age. He had a cloak to knee level which was tied at the front. He was wearing a white shirt with a ruffle down the front.

He gave off the most appalling sense of evil that I have ever experienced in my life. The feeling was that I was drawn to the window. As the dream went on so the man began to look up at the window. He wanted to reach me and the only way he could do that was for me to open the window. Every dream I had I was getting nearer to the window. At first the dreams were only every month but then they became more frequent until I was having them every night. I used to wake up screaming and covered with sweat.

We stayed there just over a year. I could not stay there any longer. By the time we moved I had opened the window slightly ajar. At the same time I became very ill. When we left the house I was so ill that I couldn't pack to move, I had to ask the removal men to do it. I was really glad to see the back of the place.

In the summer of 1979 my sister came to stay from abroad and stopped for a week with her two boys. I was so anxious to leave that we went into temporary accommodation. After we had sold the house, I said, 'I'm really pleased I got out'. My sister remarked, 'If you had stayed in that house, I wouldn't have visited you again'. I said, 'What do you mean?' She said, 'When I was there, I kept having the most appalling nightmare'. She began

The feeling was that I was drawn to the window. ... Every dream I had I was getting nearer to the window. (Lodge Park).

telling me her dream and I stopped her halfway through and finished it. It was exactly the same as mine. She was drawn to the window and a man wanted her to open it.

I hadn't told either her or my mother about the dream. I was afraid that if I told someone, it would come back. The only person who knew was my husband and he didn't believe in anything so he said I was having a nightmare.

Laying a ghost (Crabbs Cross)

Crabbs Cross is on the boundary of Warwickshire and Worcestershire on ancient cross roads on an even more ancient prehistoric ridgeway. The traffic island in its centre is known as 'Boney's island', probably after the amount of barefist boxing that went on there. The sport was illegal but, if a magistrate from one county arrived to stop the fighting, the pugilists had only to step over the border to continue fighting.

Houses mushroomed in Crabbs Cross and Hunt End in the 1840s and 1850s, when two needlemaking factories were built, Welch's and Townsend's. The Townsend factory developed into Royal Enfield, famous for its motorcycles.

The area has an unusual mix of Victorian and modern housing, side by side. Becky* lived in a modern house:

I moved here in 1986 and I absolutely loved this house. Even after my husband left me in 1991 I carried on living here alone for another six years and never felt afraid. One night I had a really weird dream that I was standing somewhere in the area around where my house was, only there was nothing but rambling fields and hills and I knew that it was definitely many, many years ago. I had never been that interested in the history of Redditch but the image in my dream was so clear that I felt the need to go and hunt out some old maps of the area and this really started my passion for local history. I started reading lots about the area and surrounding villages etc and it was about this time that I had a strange encounter.

A couple of times I started to feel as though I wasn't on my own in the house and I'd 'feel' a shadow behind me but when I looked around there was nothing, obviously. Whenever this happened I would feel jittery and a bit uneasy and I used to tell my friend who lived two doors away all about it. There was one occasion in particular I remember that I ran to her house shaking because I had been standing at the kitchen sink when I heard an almighty 'BANG' right behind me, like a door slamming, although nothing was out of place. I remember on that occasion my friend coming round with a bottle of Lourdes Water and chanting Hail Mary's - it's really funny now but at the time I was pretty shaken.

One evening, I was sitting in my living room, chatting with a friend who was visiting me, when I noticed three small orangey-red lights dancing around on the fireplace. I stopped mid sentence and said to my friend, 'Oh look at that, what is it?' and I pointed to the lights. But she just couldn't see them, and then as quickly as they appeared, they just disappeared again. That wasn't scary, just weird.

The scariest thing happened one night while I was sleeping. A few times I had felt vibrations in the staircase which woke me up, and heard creaks as though somebody was trying to come upstairs without waking me, and each time this happened I was terrified, and then it went away again. However, one night I wasn't actually asleep but I was very tired and lying in bed, thinking about things, when I felt and heard the movement on the stairs again. I can honestly remember saying to myself, 'Calm down, it'll go' and I lay in the dark, waiting - but it didn't go. I felt the floorboards in my bedroom moving as they would when being walked across. My heart was absolutely racing and I was burning up really badly - I could actually hear my heartbeat thudding through the mattress. I lay there still and I remember thinking, 'Oh my God, this isn't happening' and I have to emphasise that I was extremely awake. All of a sudden somebody sat on my bed - I felt the mattress dip and I 'dipped' with it. Somebody then climbed into my bed, snuggled up to me, put an arm under my waist and I heard a man's voice whisper 'Budge up' right into my ear. At this point I completely freaked - I bolted up, screamed and dived out of bed, switched the lamp on - and nobody was there. I was completely terrified and couldn't get to sleep for the rest of the night. I experienced a lot of trouble sleeping in the dark for a long time after that.

The factory apparition (Park Farm South Industrial Estate)

Studley Road runs from St Bedes Roman Catholic School, south-east of the town centre, to Studley. Just over halfway along its course it passes the grounds of Kingsley College, and on the other side of the road is part of an Industrial Estate, known as Park Farm South. The latter was built on the site of the old Shakespeare's farm.

In one of the factories there, many of the workers are talking about an unusual visitor. One employee says:

We have all seen it, even a couple of women who didn't believe in ghosts. They laughed at us when we said we thought there was a ghost in the place, but now that they have seen him they have changed their minds!

He walks around, he has got a trail and he takes a certain route. Sometimes it goes very cold, then you know he is about somewhere. His tour takes him behind me, and I can just see a tall, dark shape in a black coat. Just once, in January, I saw him more of him for a fleeting second, his arms were folded, he had dark hair and he was looking at us. He would have been about 40 or 50. That's the only time I have ever seen his face. He goes upstairs a lot, at Christmas he was upstairs and he was terrible, banging and throwing things about, it sounded like the clappers up there. He likes to be present when there are a lot of people around, he doesn't show his face when not many people are about.

I was sitting at the end of the production line, fixing lights on to strips, when suddenly the strips shot up in the air, then they came down again. The music goes loud and soft for no reason and sometimes, you can't switch it off. Things that are at the back of the shelves jump off and land on the floor.

We have been told that the factory is on the site of a large garden belonging to the farmhouse. We thought it might be the gardener.

There's a nice atmosphere though, you don't ever feel that he's nasty.

The Wobbling Apparition (Beoley)

The old Roman Road, Icknield Street, runs through Beoley. The Redditch historian writes that Beoley may have been the local service station for the legionaries travelling along the Street. Where the old Roman Road crosses the A4101 seems to be a favourite spot for hauntings. The archives tell of the Beoley goblin who jumped on horses' backs so that they refused to go up the hill, and the charcoal burner who was burned to death on Beoley Hill - his screams can still be heard when the wind is high. Over the past ten years ghosts have been seen wearing evening dress, a deerstalker hat, a cagoule and wellingtons, there have also been the inevitable monk or two. At a meeting of the Alcester Merry Wives in January 2005, one of the ladies told how, in the 1920s, her mother was walking from Redditch to the Village Inn at Holt End with a group of friends when it began to rain. They were sheltering under a tree near Beoley Church when the ghost of a white lady appeared.

The houses were once clustered round the church but the population has now moved away to Holt End, leaving only Beoley Church, Beoley Hall, a few farms and green fields. Beoley Church is on a hill and the satellite village of Church Hill is spread out at its feet. Anne lives in Church Hill but she works in Birmingham and her daily journey takes her near to the Church:

I was driving to work at halfpast six in the morning of Tuesday, 8th February 2005, when, as I turned left to go into Dagnell End Road from Icknield Street, something caught my eye. In the other part of Icknield Street that runs past Beoley Hall, I saw a white lady walking away from me down the middle of the road. I couldn't see her face as she had her back to me but, although it was dark, I could see that she was all in white, with a crocheted shawl over her head and wrapped tightly around her, It ended in a v-shape just below her bum. Beneath the shawl was a cotton-type dress that came down to her calf, the bottom part came out slightly and was a grey colour. She was hunched, she could have been elderly or hunched up from the cold. As she moved forward she was swaying slightly from side to side, almost like a wobble. You see pictures of old Italian woman with a shawl tightly over their head, she was like that. Something in the clothes she was wearing told me that she was not from nowadays, plus the fact that you couldn't see her walking. I thought it might be somebody who needed help. I stopped the car, took hold of the steering wheel and pulled myself forward on to the windscreen to get a better look. I sat there for a good three minutes. Then she disappeared.

As I drove off I looked back and she was still not there. It frightened me to death. I was so cold with goosepimples. I thought 'I've got an awful cold, am I hallucinating with a temperature?'. I knew I just had to get away, I drove like a mad woman along Dagnell End Road. I was in a blind panic, if a car had been coming up the road I wouldn't be here to tell the story. I argued with myself so much afterwards. Was it real or not real?

After work, I drove back to see if anything could have caused the apparition. I could see a bollard but that had nothing to do with it.

The Phantom Car (Ipsley)

*I*n the Domesday book of 1086 there is a fleeting reference to Ipsley. It was a large parish, on the 1830 Ordnance Survey map it extends from east to west for about two miles, from the old Gorcott Hall to Headless Cross. Most of it covered a desolate, marshy area, subject to Will o'the Wisps, and it was not until the Redditch Development Corporation arrived in 1964 to cover the farmland with houses, that it became heavily populated. Now it's surrounded by the new town, although Ipsley Alders has been preserved as a nature reserve.

There's an old story about Ipsley churchyard. A woodcarver was working in the Church one New Year's evening and he had taken his little daughter, who was playing outside. Suddenly, he heard her screaming. She said that an angel on a tombstone had begun to turn the pages of the book she was holding. With that, the woodcarver chopped off the angel's hand with a tool that he was holding. Since then, every New Year's Eve, a ghostly hand grows back on to the arm.

Fiona and Bob moved to Ipsley at the end of the twentieth century, their previous house was 'Rose Cottage'.

Rose Cottage was always a comfortable house in which to live. However, in the lounge we would sometimes get a strong smell of perfume, which couldn't be accounted for. A very old friend of ours noticed it and identified it as gardenia. None of our own family used the perfume or could identify it.

Someone would walk all the way round the house many times. Whilst sitting at the dining table we would see just the back of a man (shoulders and half the hat) who appeared to have gone the wrong way round to the back door. We became fairly used to this and did not take any notice. Sometimes someone visiting would see it and say, 'Someone has just gone round to your back door'. We would often go to look and I would say 'It was probably a shadow' which saved trying to explain something for which there was no explanation.

One day, when my daughter was twelve, my wife was about to take her to school. The garage was at that time eight pine posts with a roof. The car was a three-wheeler with no reverse gear. To go backwards one had to switch off and start the engine backwards with a dyno-start and then stop again and carry on as before. Having exited the shelter my wife started the reversing procedure when our daughter shouted 'Look out mum, there's a car behind you' - in the space she had just vacated! The said car seemed to drive right through them and out through the five bar gate - which was oak!

Needless to say, my wife was more than a little shaken, and was still shaken when I arrived home from work. She told me all about it and we decided not to bring the matter up in case it had an undesirable effect on the twelve-year old. However, when the time seemed to be right, I asked my daughter, 'What was this business about the car?'. She was not by this time unduly worried, so I asked her to roughly sketch the shape. It was bulbous and curvy, and as near as I could make out, something like an old Austin A70. I asked my wife the same question separately and she came up with a similar shape.

All very odd. The car shelter was not old, where it stood there had been pigsties some years before, the shelter had no history, I put it up myself, so nothing has a logical explanation. When someone asks if I believe in ghosts, frankly I don't know what to say.

Rose Cottage, alas, has now been demolished by some greedy developer.

Caught short! (Foxlydiate Hotel, Webheath)

The Foxlydiate stands on the site of a large house that was pulled down and re-built as the Fox Lydiate Hotel in 1938. The original pub was over the road and known as the 'Fox and Goose' but was demolished in 1947. The young lady who tells the following story goes by the name of 'George'. She was only six years old when she visited the hotel with her parents and took herself off to the loo:

You know the corridor down to the ladies loos? - Well, I was walking down there on my own and I particularly remember feeling very cold. Then, I distinctly saw a grey shape walk from the wall by the kitchen and out of my view. I ran round the corner, thinking it was a person, but saw the silhouette of a lady with long, wavy hair down to her waist. I screamed, wet myself (remember, I needed the loo) and ran back the way I came. I still can't go down that corridor on my own and I even take my mum if I have to go on an urgent visit!!

Body Parts (Blackstitch Lane, Webheath)

Webheath is on the western edge of Redditch and has modern housing built round a Victorian core. Strange to say, the next ghost was seen in one of the new roads and not in the old:

On Friday, 29th April 2005, my grandson was coming home from visiting friends in Flyford Flavell to his home in Oakenshaw. Although it was 2 o'clock in the morning, he hadn't been drinking - my grandson is a very sober young man and sticks to fruit juices and mineral water. If he has one glass of wine, that's it. I believe he was making a slight detour to drop off one of his friends.

He was driving along in the Blackstitch Lane area when, all of a sudden, he realised that he could see a dark figure about two feet out into the road from the gutter. He slowed down and he had to move out into the middle of the road to avoid him. The figure was wearing a shawl or something which covered its head over a flowing gown. My grandson couldn't make out whether it was a man or a woman. As he drew level with the figure he looked out of his side window and, to his horror, he realised that he could only see part of it - the figure didn't have a complete body. As he passed he looked in the wing mirror and the shape was still there. If it had been a real person he would have jumped back on to the pavement before a car hit him.

It really shook him up.

Odours of sanctity

Perfumes are thought to be of great significance in the spiritual world. After death, the bodies of saints should not, properly, decompose in the normal way but retain an 'odour of sanctity'. Lyn, who lives in Redditch, is haunted by strange smells.

When my mother-in-law passed away I had this really strange smell for the whole day of her funeral. It was very distinctive. I thought it was me. I thought, 'What have I been using?'. I said to my husband, 'Can you smell anything?' but he couldn't. Very occasionally, it has come back, I think mother-in-law's around again.

When my cousin died there was this very strange, sweet perfume on the night of her funeral. It was there when I went to bed. She used to wear a perfume of the same scent but I don't know what it was.

I had a strong smell of moth balls after my grandmother died. I can still smell it occasionally. She used to be a milliner, and she had big wooden boxes full of feathers and decorations for hats. We used to love to play with them when we were children. You get the smell of mothballs in them although I don't think it was actually mothballs, more the preservatives.

I find that the perfume is one that was associated with the person when he or she was alive.

Uncle Harry's Glasses

We conclude the Redditch section with a strange tale from a local lady.

In my early twenties I had a good friend called Linda who decided to pluck up the guts to go and see a psychic or a clairvoyant or something. The woman told Linda that there was a woman with her when she came into the room. She described the lady as, 'young and pretty and wearing a beautiful white dress'. It didn't mean anything to Linda and the psychic added 'Find your Uncle Harry's glasses and you'll have the answer'. Well, when she told us about this at work, we used to make jokes about it, and 'Uncle Harry's Glasses' became a sort of punchline whenever anything out of the ordinary occurred - ie Uncle Harry's Glasses would know the answer, that sort of thing; very childish I know but it gave us a few laughs.

Anyway, one Sunday afternoon Linda phoned me up in a very distressed state. Linda did in fact have an Uncle Harry (I suppose the chances were pretty high - the name Harry featured quite strongly in my own family and I guess most people had an Uncle Harry lurking around somewhere). Linda's Uncle was an old man who had been in hospital for a long time, and it was decided that he should be moved into a residential home as he was incapable of taking care of himself.

Linda's mum (whose uncle it was) and Linda had the awful chore of having to clear up his bungalow in order to hand it back to the Council. Linda told me that there was a load of junk on one of the window sills and she was just putting it all into a box when she knocked a framed photograph on to the floor. As it came crashing down Linda's mum looked round and saw a pair of reading glasses on the windowsill behind where the photograph had been. She picked them up and said to Linda, 'Here's Harry's glasses, he's driven us mad trying to find them'. Linda said she felt a bit prickly at that point and looked at the photograph. It was an old black and white wedding photo of her Uncle Harry standing with someone who was clearly not her aunty. She asked her mum who it was and her mum (who was oblivious to the fact that Linda had been to seen the psychic) told her, 'Oh, that's Harry's first wife. They were only married about six months when she died - they buried her in her wedding dress'.

12. Stourport-on-Severn and Hartlebury

ourport-on-Severn is one of those towns that hides its light under a bushel. It's full of interest, yet rarely features among the tourist attractions. The town was created by James Brindley in 1765 as a small port on the river Severn and much of his engineering work - his basins, his locks - are still there. Stourport has one of the oldest Methodist churches in England (open to tourists on Saturday mornings) and the Church of England has one of the largest graveyards. The new Church of England has the ruined arch of the old one next to it. The old one took half a century to build and then only lasted ten years before it blew down.

Until the Beeching axe fell in the 1960s, there was a railway station near the centre of the town so that, in the days before everyone had a car, holiday-makers from all over the Midlands and especially Birmingham, flocked there. It still has a holiday feel, with caravan sites, plenty of fish and chip shops and a small permanent fair. There are also quiet river walks for those who like a peaceful, rural holiday. Many people who take a holiday at Stourport decide to settle there in retirement.

Across the river Severn on the southern side of the A451 are the caves of an ancient hermitage. In medieval times there was a ford here, where monks established a monastery to help travellers. Old manuscripts imply that they grew rather greedy about their renumerations. The level of the river Severn has risen by five to six feet since the building of Lincombe Lock in 1844 so the ford has now gone but the weathered remains of the caves still exist.

On the northern side of the A451 in Areley Kings, is the ancient church of Saint Bartholomew. In about 1200, Layamon, who was the priest here, wrote the first great literary work of the English language, translating the heroic tales of King Arthur from the French original.

Ghoulies and ghosties and long-leggety beasties

This charming and compact town has many ghosts. The Bridge Inn overlooking the river is one of the oldest pubs in Britain and two licensees have seen a lady in a crinoline dress wandering through the premises. Before the Drill Hall was converted into flats a ghostly sergeant was seen several times noiselessly shouting and banging his fist on a desk. Family-owned shops along the old High Street have had various problems. The Stourport historian, Margaret Dallow, says:

Grinnall's Greengrocers, near the Swan Hotel, had to be exorcised in 1985. Part of the former premises was occupied by the Mormons, who were previously evicted from the premises, declaring that they would return one day. In 1984, the upstairs room, which were occupied as offices, began to experience strange happenings, doors opened unaided, kettles switched themselves on, lights flashed on and off, while female staff complained of ghostly hand touching their shoulders as they climbed the stairs.

She, herself, had a curious experience:

As a keen photographer, despite always taking two films with me, I often run out of film. This happened in the 1980s. I was looking over some old cottages that were being renovated, with an elderly couple. The man drew my attention to an initialled and dated lintel by the front door of the end cottage. Having used up my film I went back home, picked up another film and spent the next quarter of an hour searching for the brick - I never found it. A few days later, when I knew workmen were about, I approached them and asked about the brick. None of them remembered seeing it and the front of the cottage in question had not been touched. Very, very strange.

The weekend visitor

In 1979 a young couple moved into one of the Victorian houses in Brindley Road:

We thought something was not quite right when we first moved in. Where the kitchen is now, was the bathroom, and when the cats went in, they meowed and hissed.

Over the next few years we made a lot of alterations to the house. Then, about three years ago, things got worse. We felt as if someone was in the house with us. My wife heard somebody walking up the stairs when there was nobody in the house. I thought that somebody was behind me in the kitchen area and my wife said that she had the same feeling - she thought that I was behind her. It usually happened at weekends.

Someone told us that if we experienced anything more we would get help from the local vicar, so about three years ago we contacted her. She brought us some forms and it took us about two hours to fill them in. She wanted to know if we knew the people who had lived in the property before. Did we know anybody who had died in the house? We did know the people who lived in the house before, they were Methodists, and although they have all passed on, they didn't die in the house. She brought a gentlemen along and they blessed the property.

About three weeks ago it started up again. I put down my brief case, which has a combination lock - I always put it back at a certain number and when I picked it up, the number had been set at 666. Nobody could have touched that brief case, and I was the last one working with it. Nobody except me had been in the house. It made me feel quite odd.

The couple have evidently now moved from the property as the house is occupied by another family.

Uncle George says 'good-bye' (Wilden)

On the Kidderminster side of Stourport-on-Severn, scattered along a steep drop to the river Stour, is Wilden. Bewdley has stolen much of Stourport-on-Severn's thunder by claiming Stanley Baldwin, the prime minister of the 1920s and 1930s, as its own. In actual fact, he spent many years in Wilden where his family owned large iron works. Not only is there no plaque on Wilden House where the family lived, the house itself has disappeared altogether.

Stanley Baldwin's family and the Burne Jones's were related with the result that the little church at Wilden is the only one in England with a complete set of Morris windows. From the outside, All Saints Church looks like an ordinary little Victorian church but its interior is ablaze with colour.

From Wilden comes an intriguing anecdote:

My uncle George lived near the brow of the hill in Wilden, Stourport-on-Severn. He was a builder and had been in the army, consequently he was a very down-to-earth man, but in his younger days he had had an experience that he could never explain.

Uncle George went for a walk with two sisters and when they were returning to the house, they met their uncle at the gate of a stile. The uncle lived nearby and had been so very poorly that they were surprised to see him out of bed. They said to him, 'What are you doing here?'. He said to them, 'I've just come to say, 'Good-bye'. They all saw him and he was as solid as you and me. When they reached home they heard that he had just passed away.

HARTLEBURY

Half a mile to the east of the outskirts of Stourport-on-Severn, is Hartlebury Castle.

The original castle goes back to about 1255, when it was built as a military stronghold, complete with moat. During the civil war of 1642-46, it was occupied by the Royalist army and was particularly important because the royal mint was here, making coins to finance the war. The castle surrendered at the end of the war, for a time it was used as a prison, but later demolished. It was rebuilt in the late 1600s and 1700s.

The Bishops of Worcester have lived here for four centuries. Many of them have been at the heart of great British events, some even helped to change them. Bishop Stillingfleet was chaplain to Charles II. Bishop Fletcher was present at the execution of Mary Queen of Scots and made a clumsy attempt to convert her. Bishop Sandys supported Lady Jane Grey and went to prison for it. Two of Worcester's Bishops, John Hooper and Hugh Latimer, were burned at the stake in 1555. John Hooper was also Bishop of Gloucester and was therefore burned outside Gloucester Cathedral. Before a fire was lit, gunpowder was usually tied round the victim's neck to ensure a quicker death but in Bishop Hooper's case, it failed to explode and he died a terrible death.

Bishop Latimer was a popular preacher who campaigned for Henry VIIIs divorce against Catherine of Aragon and the break from the Roman Catholic Church. He was appointed chaplain to Henry VIII but quarrelled with the king, resigned the bishopric and lived at Hartlebury in grinding poverty, selling his books and even his clothes for food. Henry VIII died in 1547 and by 1553 Catherine of Aragon's daughter, Mary Tudor, a staunch Roman Catholic, was on the throne. 'Bloody Mary', as she was became known, executed about 300 preachers and even dug up and burned the long-dead bodies of Protestants. She clapped Latimer under close arrest and two years later he was taken to Oxford where he was tried and condemned for heresy. As the bonfire was lit, Latimer spoke his famous words: 'We shall this day light such a candle by God's grace in England, as I trust shall never be put out'. He was right. As he predicted, their deaths inflamed the growing hatred of Mary and turned many against Roman Catholicism.

Until the early 1840s the Bishop of Worcester had two residences, Hartlebury Castle and a house near to Worcester Cathedral, still known as 'The Bishop's Palace'. Then in 1841, Bishop Pepys arrived with his wife and four children ready to move into the Worcester Palace, only to find he was locked out! The previous Bishop, Bishop Carr, had left such huge debts (j100,000) that creditors had even tried to seize the dead body of Bishop Carr to sell for dissection and Bishop Carr's friends had had to pay them off so that they could bury him. The house and its contents were impounded. All Pepys' belongings were piled up on the pavement outside and a crowd gathered as he argued with the creditors. Finally, he gave up and lodged at the house of a local solicitor. After that it was decided that two places of residence were too costly and one of them must be sold. Pepys decided to keep Hartlebury Castle - a strange choice as the Palace is almost next to the Cathedral and would have been much more convenient.

The famous library at Hartlebury Castle was created by Bishop Hurd in 1782. He was George IIIs favourite bishop and was offered promotion to the post of Archbishop of Canterbury but he declined. Margaret Dallow, the historian, says:

At the top of the main drive of Hartlebury Castle is an avenue of trees, and here the sister of Bishop Hurd has been seen 'floating' along towards the parkland gate almost opposite the old mill.

A few years ago a regular visitor went to the Castle with her husband and children:

I have been to Hartlebury Castle several times. At this particular time there was a children's trail and while we were doing this the curator asked us if we had been before and we said, 'Yes'. He asked, 'Have you ever been in the library?'. We told him that you have to go with somebody and it's usually closed. He asked us if we would like to have a look and he took us there.

The library goes right the way across from one side of the room to the other. It's very long, it must cover 40 feet. All the Bishops of Worcester have used it. I went up to one of the windows and I was just looking at the view outside when I found that I couldn't breathe. My chest went so tight. It was just like somebody putting a weight on my chest. I said, 'I have to get out'. My husband said, 'Are you alright?'. I said, 'I have got to move away from the window, one of the Bishops obviously died here'.

The curator told us that one of the Bishops walks from one end of the room to the other most nights and disappears through the wall where there was once a doorway. He told us, 'I haven't seen him but a lot of people have'.

There's a sequel to this story. After reading this account, David Kendrick, the Collections Officer for the Worcestershire County Museum, remarked:

I have made enquiries with members of staff who accompany visitors through the State Rooms but there is no recollection of this lady's visit - at least not in the terms she suggests in the text. There was a 'lady and husband' who visited last year when the lady experienced something at 'the top of the stairs' - probably the top of the main museum stairs where a similar experience of 'presence and chill' took place several years ago.

The top of these stairs led into the servants' dormitories where there may have been deaths and certainly some unhappiness. This would seem more likely than at the top of the library stairs as, until 200 years back, one would have been standing in mid-air!. The library is more recent than much of the castle having been built on to the back of the Great Hall and Saloon in the 1780s by Bishop Richard Hurd. The detail of the blocked door is not correct - the doors at both ends are still functioning; one for us, one for the bishop, so neither are 'blocked'. There is no record of a bishop (or anyone else) dying in the library in the book written by Bishop Pearce which lists the lives of the bishops from 854 up to the 1920s. To be truthful, I am very disappointed that we cannot support this story - we could really do with a decent ghost here! Quite why with the long history of Episcopal occupation and with one bishop burned at the stake (Latimer) and another (Cantilupe) siding with de Montfort in the 13th century Barons' Revolt we don't have one is a gross supernatural omission!

Just one thing springs to mind. The lady's account says she was talked to and accompanied by 'a curator'. The three curators here, - Robin, myself and Anita Blythe - don't usually take individual visitors around the State Rooms or galleries. Yet the comments made by the 'curator' about the library being only accessible when accompanied (by a Visitor Guide or Attendant) are quite correct. I wonder if it was the 'curator' who was from another plane ......?

The Holy Ghost (Hartlebury Church)

The tower of Hartlebury Church was built in 1587 by one of Worcester's most colourful bishops, Edwin Sandys, born into a wealthy family in 1519. He held Protestant views and helped to put Lady Jane Grey on the throne, consequently when Mary came to the throne, Edwin was clapped in the tower. Queen Mary allowed him to be set him free by mistake, soldiers were sent to re-capture him but he managed to escape to France. When Queen Elizabeth came to the throne Edwin was able to return to England and was appointed Bishop of Worcester, then eventually Archbishop of York.

During his travels he stayed at the Bull Inn, Doncaster. He had recently discharged from his service a notorious character by the name of Bernard Maude. Maude and his new employer plotted to involve Sandys in a great scandal. They hid the innkeeper's wife in the bedroom cupboard, she waited until Sandys had gone to sleep then she climbed into bed with him. Enter Maude and accomplice. They demanded property and j800 to keep quiet but Edwyn refused to co-operate. A fight ensued with Edwyn victorious. This came to the ears of Queen Elizabeth who insisted that Maude and his employer went to gaol.

Sandys was a great benefactor and founded a school at Hartlebury. He arranged to have the tower added to Hartlebury Church the year before he died in 1588 and it still exists, although most of the church was rebuilt in 1836/7.

About six years ago a local lady was having an organ lesson with the organist, when:

We were sitting at the organ stall with our backs to the main church, when we both went freezing cold. I turned round and I saw, in the Lady Chapel, a tall, black figure. He had the stature of a man and was wearing a hooded cape that reached the ground but he seemed to have no feet. He was facing the altar and was turned halfway towards us so that I should have seen his profile but his face was fuzzy. I was so frightened that I turned away and when I looked back a few seconds later he had gone. I didn't tell the organist.

A few weeks later a small skull was discovered when part of the old church was dug up to provide a toilet.

Mary, the organist, was giving lessons when a series of strange incidents occurred:

I'm the organist at Hartlebury Church and, in the past, I've taught various people to play the organ. A few years ago I was teaching a young gentleman. At the front of the church are big old doors that you open with a large key. There is a large middle door and two smaller. These are always kept locked. We would go down in the evening and let ourselves in at a little door at the side with a Yale key. My student and I had no idea that anything had been experienced in the church before. What happened came 'out of the blue'. We were both chatting when we heard one of the big doors behind us unlock. I said to my student, 'What's that?'. He replied, 'Someone has just unlocked the door, perhaps it's the bellringer, John'. We carried on with the lesson. Just before we went, my student remarked, 'I'll just go and say 'good-bye' to John'. He came down the bell tower and said, 'That's funny, there's no-one there'. We tried the big door and, sure enough, it had been unlocked. I told him that I would go and tell the church warden. The warden said, 'It should be locked, I'm sure that I locked it when I looked in last night and the only other person with a key has gone on holiday'.

A week or two later we heard three enormous bangs as if one of the large doors in the Church had been slammed shut behind us. It was so loud that it reverberated inside. The first time it happened my student went to check the doors and they were all locked. It happened again a few minutes later. Again, he went to have a look round. He said, 'Perhaps someone is messing about, my girlfriend is in the car outside, I'll ask her if she's seen anyone'. She said that no-one had been about. By this time we were a little nervous. Then it happened again. Now, my student was a big bloke, about six feet tall but we both moved so fast that we wedged in the door trying to get out.

When we mentioned the incident to other people, the cleaner said that she often heard footsteps. She just says, 'Welcome, whoever it is'. Apparently, there have been one or two other instances. I have always felt uncomfortable in there on my own. There's one corner of the church I don't like, it always feels cold.

I did get locked in once. I have always blamed my daughter but with hindsight, I don't think she did lock me in. I had gone to practice and taken my daughter as I don't like being in the church by myself. We went in through the little door at the side. I always propped it open, with a chair against it. There's another door through into the church and I prop that open with a chair, too. After a little while, my daughter asked, 'Can I go out to play?'. I said, 'Yes, but whatever you do, don't shut the doors.

When I had finished practising I went to go out through the door. The inside door was locked and so was the outside door. You can't unlock them from the inside. I had to shout really loud, 'Emma! You've locked the doors and I can't got out!'. She couldn't open the door either and she had to go and fetch the vicar. I said, 'You silly, silly girl, I told you not to lock the doors!'. She swears that she didn't.

No-one has attempted to identify the dark figure but the possibilities are many. Could it possibly be Father Garnet, who was once a priest at the Church? He was implicated in the gunpowder plot of 1605 and was hung on 3rd May in St Paul's Churchyard. He was supposed to have been hung, drawn and quartered but, after he had been hung and before he was dead, the crowd surge forward and, taking pity on him, some pulled on his legs so that he was dead before he was cut down and taken to the block.

Several miracles are said to have happened after his death. His head was deposited in a straw-lined basket but all of a sudden, a bloodstained husk of corn leaped out of the basket and into the hand of a young man, John Wilkinson. Folk swore that the bloodstained husk assumed the pale face of Father Garnet with a bloody circle round his neck. The husk was smuggled out to Catholic France but lost during the French Revolution.

Before severed heads were put on poles it was customary to have them parboiled, which blackened the features, but Father Garnet's head remained miraculously white. This drew such a constant crowd of spectators that the government ordered the head to be faced upwards.

HEIGHTINGTON - The inexplicable slap

About three miles west of Stourport-on-Severn and the same distance south-west of Bewdley, is a scattering of houses known as Heightington. Before Bewdley bridge was built in 1447 it was a place of some importance, as it was on the main route from Worcester to Wales. Travellers crossed the river Severn at Redstone ford (now below Stourport-on-Severn) and made their way to Cleobury Mortimer and on to Wales.

Eight hundred years ago King John is reputed to have worshipped at the tiny chapel of St Giles when he hunted in the Wyre Forest.

Heightington is a well-known beauty spot as it lies on high ground with magnificent views, to the east is the Severn valley while to the west is a spine of hills from Abberley to Malvern.

Near Heightington is an old farm crammed with ghosts. Mary* says:

The house was built in 1740. Everybody who comes here is confused because the back is at the front and vice versa. The Vicar of Cleobury lived here for some time, also the Yarrantons and the Wainwrights who emigrated to Australia. In 1922 my husband's parents bought the house. I have been told that some of the beams in the house are made from ship's timbers.

Whenever anybody came to stay here for a short period, every time they used the bathroom they could feel somebody had slapped them around the face. That happened to two or three people. I now reckon that was my mother in law who wanted to prove she was still here.

We went through a session of problems with pictures on the wall, we would get up in the morning and they would all be lopsided. A picture would sometimes fall off the wall and on to the floor for no reason. I heard lots of conversations in the room above. Two years ago I woke up at about two o'clock in the morning and I could hear a really gentle conversation between a man and a woman. I couldn't make out what they were saying.

One morning, I had been putting some washing by the stairs and I was just about to go into the bedroom when I saw a little girl aged ten or eleven standing on the landing. She was beautifully dressed in a calf length, velvet pink dress, with smocking across the top. She had long fair hair, some of it at the back in ringlets. She was wearing white tights and black shoes. She looked very real. I turned and when I turned back she had disappeared. She was here and then she wasn't.

The house is full of ghostly animals, especially cats. There have been so many cats and dogs here over the years. I'm often tripping over them, then I find they're not real ones. I was making the bed one morning, I looked through the bedroom door on to the landing and I saw something white

He (the Cavalier) has a black cape-type thing round him, a hat and a plume, he's aged from mid to late 30s and is very tall and very thin. (Heightington).

there. I went and had a look and it was a beautiful white cat. It was quite solid. It was curled up as if it was asleep in the sun. It started to go up the second flight of stairs into the attic and then it gradually disappeared.

For two years I occasionally saw a fair-haired young lady in her mid-twenties. She wore a long crinoline-type dress in cream and she was always walking down the stairs. Sometimes she had a candle in her hand. She was lovely. We had a really nice feeling when she was around the house.

I wasn't the only one who saw these ghosts. One afternoon, I was sitting in the lounge with three friends when we could all smell the smoke of a pipe. It was a fruity type, a sweet tobacco. Only my husband smoked and he isn't allowed to smoke in the house. My friend, Susan, said that she could see an old man sitting in the corner smoking a pipe. She said that he was dressed in rough country clothes, hessian type, and he wanted a glass of whisky.

When my son was about two or three he used to say to me, 'Mum, I have seen something up in the attic'. He couldn't really describe what he had seen. This went on for a good 12 months.

Both my mum and I have seen a Cavalier. Years ago we would have been absolutely petrified but now we were so used to these apparitions we were just fascinated. He has a black cape-type thing round him, a hat and a plume he's aged from mid to late 30s and is very tall and very thin. There's an old story round here that some of the fugitives from the Battle of Worcester took refuge in our barn. He was thin because they were short of food. Mum was sitting in the chair in the lounge and I was upstairs getting changed ready to go to work. As soon as I came downstairs my mum said, 'I have just seen a Cavalier in here'. Not many weeks after that, about 2 or 3 weeks, he was here for a couple of minutes. He looked very real. He just stood there, looking round then he suddenly disappeared. Mum and I then had a discussion comparing what we had seen. He only comes into this room, I haven't seen him in any other part of the house.

Over the Easter period, four or five years ago, my neighbour from a mile up the road went on holiday and my son and I looked after her animals while she was away. In the 1820s there was a murder there and the body was thrown into a pool at the side of the house. I have been told that if you go anywhere where there is spectral activity it can attach itself to you.

Later that evening I saw a figure in my kitchen and assumed it had come from my neighbour's house. It was a tall man, with a black cloak and a big black hat. He looked like the Grand Inquisitor in the Gondoliers. I thought, What's he doing in my house? He disappeared after five or ten minutes. It was quite eerie. It sent a chill through me.

I was quite unnerved by this experience.

13. UPTON-ON-SEVERN

he King of Mercia gave Upton-on-Severn to Winchcombe Abbey in about 800 AD, but the laws of inheritance were very complex and a century later a descendant of the donor, Aethelwulf, claimed that Upton-on-Severn was his. Eventually, he gave it to Worcester on the condition that the monks at Worcester should pray for his soul after his death and that there should be peace between his descendants and the Bishop of Worcester for ever.

As a busy inland port, Upton-on-Severn was a wealthy town. The Georgian houses and inns were substantial and well-built, and many of them are still in existence, such as the White Lion, where Henry Fielding stayed and was so enchanted that he set the final climactic scene of Tom Jones there. The town was rich enough to have three new churches. The first was built in the fourteenth century, then in the 1700s it was pulled down and rebuilt except for the tower which acquired a dome, a cupola and a lantern. This second church was pulled down when a new church was built on a different site in 1879, but again, the tower was left standing and is now nicknamed 'The Pepperpot'.

Annus horribilis

Only a stone's throw from 'the Pepperpot' is The Health Centre in Old Street. It was once Malvern Hill Council District Office & Tourist Information Centre. Barbara* worked there in the late 1970's and early 1980's.

It's a very old building and lots of people have said how spooky it is. At the back of the office was a room and it was always cold. The place could be almost burning up and still that room didn't feel warm.

I was working there in the May of 1980 when I felt a sharp tap twice on my shoulder. I turned round and to my surprise, nobody was there. On the one side of the office is a large window and on the other wall is a smaller window. I was standing with my back to the radiator (to be honest, I was warming my backside) and looking out of the smaller window when again, I felt the same sharp tap on my shoulder, twice, just as before.

I thought, 'Somebody is trying to tell me something'. I felt that something terrible was about to happen. Sure enough, a day or two later I had a near head-on collision in my car. I had quite severe injuries and the Council tried to make me redundant. It was my annus horribilis.

The terrible Captain Bound

Alan* lives in an old house near the centre of Upton-on-Severn. He has had several strange experiences, for example:

One night we heard what sounded like someone doing the washing up. It went on for ages. My partner heard it as well. She said, 'Who is doing the washing up at this time of night?'.

We thought it was our lodger making a statement because I had asked him to do some washing up occasionally. I was going to get up but then it stopped a few seconds later, so I went back to sleep. The next morning we discovered that the lodger wasn't there. He was out

It could have been the rattling of chains that we interpeted as washing up. There was a very metallic sound to it, like pots and pans.

The strangest experience of all occurred soon after he had moved into the house:

One evening I was feeling a pressure in my head, I thought I was going to get a headache and went to bed early. I woke in the night and thought I was having a dream. I was floating and I could see my body lying on the bed. I remember thinking, 'I am having an out of body experience', so I floated into the front room and started counting the folds in the curtain and noted where the shadow of the curtain was hitting the carpet. I made mental notes of objects and projections - being a builder I could assess the measurement of things. If I remembered these details I could compare them against the real thing the next day to see whether or not I had been dreaming.

Then a mellow voice said to me, 'Go and get William Bound'. I had never heard of William Bound. The voice repeated, 'Go and get William Bound'. I flew out of the house to Callow End, it was such fun and I felt such freedom. I stopped at Callow End and looked round, it was dark. Then I flew on to Worcester and round Elgar's statue. Then the voice came back saying, 'OK, you have had your bit of fun, now you have got to go and find William Bound'. In an instant I was back in my house. I could hear a baby crying, the sound was coming from the attic. It had a ghostly feel about it and I didn't want to go anywhere near it. I was getting frightened. I began to pray and as I did so, I felt my body getting brighter and a Christ-like presence came into the room. At this point I went though the ceiling and up into the eaves of the attic and came back down holding the baby.

Then I said to myself, 'Oh, he's not black'. I don't know why I said that. This Christ-like presence and his light took the baby away. When this was done I felt exhausted and heavy. I walked back to my body, lay down beside myself and heaved myself back in.

I woke up next morning totally exhausted thinking I had had a very vivid dream. However, when I checked the creases in the curtain, the shadow on the carpet and all those things I had memorised in great detail the night before, everything was correct.

Two days later, a friend came with his wife. His wife said to me, 'I didn't want to say anything about this before, but the last time I was here, that night I had a horrible dream that there was a dead baby in your attic. I thought I ought to tell you as it was so vivid.' I was shocked by this.

I forgot the name until a couple of years later someone mentioned Captain Bound. Suddenly, the name came back to me. I jumped up and said, 'That's it, the name was William Bound'. But why William? Captain Bound's name was Thomas and he had neither a son nor a brother named William.

Evidently, Captain Bound lived in a house which is very close to mine, and there all kinds of rumours about him. Legend has it that he got a maid pregnant and locked her away at the top of the house. I wonder if the rumours are true, and that the maid he got pregnant was black - it's a fact that black servants were employed in those days. That would explain my remark, 'Oh, he's not black'. Perhaps the baby was murdered at birth but the mother thought of him as 'William'.

Thomas Bound lived in Upton-on-Severn during the middle of the 1600s. As a young man, he was a God-fearing Parliamentarian and became a church-warden in 1640. He fought for the Parliamentarians in the civil war of 1642 to 1646 and was made Captain. He acquired enough money to buy the Manor of Harvington in 1652. Perhaps the atrocities of the Civil War warped his mind because he turned to a life of crime. A female body found in one of the top storey rooms of The White Lion was thought to be one of his victims. E M Lawson wrote in 1869:

He was a terrible wicked and cruel man, who married three wives and murdered two, and forged the will of an old lady to get her farm at 'South-end'. The old lady's ghost then began to haunt him and he drowned himself in a pool by the causeway. His ghost then began to haunt the area and was very troublesome. The minister laid him under a great stone that formed part of the little bridge by the pool but he was soon loose again.

The phantom hitch-hiker

A collection of ghost stories would not be complete without a phantom hitch-hiker. To quote Barrie Roberts, 'The problem with phantom hitch-hikers are that there are so many of them.

Mr Raymond lives in Upton on Severn and as a musician, he regularly travels

167

through the Midlands. One September evening he had an experience which changed his perception of the paranormal for ever:

About ten years ago, I was meeting a band in Hereford to go to a gig. It must have been around September because it was just beginning to get dark earlier. I went to Ledbury, then I took the A438 to Hereford. Just as I was exiting the little roundabout on to the road for Hereford, I saw a man standing by a little bridge and he waved me down. Thinking he was in trouble or needed a lift, I stopped.

I opened the door and asked him, Where are you going? He replied, 'Where are you going?'. 'To Hereford' I replied. 'That will do', he said. So I let him in the car. He must have been in his mid-fifties with a long, black coat. This would be in twilight but I saw a glimpse of his face and I thought he looked like Van Gogh, stubble and all.

I drove on and I asked him, 'Do you live in Ledbury?' He said, 'No'. Then he said, 'Is this the way to Wales?'. I told him, 'You can get to Wales this way but which part?'. 'Mountains', he said, 'And hills'. So I said, 'You live in the Welsh mountains?' to which he gave a vague reply. Then I said, 'Brecon Beacons are this way, and you can get to all different parts of Wales from Hereford, so I will drop you in Hereford'.

Then he said to me, 'Have you ever been out of your body?'. Thinking this was a fairly strange question to ask someone you have only just met, I declined to answer it, saying, 'No'. He continued, 'I seem to have problems where I keep coming out of my body. I don't know what's going on half the time. I feel all light-headed and floaty' and he started to describe to me how he felt.

I then got the impression that he may have been abusing drugs so I asked him, 'Have you been taking LSD?' to which he replied, 'What's that?'. I asked him if he had been taking magic mushrooms or any of the hallucinating drugs but he didn't seem to know what drugs were. Then he said, 'Do you think it's the work of the devil?'. I replied that I very much doubted it, I didn't think there was such a thing as a devil.

I thought this was a very strange conversation to be having and tried to ease the situation. I asked him, 'Are you ill? Have you seen a doctor?'. He replied, 'No, but I have seen a priest'. I asked him what the priest said. He told me that he was there but he didn't know.

Having had enough of this conversation I tried to steer it to more mundane things, but it seemed to me that that he kept trying to steer us back to his topic. We spoke for a little while about normal things. I told him I was a musician and I was going to Hereford to perform.

He said, 'A musician? What do you play?'. I told him 'A guitar'. At this point he got very uninterested as if he didn't understand what I was saying to him. After a while, the conversation returned to his subject. I told him that

I had heard about out-of-body experiences but that it had never happened to me. It was the wrong thing to say, because he then said, 'So you have heard of it then?' and it strengthened this particular conversation.

I told him he may be deficient in something like a certain mineral. 'It could be something you are not getting in your food'. After all, he was a very thin man. I told him how I had a problem with my ears which made me feel all floaty and off-balance. Maybe he has something similar. I told him that when he got to Wales, he should get a doctor to check him out and look in his ears.

I came to the point where I knew something was wrong. It was now getting darker but we went through a village that was well-lit and I was able to get a good look at his face for one or two seconds. Then everything changed for me. His eyes were slightly bulging and he had no pupils. This completely threw me, I became very uneasy and frightened. I was speech-less and silence fell. I began to worry, I had never seen anyone so sinister-looking. Although his personality imposed no threat, my mind was going wild thinking, 'Is he mad? Is he going to attack me?'. A strange energy came over me which I thought was my own uneasiness.

I wanted to drop him off but was worried that I had said I was going to Hereford and I thought he might turn nasty if I dropped him off beforehand, although he showed no sign of any malicious tendencies whatsoever. He seemed quite gentle.

I couldn't stand the silence so I thought of something to say and started up another conversation. I toe-ed it on the accelerator to get to Hereford quicker. It felt at times as if the car was floating - it probably was, the speed at which I was going!

To my relief, the outskirts of Hereford were in sight. My next worry was that I didn't want him going to the gig with me. I thought he might go with me and then want a lift back, so I needed to get rid of him before my destination. I drove into the outskirts of Hereford and looked for a suitable place to drop him off. I pulled over in a street of terraced houses. I said, 'This is as far as I'm going mate, I have to let you out here'. He tried to get out and said he couldn't operate the door handle.

I didn't want to lean over him to open the door so I got out of the car and walked round to open his door from the outside. The man got out of the car and stepped on to the pavement in front of me. I slammed the car door, looked back to say 'Cheerio' and he had gone! I couldn't understand it. I looked round the car to see if he was hiding behind it. I even looked under the car. There was nowhere he could have gone. There were no alleyways or streets leading off nearby. Confused, I got in the car, drove 100 yards up the road, turned round and drove back. I drove back and forth to see if I could see him. But he had gone.

I went to the gig. When I got there I first met the drummer who said to me, 'You look like you have seen a ghost. Are you alright?'. I replied, 'I don't know, I think I have just given one a lift'.

When we played the music, although I was playing with them I didn't feel I was with them. They all commented that I had a weird energy about me that evening. When the gig was over I went to Malvern to get a meal. The chef, being a friend of mine, said to me, 'I mean no offence but you have a really strange energy about you tonight'. I was still not sure what had happened. I shall never forget his face and those eyes.

Over the coming week it began to dawn on me that the situation was more weird than I had first thought. The man was completely solid, yet how did he disappear in a second?

I have a friend who lives about 40 miles away in the direction of Hereford. When I began to tell him what had happened, he said, 'I know what you are going to say, but go on'. He told me that, some years ago, on the Herefordshire/Worcester road, he had seen a person in a long black coat standing on another bridge waving cars down on many occasions. He didn't give him a lift as he had the children in the car. At one time he did stop, reversed the car back to the man and he disappeared. My friend also remarked that about 20 years ago there was an article in the *Herefordshire Times* about a ghost that appeared on the road and flagged cars down.

14. VILLAGES

n the days of the Anglo Saxons, when King Offa ruled Mercia, a Christian woman named Aelfgyth founded a little church in a beautiful spot surrounded by hills. The village grew and became known as Alvechurch. The Church was rebuilt and renovated many times and is now known as St Lawrence. The Bishops had a Palace here and in 1361, when the plague hit Alvechurch, Reginald Brian, Bishop of Worcester died here. Pestilence Lane is said to lead to the burial pit of the plague victims.

A curious story comes from Alvechurch. It has always been believed that if you see the ghost of a person who is alive, that person will die very shortly. There are many incidents recorded in old archives where this has been so. Here is a more recent example from the 1970s.

I was sitting in the dining room one evening and my 21-year old son was in the sitting room, next to it. He came in through the doorway from the hall and stood there for about two seconds, just inside the doorway. Then suddenly he just disappeared. He vanished into thin air. I just sat there. I couldn't believe it. I went into the sitting room and he was still there, it was obvious that he hadn't moved for some time. One or two weeks later he went on holiday with some friends to Aberdovey and while he was there he was drowned.

ASTWOOD BANK - The Bell Inn, Polly and the Bell

From Redditch, the A441 runs to Evesham, chiefly an old toll road. The toll road was supposed to go all the way to Evesham so that the growers could get their produce quickly to the Birmingham markets, but when the road reached the Dunnington Cross Roads the money ran out and so it ended there. About three miles from Redditch, at Astwood Bank, were two inns standing side by side, the Bell and the Woodman. The Woodman was a very old coaching inn dating back to the 1700s. It was said to be haunted by an ex-licensee, Brian Onens, who walked with a limp. After he had died the locals would hear a man with a limp walking overhead although no-one was up there.

The Woodman was demolished in about 1964. Locals say that no houses were built on the site because it was afraid that the occupants would be haunted by the ghost. Whatever the reason, the site became part of the car park and lawn of the Bell. The ghost seems to have moved next door and changed its gender, for a mysterious lady has been seen in The Bell several times. For example, when John Heath was helping one Christmas, he had a long conversation with a young lady in a cream trouser-suit, not realising she was the ghost.

Lin was manager of the Bell in Astwood Bank for many years. A curious fact is that although she was too busy to take an interest in the history of the inn, she instinctively named their ghost 'Polly'. Mrs Pollie Croft was the licensee from 1918 to 1920. Lin says:

Our ghost used to move things round. We would put the glasses straight at night and when we arrived in the morning they would all be moved round. If we laid the tables at night the cutlery would be all over the place when we came the next day. She would turn the taps on at night. I would come in the morning and the taps would be running.

Polly used to take the money and move it. I would lock it away, very carefully, but it would still disappear. At first, I thought that someone was taking it but there were times when some had gone missing and nobody had been in the Bell except for me. I never saw her doing it. I used to stand there and say, 'Come on Polly, where have you hidden it, put it back'.

We reckoned that she lived in the cellar. We had a young lad who absolutely refused to go down there. On a Saturday afternoon one of the regulars went into the back room to use my telephone and he saw her coming up the cellar steps. He was as white as a sheet when he returned.

I was in the pub on my own lots of times but I was only frightened once. Usually, when I worked late at night, I was with a Chinese gentleman but on that particular occasion, it was his night off and I was alone. It was about 11.30, the pub had closed and I was very tired so I stretched out on a bench in the lounge. Then I saw her. She walked out of the cellar door and came up to the lounge door. She was wearing a cream floor-length gown with a nipped-in waist and a large white hat. The room went icy cold. I went off, and left her. Although I knew about her and knew that others had seen her this was the first time I had seen her myself. That's the only time I was ever worried.

A waitress was in the restaurant on a weekday evening, it was early - about seven o'clock - and the restaurant was empty when she saw a lady in a grey floor-length dress and a large hat sitting at one of the tables. She went to go towards her but the lady disappeared.

Although I was the manager, I didn't live in but I often went into the living quarters. I never felt uneasy there, only downstairs and especially in the cellar.

The living mist

Less than a mile from the Bell Inn along the A441 is the 'Why Not Inn', named after a famous race horse, not that this provides any possible explanation to Mrs Harris's strange experience:

On Thursday, 14th October 2004 at approximately 9.45 pm, we were travelling into Astwood Bank. Just before the Why Not pub, my husband and I saw a column of mist, which was upright, like a person. It travelled from one pavement across the road in front of the car. As we got near it, it passed through the driver's side of the car. The rest of the road was completely clear. I would love to know if anyone else has seen anything like this and at this spot.

The gardener

Ghost stories are seem to be very popular with cubs and scouts and this one was told by a Scout Leader at a meeting of Astwood Bank Scout Group.

My father loved his garden and he was always working there. Six years ago, on August Bank holiday, he died. I stayed with my mother to make sure she was alright. I got up in the night to go to the loo and to my surprise, the light was on in the living room. I went to investigate and found my mother there. She said, 'I have just seen your dad sitting on the bench in the garden'.

She moved to a flat in Church Hill. Now, every Christmas day my dad and my husband would have their Christmas dinner and afterwards they would have a glass of port and one of the big fat cigars. The first Christmas after my father had died, she smelt cigar smoke. A neighbour came round who never knew my dad and she said, 'There's a smell of cigar smoke in here'

BARNT GREEN HOUSE - The ghost in the river

Until the railway arrived in about 1846 Barnt Green was only a scattering of houses and even then, for half a century, the station was in the middle of a field. It is now a thriving dormitory town. Barnt Green was part of Alvechurch until 1450, when it was taken over by the Cecils, a historic English family often prominent at court. Five centuries later, Mike Lowe and his family were living there. Both Mike and his father 'had a little experience':

When you are going from Alvechurch to Barnt Green you go past Lower Bittell Reservoir, then you turn left at the T- junction and pass under the high bridge on the road to Rednal. Just past the bridge, on the left, is an old black and white building. That's Barnt Green House, which goes back to 1602, now known as Barnt Green Inn.

When my story begins I was about fifteen or sixteen. Of course, I wasn't married then and we're just coming up to our 37th wedding anniversary so that gives you some idea of the date.

My father at the time was working nights at the Austin factory, cycling there and back again from our house in Barnt Green. He would come in each morning and say, 'Alright son?' and I would say, 'Are you OK?' and we would both say 'Yes' but this one morning he said, 'I have just had a little experience - I have seen a ghost. I was cycling home from work and this white figure crossed the road in front of me, just by Barnt Green House'.

About two years afterwards, when I was about eighteen, I used to follow Birmingham City Football Club, going to places as far away as Ipswich. Late on a Saturday night you could only catch a bus to Northfield so that I had to walk from Northfield to Barnt Green. One night I was walking along the old road from Rednal to Barnt Green, approaching Barnt Green House. I had just gone past the cricket club, then a dip in the road and a nasty bend, and I was about 100 yards before the entrance to the House, when a white figure crossed the road and walked through the hedge, right by an oak tree which, incidentally, is still there. She was tall and thin and quite solid, she wasn't floating and seemed to be walking quite normally. Then she walked through the hedge.

I wasn't frightened, more curious, so when I got to the bit where she had gone through the hedge I stopped and looked over the hedge. At first I couldn't see her and thought she had disappeared, but then I did see her again. She had gone down into a hollow out of sight and come up again. Where the figure went down is the river Arrow, opposite Barnt Green House, and she had reappeared on higher ground on the other side of the river. She had followed the ground down, walked straight through the river and up. I was watching her for about five minutes.

Then suddenly, I remembered. When I was at Barnt Green School, in one of our history lessons we had been told that there is a tunnel between Barnt Green House and Cofton Church. We had been taken to the house and shown the entrance to the tunnel which was bricked up. Then we had been taken to the crypt in Cofton Church and shown the other end of the tunnel, which again was bricked up. It clicked! I realised that the white lady was following the line of the tunnel above ground.

I got home and when I saw my dad the following morning at breakfast I was able to tell him I that I had seen the ghost as well.

Apparently, the 145 Bromsgrove to Birmingham does the usual route Burcot/Blackwell/Barnt Green and I have heard that one or two drivers over the years have also seen the white lady.

BROMYARD - The witch

Bromyard is on the borders of Herefordshire, set in miles of farmland between Worcester and Leominster. It has a superb church with spectacular Norman doorways dating back to the 1200s. On the Worcester side of Bromyard a track leads off from the A44 running through an open area topped by trees, known as Bromyard Downs. In the 1300s, Bromyard had a famous witch, Alison Brown, with a fearsome reputation for curses. Did the four friends in the following story come face to face with Alison?:

My husband and I and two of our friends had been to Leominster to see some other friends. My husband has been dead nine-and-a-half years so this must have happened about ten or eleven years ago. We were coming back over Bromyard Downs about ten o'clock at night on a Sunday evening. It was a perfect evening, it was dark, but there was a full moon. All of a sudden a figure appeared from the bushes on the other side of the road. It sort of came out in front of us. It had long hands and long fingers and it tried to stop the car. I thought it was a woman - she had long black hair and her dress was black, she was all black. We were quite taken aback. We really didn't know if it was somebody who had an accident and was asking for help or somebody holding us up. We didn't know what it was. There was nobody else on the road, we never saw another car in trouble, in fact we never saw another car at all. My husband put his foot down and we carried on.

It could have been somebody dressed up but there was nobody around at all. There were no houses. It was right out in a quiet part. Why would somebody be dressed up in the middle of nowhere? It was just so spooky. It was so peculiar. It just wasn't nice. It was the only time I have ever seen anything like that at all. I see no reason why somebody would be dressed up to look like an apparition to be there all by themselves.

Phantom Music

The next little anecdote comes again from the A44 Bromyard Road, but this time from a building much closer to Worcester:

For a short time I was working at ATTECS on the Bromsgrove Road. They were having a big sales promotion and I was working late because a job hadn't been finished. There were just two of us on the site. I heard music like that of an army band coming from the direction of the kitchen and I heard feet marching past. I said to my friend, 'Where's that music coming from?'. We looked in the office but nobody was there.

We were so intrigued that we looked into the history of the place and found out that, during the war, it was a convalescent home for injured airmen and they had joined together to form a band. When I was there, there was still some writing on the wall from the wartime.

COOKHILL - The dark secret (Cookhill Priory)

If you drive along the A441 from Redditch towards Evesham, you go through the tiny village of Cookhill. Just before the point where the A422 crosses the A441, you catch a brief glimpse of an old, red-bricked house. In the garden is a small, low, red-bricked building. This is the remains of the historic Cookhill Priory. It was a Cistercian nunnery dating back to the late 1100s and refounded in the 1200s by Isabel, the wife of William Beauchamp, Earl of Warwick. She seems to have joined the nunnery, she was buried among the nuns and until the 17th century a tomb bearing her name was in the ruined chapel of the nunnery. In 1282 the nuns were in trouble for not paying their taxes and three years later they were in trouble again for not observing the strict Cistercian rules, for example they were seen wandering about the town. When the nunnery was dissolved by Henry VIII in about 1538 it had seven nuns.

The site was bought by the Nicholas Fortesque in 1542 and in 1783 the family incorporated some 14th century ruins of the old Priory church in the garden into a chapel. The house was built on part of the nun's quarters in 1763 by Captain John Fortesque. He claimed to be the sole survivor of the crew of the Centurion, which had sailed round the world. He died in 1808 at the ripe old age of 87.

The lady who give the information in the next story once lived in Inkberrow, about a mile away. She did ask for the information to be checked, but unfortunately no-one seems to live in Inkberrow or Cookhill now who can verify it:

The following story was researched by the late Woodward Jephcott and a summary of his research by the local newspaper was pinned on the church door for many years. I quote from memory:

'In the late 1800's the occupants of the Priory had a guest who was put in a lovely panelled room. When he came down in the morning, the owner's wife asked him if he had slept well. He said, 'Well, actually, I was disturbed, there was a bang behind the panelling as if something had fallen. The owner said, 'Oh, we'll get behind the panelling and see what it was'. To their surprise, when they pulled the panelling away, they found a portrait of Charles I and with it were two letters from a woman who lived in Inkberrow. The first letter said that her husband was the person who had executed the king. It explained that half a dozen soldiers had gathered together and had drawn straws to see who should do the dreadful deed. Her husband had drawn the short straw. He was paid thirty pieces of silver. The letter went on to say that her husband was dying, and 'Could the priest come and shrive him?'. Then there was a second letter which said simply, 'Too late, he's gone'.'

The portrait and the two letters went to the vicar who kept them in the vestry. At one point the church was broken into by travellers who lit a fire to keep warm and what did they burn? - the portrait and the two letters.

I used to live in a house in Inkberrow. When it was in the hands of the previous owners, the roof had to be repaired. The roofers said to the owners, 'Did you know there was a room under the roof?'. They opened it up and found a Commonwealth musket of the type used in the Civil War of 1642-1646. The house was built about that time or even earlier and it occurred to me, I wonder if that was where the executioner lived?. It must have been someone with a dark secret who wanted to hide away in a secret room.'

When Nicholas Fortesque bought the site of the Priory in 1542, he also became Lord of the Manor of Cookhill. He was a member of the King's household and head of a most colourful family. His grandson was a zealous Roman Catholic and narrowly escaped being imprisoned after the gunpowder plot. Nicholas's great, great grandson fought in the civil war for with the Royalists, unfortunately on the losing side, so that all his estates were confiscated. However, when Charles II came to the throne he was given them back again. There's a whiff of a scandal here, because the eldest son was disinherited.

I'm not seeing this

Cookhill and the Priory remained in that family until 1823. Cookhill church was built in 1876 and the village hall is next to it. A few years ago, Judy used to go to Keep Fit at Cookhill Village Hall.

It finished at nine o'clock. About eight years ago, I came out of Keep Fit and was driving towards Astwood Bank, not far from Cookhill, when I saw this white mist float across the road. I could make out quite distinctly that it was in the shape of a young girl, early twenties I would say, and she had with her a large long-haired dog. She looked like the heroine that you get in these historical films - earlier than Victorian - where she comes down the staircase with her hair and her dress fluttering in the wind.

I braked, but I didn't stop completely. I had my eyes on the road so I didn't see exactly what happened when she reached the grass verge on the opposite side but I took a quick look sideways and she had disappeared.

At first I thought, 'Oh how beautiful', but then I thought, 'This is weird, I'm not seeing this, I don't believe in this sort of thing'.

CROWLE:- Death shall flee

The huge Crowle estate was given to the Bishop of Worcester in the early 800s by the King of Mercia. Over the years, all kinds of important people have owned parts of it, and more than 30 acres was given to the hospital of St Wulstan, now

The Commandery in Worcester. Peter de Wick had a piece and in 1220, he built a mill on it and flooded land belonging to Hugh de Crowle, so that Hugh took him to court. The church arrived in the 1300s but was completely rebuilt in the 1880s, however parts of the earlier church remain, notably in the porch, the font and the pulpit.

The following anecdote comes from a college lecturer who has lived in Crowle for about 20 years:

This is a very old community and many of the buildings date back to the time of the gunpowder plot. There's a local story that some of the gunpowder plotters fled overland across the surrounding countryside on foot, after their scheme to blow up Parliament and James I had been exposed. Guy Fawkes had been captured and tortured. In ones and twos the rest of the traitors fled on foot, trying to make it across Worcestershire to a Catholic safe house.

An elderly neighbour confided to me that he did not like to linger in the darker country lanes after nightfall, following an experience which happened to him when he was a youth in the 1920s. Walking home one winters night down a particularly dark lane, he had heard the sound of ragged breathing and someone running despite sounding exhausted.

Suddenly a man vaulted over an old five bar gate some little way in front of him, and stood for a second in the lane. He was wearing a cloak and a big black Cavalier's hat. No sooner had he hit the ground and straightened up than he vanished into thin air.

My friend never lingered in those dark country lanes after that!

Within the triangle formed by Warwick Coventry and Stourbridge were the families of 19 conspirators of the gunpowder plot. There were the Lyttletons of Hagley Hall, the Talbots of Grafton manor, the Habingtons of Hindlip Hall and the Throckmortons of Coughton Court. The Throckmortons were related to Robert Catesby who originated the plot, and Catesby had rented Clopton House at Stratford. The conspirators in London fled on horseback, but there were many associates around who would have been trying to escape from the arm of the law on foot, perhaps fleeing from one house to find safety in another.

However, perhaps the ghost was not a conspirator of the gunpowder plot, but someone fleeing from the Battle of Worcester in 1651. A Cavalier's hat and cape suggests a Royalist. Estimates vary, but the defeated army was reckoned to number 16,000, with 4000 killed in battle and 7000 prisoners taken. This leaves 5,000 soldiers making a hasty escape across country.

The ghost dog

Here's a curious little tale about a much-loved pet who passed away:

My dog and I saw a ghost dog. Years ago, when I lived at home with my parents, we always had golden spaniels. We lost one so we had a new one who was about two years old. The family always used to sit in a semicircle watching the television. In front of us was a square coffee table with a long chenille tablecloth over it. The new spaniel had not joined our household for very long and he was sitting alongside my chair when I saw what I thought was our present dog move the cloth and come out from under the table. Then, to my surprise, I saw our present dog down by the side of me. He was looking in the same direction as me so he must have seen it too, and as he stood up I noticed the hairs on his hackles rise.

ELCOCKS BROOK - Spooks in the Brook Inn

About two miles west of the southern tip of Redditch, along a country lane, is the 600-year old Brook Inn. Originally called the Elcock, it has been known as the Elcoat and the Elcott. The oldest part is not the cottage itself but the annex on the right (when facing the inn) which is now used as a cellar. This is a pub which has everything, not only is there good food and ample parking but it can also supply you with a ghost: Louise and her husband, Andy, the present licensees, have been there almost 18 years and Louise says that during that time -

So many things have happened here I don't know where to begin. You can go a couple of weeks and nothing happens but you never go more than a month without something strange going on. At the end of the day we normally sit and have a drink with a couple of regulars and the staff, and several people have mentioned that they have seen something strange.

Things go missing. My husband's sunglasses were missing for well over six months. They were an expensive pair and he searched everywhere. Then one day, he just opened a drawer and there they were, right on top of everything.

We have had things like cups smashed. One of the bar staff and my mother-in-law were cleaning behind the bar when suddenly, one of the coffee cups jumped off the shelf and smashed on the floor. In the catering kitchen utensils have suddenly gone on the floor for no reason.

We have live music on a Friday night. About two years ago we helped the two performers out with their equipment and we said to them 'Would you like a drink?'. Hanging over the bar is a large brass bell which can be heard all through the premises. We were sitting in the old part of the pub, a few yards from the bar when suddenly it gave this enormous clang. I went over to it and the string was still moving.

On one occasion, Andy and myself were behind the bar, and one of our staff who was clearing the tables in the old part of the pub looked across the room and saw that a taxi driver had just walked in. He said, 'OK, I'll be with you in a second'. When he looked up again nobody was there. There was nowhere he could have gone, he must have walked through the wall!

When I first came I was aware that somebody else was here, but I didn't say very much. The cleaners say that they are aware that somebody is watching them through the mirror but when they stop and look at the mirror, nobody is there. My husband was very sceptical about ghosts before we came here, now he's not so sure. We have both seen a shape out of the side of our eyes several times. It looks as if we had drawn an outline of a person and filled it in with pencil. My husband thinks the shape is a male and I think it is a female. When we're lying in bed, we can feel someone come into the room and one of us will say, 'We've got company' Then you feel as if somebody sits on the bed.

Everybody in the family has had an unusual experience. My husband was in the cellar, which is in the old part, he was bending over, tapping the beer when he saw that someone was standing by the side of him. Because he was in working, he couldn't turn round straight away, but he clearly saw an old pair of shoes and plus fours. When he was able to look round a few seconds later, it had gone. However, it might be something to do with me. Even when I was a child I was seeing things. I used to stand in the church choir and I could see my granddad.

My father-in-law was very much against ghosts. He was in the yard, getting some wood out, when he was tapped on the bottom. He thought it was his wife, and said, 'I'm coming, I'm coming', but when he turned round, no-one was there.

When she was small my daughter used to have an imaginary friend, we even had to lay a place for it at the table. One night, I got out of bed to go to the bathroom. My daughter's bedroom is right opposite the bathroom. When I came out she was standing there, she said, 'I'm watching the old lady that's outside the bathroom, mum'. She felt it was granny.

Our dog, Sandy, seemed to be susceptible to it. He would stare at a certain part of the room, but we couldn't see anything. It was always the old part, nearest the cellar.

All this has gone on for so long that people just accept it. I feel that it's not an evil presence, but a nice, comfortable one. This place has a lovely homely atmosphere. I wouldn't be without it.

ELMLEY CASTLE - Locking the ghost out!

Elmley Castle is a small village at the foot of Bredon Hill, principally a wide main street lined with houses on the west side and a row of trees on the east side. King Offa gave Elmley to the Bishop of Worcester in 780. The delightful church is well worth a visit. It has Norman parts including some herringbone masonry, a 12th century font, pieces of ancient glass in the windows and the two monuments to the Savage family are two of the best in the county. In the church-yard is a 16th century square sundial.

The village takes it name from the castle built in the 11th century by Robert le Despencer. It must have been a fantastic place, built on a spur of rock projecting from the northern slopes of Bredon Hill. The castle became the home of the powerful Beauchamp family. In 1216 it was owned by Walter de Beauchamp but he fought on the side of Simon de Montfort against King John. Instead of chopping off his head, the King packed him off to the Pope in Rome to obtain absolution. Three nobles were put in charge of the castle while Walter was away, but perhaps this was when it began to fall into disrepair, because 80 years later it was almost valueless. In 1317, it was given to Hugh le Despenser the Elder and he was ordered to fortify it, but his friendship with Edward II turned the powerful barons against him and they managed to get him banished in 1321. Later that same year the castle was attacked by the Earl of Hereford and much damage done. The castle was barely habitable and by 1544 it was a complete ruin.

Such an old village will have many a strange story to tell and this is the traditional haunting place of 'The Hopney Bitch', half-man, half-dog, that wanders across the wide main street.

The couple in the next story tried to lock out a ghost!

My parents had a cottage there in the 1970s and they had a poltergeist for years. Things used to go missing, they could hear footsteps going up the wall next to them and various objects used to fly across the room. I've seen a mug fly across the room. One Christmas time, my father was lying in bed early one morning and he could hear the pots and pans rattling and he could smell cooking. He called out, 'Mother, is that you downstairs?' and the reply came right from his elbow, 'No, I'm in bed right beside you'.

Although the entrance gate was only about three feet high they put a lock on it, hoping it would keep the ghost out!

FECKENHAM - Rosa Returns

Walking through the one main street of Feckenham Village, with its half-timbered and Georgian houses, it's difficult to visualise how important the village was, for it was once the administration centre for the huge Forest of Feckenham.

The word 'Forest' in this sense does not necessarily mean trees, but only refers to an unfenced area where the king kept deer. The 'forest' could be scrubland and heath as well as woodland.

Henry II enlarged Feckenham forest so that it covered a third of Worcestershire. Such scandalously strict laws were imposed on the forest that many villagers left the area. You could not hunt in the forest, you could only gather fallen timber, you could not graze your pigs or cattle in it nor build a house. The punishments for breaking the laws were severe and on the southwest side of Feckenham church are the remains of a ditch which once surrounded a prison in which the offenders were incarcerated.

King John had a Royal Manor House or hunting lodge here, used in the 12th and 13th centuries. It was bought by the Abbots of Evesham in 1356, fell into disrepair and all that remains is a hump on the edge of the football field. The punishment for shooting the king's deer, was death, but it was not often the full penalties were imposed, as the following incident shows:

In 1278, two of the workers from Bordesley Abbey were caught shooting the king's deer. The punishment was death. The forester marched them back to the Abbey, to be punished by the Abbott. However, as they neared the abbey they were spotted by two monks who managed to run out and bribe the forester with half a mark (about 36p) into releasing them. Then the forester was in trouble for letting his prisoners go, but the case took a year to come to court and as the forester was very poor and had no money to pay a fine, the case was dismissed.

The forest gradually disappeared as corrupt officials sold off land for the wood needed to smelt iron or evaporate the salt water at Droitwich. Henry VIII used a lot of the timber to build his fleet of warships. By the late 1500s, most of the forest had disappeared.

One of the prettiest houses in Feckenham was once occupied by the lady who told the following story:

> We lived in a house in Feckenham. All the time that we lived there, we had a ghost. I don't know why but I always knew her as Rosa. We never saw her but we could hear her moving about.

> She hated us to have anything done in the way of alterations. We had the Butler's pantry made into part of the kitchen and she didn't like that very much. We could hear footsteps walking around upstairs and coming down the stairs. Then we could hear her moving about upstairs, it wasn't banging, just movement. It also happened when we had some new windows put in.

I didn't find it terribly worrying. She was never any trouble. I would just say, 'Oh, there's Rosa again'.

Looking through the Feckenham Parish records, a Rosa Ireson died in that house or nearby in 1879 aged 17 months.

Beholding the light

Mr Thomas is a great enthusiast for ghost stories and has persuaded several of his acquaintances to provide a story or two. He had a strange experience himself one dark night:

About seven years ago I went to Stratford-on-Avon for the day on my bike. It was late when I started back, I know that I didn't get to Feckenham until past midnight because it was one o'clock before I got back to my home in Hanbury. One of the reasons I was so late was that my carrier bag stand had broken on the way home. I had to stop and tie it up, it was a good job I had some string on me. It was almost pitch dark. Because the stand had broken, I was riding along very slowly. There's only a low light on my bicycle normally and because I was going slowly, it was very dim.

Just before you get into Feckenham from Alcester, right by the power station, there's a hill. I was going up the hill when I saw a man on the other side of the road, walking down the hill towards me. He seemed to be glowing. I couldn't believe how bright he was. I thought, 'How can I see that man so clearly when it's dark?'. He was tallish, middle build and he wasn't an old man because he was walking quite fast. I had the impression that his clothes were old-fashioned but, to tell the truth, I was too scared to look carefully. It gave me goose-pimples. After he had walked past I stopped and looked round, but he had gone. Thinking back, I hadn't heard any footsteps.

HANBURY - and its hauntings!

As long ago as 836 the King of Mercia granted a monastery at Hanbury certain privileges. There was a priest here at the time of the 1068 Domesday Survey, and the earliest part of Hanbury Church, the south arcade, dates from about 1210. We get a glimpse of village life from old documents that show that in 1377 Thomas Elvin wanted to move away from Hanbury but he was ordered by the Lord of the Manor to remain there, with all his goods and chattels.

Local historian, Robin Cook, says that Hanbury is full of old legends:

On Midsummer night, at the stroke of twelve, a ghost is supposed to walk up the tower. One or two strange things have happened in and near Hanbury Church. I, myself, have seen black candles on the graves. When I was a young lad I was with a group of friends when we decided to catch the ghost at Hanbury. We fortified ourselves at the Square and Compass but ran away at five to twelve!

Old Nick is said to have been seen at Cruise Hill. If you go towards Hanbury at Upper Bentley there is a nasty bend, opposite this turn there used to be a barn and Old Nick was supposed to haunt it. A headless horseman has been seen riding up the road towards the old Bentley Manor. If you go along the Hanbury to Droitwich Road and turn to go into Droitwich, there is a lay-by on the right hand side. Something white floats across the road. Some gypsies encamped there and it frightened them away.

Sir George returns (Hanbury Hall)

There is much to see at Hanbury Hall which was built by a barrister, Sir Thomas Vernon, in about 1700. It has a schoolroom, an orangery and an ice house, and over the fireplace of a small study is a finely carved chimney-piece, said to have been brought over from Tickenhill House, Bewdley. Its pride and joy is a wonderful Baroque staircase with painted walls and ceiling by Thornhill. The Vernon's were, apparently, not a devout family as there are no religious scenes here but Thetis, Achilles, Ajax and Ulysses with Mercury on the ceiling. The ceilings of the hall and dining room are painted in the same manner. When Sir Bowater George Vernon died in 1940 he left instructions that he should be buried in Shrawley Woods, away from 'prating priests'.

One of the present Hanbury stewards talks about his death:

In 1940, while Britain was gripped by the Second World War, Sir Bowater George Vernon shot himself in the Blue Bedroom at Hanbury Hall. Sir George, as he was known, was suffering from ill-health so perhaps his medication was not suiting him. We shall never know why he felt he had to commit suicide as he left no explanation behind. His only instructions were to be buried in Shrawley Wood with his gun and without a religious ceremony. He was also careful to remove his false teeth!

I am one of the room stewards at Hanbury Hall, now open to the public, and have been on duty in the Blue Bedroom many times. On one of these occasions a visitor came up to me and said, 'As soon as I came into this house,' at this point I thought she was going to say, like most visitors before her, that the house was homely and friendly - however she went on - 'I had a very strange feeling. My husband insisted it was the wall paintings on the staircase but I'm sure it isn't that'. I told her that she was the only person

Occasionally, Sir George makes an appearance.
(Hanbury Hall, page 188)

to say that to me. After staying in the room for a few minutes she left to carry on her tour of the house.

After an hour so the lady was back with me looking very agitated. 'I felt I had to come back to see you. We've been in the Long Gallery to read the history of the house. Sir George shot himself in the house didn't he?' I confirmed this and she went on - 'it was in this room wasn't it? I sensed it straight away!'. The lady became very emotional at this and was very close to tears. She had obviously picked up on something in the Hall's atmosphere and 'felt' a bad vibration. The poor lady was very distressed and after apologising to me she left the room, and the Hall very quickly.

Occasionally, Sir George makes an appearance. In July, 2003, another steward was disconcerted by the following incident:

About four weeks ago a young man joined the Hanbury Hall team. He was on work experience or some similar scheme. We gave him a Hoover and told him to vacuum the runner in the Blue Bedroom. He went in and came straight back out. We said, 'What's the matter?'. He said, 'I'd better wait until that man comes out before I start vacuuming'. We said, 'Which man?' and he said, 'The man in the blue bedroom'. We said, 'There shouldn't be a man in there'. It was first thing in the morning, before the hall was open. We went to have a look and nobody was in there.

We took him down to the library and showed him pictures and he picked out a picture of George Vernon (who shot himself in the blue bedroom) and was certain that that was the man he saw.

Everybody was so unemotional and matter-of-fact about the event. You would have thought it was the sort of thing that happened every day.

Scandals at Hanbury Hall

Emma Vernon has appeared in almost every paranormal book covering Hanbury. Thomas Vernon, who built the hall 'died without issue' in 1721, consequently on his death the manor of Hanbury went to the eldest son of his first cousin. His grand-daughter was Emma Vernon, born in 1755. She was an only child, and when she was about 22 she married Robert Cecil from the famous Cecil family, prominent at court. After three years of marriage, she eloped with the local Curate, William Sneyd. Robert Cecil buried himself in Shropshire and there married a farmer's daughter. He inherited the title, Marquise of Exeter, so the farmer's daughter became a countess. William Sneyd died of consumption in Portugal so Emma returned to England, homeless and penniless. She turned to a local solicitor to sort out her affairs, who married her after a whirlwind courtship. However, Emma never forgot her curate and asked that, after her death, she could be buried in the blanket in which she had nursed him. She died in 1818, and her grave still exists on the edge of Hanbury churchyard.

Every since that time there have been innumerable sightings of Emma and here is yet another from young Lucy:

One sunny spring afternoon about five years ago I was walking the dog through Hanbury with my boyfriend, Nicholas. If you know Hanbury you will know that you come up the hill towards the church, through the church gates and from there you can go round the back of the church. As I went through the gates my boyfriend was a few yards in front of me. I turned round to call my dog and, about twenty yards away, I saw a figure come out of the little coppice by the side of the church and glide down the hill.

It was a woman in a long dress down to the ground and over it she had a coat in a sort of dressing-gown fabric. She was quite petite, about five six inches tall, of late middle age and with her hair up. Her clothes were not pure white but rather a drab colour, the white had a reddish-brown tinge. She was raised above the ground a little and was slightly opaque. She glided rather quickly right down to the bottom of the hill. I was watching her for quite a while before she disappeared.

I called out to my boyfriend, 'I have just seen a ghost' and he said that he had seen her as well. So we both saw her.

The Hall was bequeathed to the National Trust with the proviso that Sir George's estranged wife was to live there, which she did until she died in 1962. She lived in a room at the Dower House and some of the local people remember her as a very sweet old lady in delicate health.

Is anybody there?

From 1964 to 1968 Terry and his family lived in a Hanbury farmhouse:

There was always a bit of a presence down there. You often caught a movement of something out of the corner of your eye and you would sit in the kitchen and something would go past the window but when you went to the door, nobody was there. You didn't see anything a hundred percent but there was always a feeling that somebody was there.

One day, my son and I were in the shed, messing with the cattle. One of them had a bad foot or something and we needed a needle for the antibiotics. I said to my son, 'Trish (my wife) has just gone past the window, give her a shout and ask her to bring us a needle'. My son said, 'Yes, I saw her as well' but when he went outside, nobody was there.

When my daughter was two she used to talk to a lady in her bedroom. We had a rep come who said that somebody had followed him into the house. He thought it was my wife's mum but nobody was about.

Shattering and crashing

On the eastern side of Hanbury is Ditchford Bank, a scattering of houses and a few farms. The name probably came from a family of French knights, the de Ditchfords, who owned several properties in Worcestershire. The area was once in the heart of Feckenham Forest, but the monks of Bordesley Abbey had permission from the king (probably Richard I in 1190) to use the timber and clear the area.

The farms are so isolated that many of them still draw water from wells. Hanbury is less than three miles east of Droitwich, so if the farmers go down too deeply, they hit the salt bed.

The inhabitants of Hanbury have many a ghost story to tell but perhaps the most interesting comes from an artist who lives in one of the old farm cottages in Ditchford Bank:

For many years we heard the crash of breaking glass, usually around October. We first heard it about twenty-five years ago, when we were moving into this cottage. My husband was helping me to unpack cases of glass and china in the kitchen while my parents were giving us a hand in the room next door. Both my husband and I heard a crash of breaking glass on the floor just beside us. My husband rushed round to look at all the windows and scouted round the house in case any glass had been broken anywhere but we couldn't account for the noise.

That was on the Saturday, on the Sunday we were both upstairs and my mother was putting the china in the kitchen cupboard downstairs when again, we heard this enormous crash. We both heard it, we shouted down to mother, 'What have you broken?' She shouted back, 'I haven't broken anything'. Ever since then it comes on the anniversary of our arrival, although I must say that we don't seem of have heard it for the last ten years or so.

We have had other inexplicable incidents. We were sitting in the dining room, having lunch, when the windows started to shake and tremble. It was not a windy day and new windows had recently been fitted. We had a visitor sitting at the table, when it happened he jumped up, hurried back to his car and went home!

I sometimes smell tobacco smoke. My husband occasionally smokes a pipe but this is quite different, it's a very strong smell. Sometimes I'm sitting down, relaxing, and a smell of tobacco wafts past.

My husband has had more than one terrifying experience. We had not been here long when it became necessary for me to be away each week and only come home at weekends. At about five o'clock in the morning, when my husband was in the house by himself, great crows attacked the windows of the house, both back and front. The windows were black with birds, and they flew into the glass so violently that he was afraid that they would break the glass. It was terrible, like something out of a Hitchcock film. This happened a number of times, so my husband did all sorts of things to try and stop them. He thought that perhaps the birds hadn't seen the glass so he put brown paper on the windows. It only happened when he was on his own, so he put dolls in all the windows to make it look as if the family were here. It got so bad that he came home several lunch times with a shotgun. He would lie in the hedgerow waiting for them to rise in the air but he wasn't a very good shot! Eventually he caught one and hung the carcass up. After that they went away. It was probably a protection of the area by the crows.

I was very close to my brother and I was quite distraught when he died. We went to his funeral in York. We were expecting some American tourists to stay with us and I tried to get in touch with them to put them off but I couldn't locate them because they were touring, consequently, I had to cook a meal for them when I came home. They were a jolly lot but I was so upset I didn't really know what I was doing. We were having dinner when one of them said, 'I must go and get my camera', and he went out to his car which was parked round the back. When he returned, he said that he had just passed someone who had come near the front door with my dog and had walked past the house. I went to have a look but nobody was there, only the dog. I asked him to describe this person and, without a doubt, he described my brother - his features, his beard, the clothes he was wearing. I tried to be as normal as possible. I like to think that my brother came back to reassure me that he was alright. I only wish he had appeared to me and not to a stranger.

The phantom

A young man went fishing with a friend at Woodrow pool near Hanbury:

It's bursting with fishes. There's a wood next to the pool, at the side of the pool is an old water house and at the top is Hanbury Hall. We enjoyed ourselves so much that we went at 9 am and were still there at 10 pm. We would have been there still later except for a strange figure that we saw.

It was a clear, moonlit night. During the late evening we started hearing funny noises and we noticed a figure at the other end of the pool, about six feet tall and bent down in the lake drinking water out of his hands. The lake just here was very deep and no human could drink out the water like that. Then it stood up and it was just like a bear. That spooked us out. We scrambled to get our stuff together and we disappeared.

KINGSWOOD MEETING HOUSE - The brown lady

On the western side of the A435, on the edge of Kings Norton and before reaching Hollywood, is Kingswood Meeting House. The trials and tribulations of the Society of Friends (better known as Quakers) have been outlined in the Evesham chapter. At Kingswood, a Meeting House was built in 1712 and a residence for a minister, but 80 years later, in 1791, an angry mob burned it down. This is another occasion when the Riot Act was read. Under the terms of the Act, the Trustees were able to claim, against the two leaders of the riot, enough money to build a new church on land that they had bought previously, in 1775.

Mrs Hill from Kingswood Parsonage says:

This church has such an interesting history. Several famous families like the Chamberlains are buried in the churchyard.

Two people have seen the ghost. The first person was in the church about twelve years ago when she saw what she described as a brown lady. She was going through a troubled time and she said that it made her feel at peace.

The second time the ghost was seen was only about 18 months ago. They were doing a lot of alterations to the Packhorse at the end of the road. I thought, 'I wonder if that's going to shake up anybody's bones?'. Our organist was sitting in her chair facing the organ, preparing for a wedding. She said to her partner who was with her, 'That lady who was just standing behind me, who was she?' Her partner said, 'There was nobody behind you'.

I said to her later, 'I heard you have seen the brown lady?' She said, 'Yes, how do you know it was a brown lady? She was behind me and she was brown?'. I told her, 'Other people have seen her!' and she said, 'Oh no!'

Coming home

We have all had or heard about telepathic experiences. Does telepathy explain the following incident?

My brother was in the RAF in the war. He had been abroad for over three years. My mother dreamed about him one night and saw him clearly in his uniform sitting downstairs in the lounge. She came downstairs convinced that he had come home, but no-one was there at all. However, the next day a letter came from him saying that he would be coming home shortly.

*Then it stood up and it was just like a bear. That
spooked us out. (Hanbury).*

191

LOWER BROADHEATH - Welcome, Mrs Smith

Broadheath has one great claim to fame: it was the birthplace of one of the greatest English composers Sir Edward Edgar, born in 1857, MO, Master of the King's Music. This is one of loveliest parts of Worcestershire, with rolling hills and little copses. No doubt it was this countryside that inspired Edgar as he walked round, dreaming up his powerful compositions. His birthplace is now a museum.

Most of the populated part of Broadheath lies in Lower Broadheath, the location of Mrs Smith's house:

We moved into this house about fifteen years ago. It's a large, Victorian house. A widow lived here previously until she was well into her eighties, then she had to go into a home. She was a small, strong-willed character, well-known and well-liked. When we first arrived people in the village said 'Oh, you've moved into Mrs Smith's house'.. They said she would be so pleased that the house had some children in it, there hadn't been a child in the house for fifty years and she loved children.

For the first six months, if I got up in the night I would sometimes feel that there was a presence on the landing. I assumed it was Mrs Smith. It was a nice feeling, as if she was glad we were in the house.

My daughter and my five-year old grand-daughter were staying about six or seven years ago. We have a little back bedroom with a very small door and the little girl slept in there. She didn't say anything to me, but she told her mother in the morning that she could see a ghost during the night. My daughter said, 'She's only five and I don't read her any ghost stories or anything so I don't think she could have imagined it'. We said how strange that was, but I didn't think any more about it. Then my mother in law came to stay. We put her in that bedroom, and in the morning, she said she had seen a little old lady dressed in white sitting on her bed. I assumed it was Mrs Smith but she thought it looked like her mother. Anyway, she wouldn't sleep in that bedroom again.

It wasn't a horrible ghost, it was quite pleasant.

RUSHWICK - The Lady of the Manor

Rushwick is both a village and a parish. The village lies on the western edge of Worcester on the A4103 and the parish includes Upper Wick and Crown East. The name comes from the Danish 'Rysc Wic' meaning 'the dairy farm in the rushes' - as it's near the river Teme the lower fields are prone to flooding. At the time of the Domesday book, it was part of the ancient Manor of Clopton and had a 'flourishing community'. The community moved away but returned again in 1957 with a large new housing estate.

In 1998 Charles Smith was driving home after work from Malvern to Worcester. As he reached Rushwick, he saw a woman standing against the wall on the near side of the road, wearing an old-fashioned, full-skirted dress. As he looked at the figure it dissolved from the head down.

Another sighting at Rushwick is told by Joan, who lived in the Manor House for many years:

It was my husband who saw the ghost in the early 1970s. We bought Rushwick Manor, then took it apart and rebuilt it. There were two inglenook fireplaces, oak beams and we found lathe and plaster walls. We think that originally it was a two-up and two-down cottage but over the years people had added to it, particularly in the 1700s as a lot of it was Georgian. It used to belong to the Smedleys and at some point it belonged to the Sandys family. The Clarke's also lived there, and during that time Mr Clarke saw the grand-daughter of one of the Smedleys. We bought it from the people who bought it from them.

My husband was one end of the corridor, laying pipes for the central heating. He looked up and at the other end of the corridor was a tall lady in a dark skirt and red shawl, perhaps in her forties. The thing that he remembered most about her was her red shawl. She was just standing, watching. She watched at him for some time, then he went off to fetch some tools and when he came back she had gone. Not long after he saw her again in a similar place.

At another time he came in from the garden and said, 'Have you been watching me out of the landing window?' Evidently a lady had been standing there, watching him.

Two of the children saw a cat on the stairs which wasn't one of ours. They followed it up the stairs into the spare bedroom but when they went in there was no cat.

I never saw anything. It was a lovely comfortable house. There were no cold spots or anything like that. I loved the house and left there very reluctantly.

SALWARPE - You aren't half white!

The beauty of Salwarpe has been appreciated by many famous men down the centuries. The great Norman baron in the time of the Domesday Survey, Urse d'Abitot, created a park for himself there. Salwarpe was owned by the monks of Worcester Cathedral in 817 but later appropriated by Earl Godwin. When the Earl was on his deathbed, Bishop Wulstan persuaded him to return it and told him that if he didn't, he would not be permitted to enter the pearly gates.

Unfortunately, his son stole it again. One of the owners was Catharine of Aragon, Henry VIIIs first wife. The powerful Talbots lived in Salwarpe Court and many family members chose the little church as their last resting place.

One of the Earls of Warwick was born at Salwarpe Court, a half-timbered house going back to the 1400s. The construction of the canal at Salwarpe sliced off part of the house and the writer, John Noake, reckoned that 'in revenge for this act of mutilation the ghost of a former occupier occasionally revisits his old haunts ... and may be seen on peculiarly dark nights ... to glide down the embankment and suicidally commit himself to the waters below'.

Ken Foster was fifteen in January 1946 and had been an electrician's apprentice for twelve months.

> We had been putting cables in the rectory, the job was almost finished and I was putting the floorboards down, hammering in the nails. The rectory was a massive place. I was in the north side of the vicarage on the top level (second floor) and there was nothing in the room but a whole lot of books piled up about 12 or 15 inches high (30 or 38 cms). It was a frosty morning but the sun was shining through the window. Then someone walked across the room behind me. I turned my head and looked round to see who was there - was it the vicar or his wife? There was nobody. The door was open right back against the wall, I could see down the passageway into the room and there was nowhere to hide. I was 100% certain someone went across the back of me. I have never been so scared in all my life. I wouldn't have minded if it had been a tramp or something.

> My mate was putting the clips on downstairs so I went down for some more nails. Actually, I had plenty of nails, it was just an excuse. There was no carpet on the stairs and I had soft shoes but going down those stairs I made one hell of a lot of noise! My mate said, 'Are you alright? You aren't half white!'. When I went back up again I shut the door. I had never had any experience like that before, it was very odd. I wouldn't tell anyone for years, the only one I told was my mother.

> We were there for three weeks and stayed there overnight. The room that we slept in was pitch black at night. The lights hadn't been put on after the war and there was non of the reflective light in the sky that you get nowadays. My friend told me that once, when he had woken up in the night, the whole room glowed - the furniture and all the objects. Yet the room didn't feel warm.

> The vicar had a dog who was a half-Collie. About one o'clock one afternoon five of us were in the kitchen having our break - there was the vicar, me and my mate and two chaps from the Water Board, when suddenly the dog started to whimper. It looked out through the window and backed off, terrified, until it was against the far wall and couldn't go any further. We all looked at the window, quite surprised but there was nothing there. Something frightened it and whatever it was, was by the window.

One day I had a bad cold or felt sick or something so I went home at one o'clock. The vicar's wife went out so the house was empty except for the chap I worked with. He was a war hero, he'd been decorated after the Second World War, but he said to me the next day that he had gone home early as well, he wouldn't stay in that house on his own.

Reverend Hargreaves was the rector then. He said, 'We think the place is haunted, we have a lot of queer things happening'. He told us that he had heard someone coming up to the house and leaning his bike against the study window, he could hear the crunch of the chippings in the drive. He walked to the front door but nobody was there. The vicar had two lads, one of them was about my age and the other was younger so they didn't say anything to the younger in case he was scared.

The vicar said that his predecessor, Reverend Mitchell, had left the rectory to go into the forces and he had gone down on his boat. He wondered if he had come back to visit the vicarage.

SNOWSHILL MANOR - One boot up and one boot down

About seven miles south-east of Evesham, is the little Cotswold village of Snowshill, where groups of limestone cottages cluster round a large green and a Victorian church. The manor of Snowshill is built from Cotswold limestone and is set in walled and terraced gardens. The manor was given to Winchcombe Abbey in 821 and was in their possession until dissolved by Henry VIII in 1539. The next four centuries saw a whole series of owners who extended and modified, adding a false front in the 1700s. However, by 1919 it was being used as a run-down farm.

Fortunately, at that point it came into the possession of the thin, bespectacled Charles Wade. It could not have fallen into better hands, and if it were not for Wade, the Manor would probably have been pulled down by now. He came from a wealthy family, he had worked as an architect and he appreciated fine art and antiques.

Charles set about restoring the house and garden to its former glory. He refused to have modern conveniences and used oil lamps and candles. He filled the house with an incredible collection of anything that took his fancy, timepieces, toys, bicycles, carts, oriental furniture and other exotics. Understandably, he chose not to live in the Manor but in the old priest's house in the courtyard. When he handed the Manor over to a museum in 1951, the costume collection alone stood at 2,000 pieces.

He was fascinated by the paranormal. One of Wade's rooms was dedicated to magic, with a pentagram on the floor and magic symbols on the walls. No-one knows if he managed to summon the spirits, but there are many stories of ghostly encounters. Jeanette's cousin was the curator of Snowshill Manor:

It's only my feeling about it, but to me it seems to be haunted. There's supposed to be a ghost in the dressing room. It contains two boots and they say that if one boot is flopped on to the side 'he' is out, if the two boots are upright then 'he' is in.

I didn't know this. When my cousin was showing me round the house for the first time We were in this particular dressing room when I had a really strong feeling that there was a 'presence'. I mentioned this to my cousin and she told me that her daughter had said exactly the same thing when standing in the same place.

Here are two more anecdotes from casual visitors:

I took my brother and his wife on a visit to Snowshill Manor. Up in the bedroom I was looking at something on the bed, a cap or something, and I was asking the guide in the room how old it was. I told her that it couldn't be all that old because it was done by machine - if it's machine-made it won't be older than 1850. She didn't really know the answer. Another guide came in and during the conversation, she mentioned, 'This room is haunted'. I said, 'Yes, there's a woman in here who stands by the fireplace'. I don't know how I knew but I just knew, I felt it in my bones.

The next story goes back to the 1960s or 1970s.

It happened a long time ago when my husband, my stepson and I went on a family outing and we ended up at Snowshill Manor.

There was a gentleman at the door taking the money. I thought he was showing us round, but when we got back to the entrance I realised that there were two gentlemen and they were twins, so we got chatting. I said to them, 'Is the lady upstairs any relation to you?'. They replied, 'There's no-one upstairs'. I said, 'Yes there is, she's sitting on a settle where the four-poster bed is. When I saw her she was sitting there and sewing. She was wearing a grey dress with a white cap and collar. I nearly spoke to her, but then I thought she must have a lot of people speaking to her so I decided not to disturb her'. The two gentlemen asked round but nobody else seemed to have seen her.

I have never really thought about it, until now. I just thought it was one of those things.

UPTON SNODSBURY - Murders and Remains

About six miles south of Worcester is Upton Snodsbury. One of the most important early pagan burial sites was found here in the mid 1800s. Unfortunately, the relics were found by labourers and ordinary folk digging their gardens, and so by the time the archaeologists realised what had been discovered, most of the archaeology had been lost. Among the finds were iron spearheads, amber beads, an iron sword, and three bronze brooches, one of them very ornate. They have been dated as belonging to the 650s.

The dead of Upton Snodsbury had to taken all the way to Pershore and it was not until 1424 that permission was granted by the Pope for a churchyard nearby. The Abbot of Pershore objected strongly as funerals were a good source of revenue and generous payments to the sacristan of Pershore had to be agreed before the churchyard could be consecrated.

Robert Palmer was a wealthy land-owner who lived in Upton Snodsbury at the beginning of the 1700s. He found life boring, so he enlivened it by combining with his brother-in-law from White Ladies Aston, Thomas Symonds, and a gang of desperadoes to break into houses, murder the inmates, plunder the houses and set fire to them. As a final exploit, he murdered his own mother and her maid, who were living alone. After that he was caught, tried and condemned to death.

The Palmers and the Symonds were well connected. Thomas Symonds was the grandson of a local judge who had been a friend of Oliver Cromwell. The families could not believe that the Palmers and the Symonds had been involved in the crime, and everything was done to prove their innocence but the case was hopeless.

When a friend of the family, the Bishop of Oxford and Dean of Worcester, Bishop Talbot, heard the news, he rode to Worcester for four hours through the pouring rain. The heavy floods nearly swept away his horse. He obtained a reprieve for Palmer and his brother-in-law for three weeks but by the end of that time realised there was no doubt about their guilt. In 1708 they were hanged and their bodies taken down, put in iron chains, hung up and left to rot. Bishop Talbot brought up and educated Palmer's young son.

The Palmers were very wealthy, but the property was confiscated because of the crime and given to the Lord of the Manor, ie the Bishop of Worcester, then Bishop Lloyd. He described it as 'the price of blood' and refused to take it. Instead, in 1713, he handed it over to maintain two schools in Worcester, one of them was known as 'Bishop Lloyd's School'.

Palmer's House in Upton Snodsbury became an inn, The Royal Oak and is now a private dwelling. Nearby is another old house, occupied by Janet:

I lived in Upton Snodsbury in a cottage that belonged to a person who worked on the land. It was built in 1897. Lots of strange things happened there.

My husband was sitting in the chair reading a paper and plate jumped off the hook and flew across the room. It had to jump off, the nails are at an angle and because its an old house, they're cemented on to the wall.

A Royal Albert saucer fell off the picture rail and a music box started playing at one o'clock in the morning. It's one of those musical boxes where you have to take a pin out to start it playing.

Before my sister died she crocheted a blanket about two feet square and I always laid it on the bed. One day I went upstairs and found it folded and put away under the bedside table.

When my husband and I came back from holiday, as we walked into the room the grandfather clock chimed one and it hadn't worked for years.

15. Haunted Schools and Secret Venues

his chapter is a collection of stories where, for various reasons, the locations cannot be given. Schools especially have asked to remain totally anonymous. We have promised not to even hint at the location of the next story, except to say that it's in Worcestershire. The people involved have been so terrified that they don't want to tell their experiences directly to anyone, so their story is told through a family friend.

Some friends of mine bought the end one of three cottages and, as the other cottages became vacant, so they bought them and converted them all into one house. It was after they had converted them that strange events began to happen, all in one particular bedroom.

The first thing was that a daughter who was sleeping there awoke to find a reflection of a person's face in the window. It was not looking in from outside but it was as if the person was in the room. The apparition had very regular features so it was impossible to distinguish whether it was a man or a woman. It had a scarf or a nun's cape over its head and its mouth was moving rapidly. It seemed as if it was trying to tell her something urgent, but it wasn't making a sound. The daughter was trying to lip-read but she had poor vision and couldn't make out what it was saying.

The second event happened to two people. Their daughter awoke to hear a loud ticking noise but there was no clock in the bedroom. The curtains were violently fluttering in the room, although the window was closed. She shouted for her mother, who ran in and switched the light on. Everything went still. Because the daughter was distressed, the mother camped down on the floor. Then the daughter felt a cat jump on the bed. They had had cats in the family, but not at that time. The cat seemed to walk up the bed, then when it came to her chest it settled down and became very heavy, so much so that she experienced breathing problems, almost like an asthma attack. The mother woke up and switched the light on but the breathing problems persisted, so much so that they had to take her to hospital the next day. She had not had a history of breathing difficulties before then. When the doctor checked her over, he couldn't find anything wrong with her.

Another member of the family moved into the bedroom and she witnessed the curtains levitating. The bottom of the curtains was raised until the curtains were parallel with the ceiling. The room went very cold. but when she touched the radiator to check that it was working she burned her arm, it was so hot. She went back to sleep but something kept pulling the eiderdown off the bed. She had to fight to keep a blanket on.

Two schoolgirl friends stayed in the bedroom. Late at night they came

... a man was standing in air, floating, in the stairwell.

out to get some food. Outside their room was a spiral staircase and when the girls started to go down it they saw a man was standing in air, floating, in the stairwell. The one girl said to the other, 'Can you see what I can see?' and the other girl said, 'Yes'. They scurried back into their bedroom but when they came out again he had gone. The strange thing is that he was standing just where the old bathroom used to be situated.

One incident happened downstairs. The wife was sleeping on the camp bed and the husband was on the sofa, and the camp bed and the sofa were pushed together. The wife woke up in the night and saw a figure standing at the end of the bed. At first she thought it was her husband, then she realised that she was holding his hand. The figure started to disappear.

I must say, though, that my brother and I have stayed in the house and slept in the haunted bedroom but nothing has ever happened to us. We heard all these stories and so we used to lie there and keep our eyes open as long as possible. I'm susceptible to these kinds of things but I always found the house very calm and welcoming. It seemed to me that nothing evil had ever happened there.

Horror at the cafeteria

The river Severn runs for 210 miles, from the hills of Plynlimon in Wales to its estuary at Severn beach. It enters Worcester at Upton-on-Severn, flows past the cathedral at Worcester, through Lincombe Lock and Weir, past the basins of Stourport-on-Severn and the merchant's houses of Bewdley, leaving the county at Upper Arley. Along its length are a range of public houses and cafeterias both ancient and modern and catering to every taste. A few years ago Julie* and her family bought a small catering complex on the edge of the river:

My mum and dad bought a café and general stores business. It was the old ferry house, which operated prior to the bridge being built over the river - the bridge was built in the 1800s. The original road went past our house at ground floor level but now it ran past the house at first floor level. There was a lean-to attached to the old part of the house, that you entered via what was the first floor bedroom but was now the store's stock room. Underneath the lean-to was the original road that was still the cobbled stone. My father concreted it over to make another stock room, it was a sin but it was very damp. The room in the lean-to was more like a short tunnel. This was the point at which the ferry used to go across to the other side.

On the road side was the stores and the other side of the original ferry house, together with a cafe built in the early part of the 1900s. Built from corrugated iron and bricks, it ran the length of the house and further on, making the house look L-shaped. We think that the cafe was originally barns that were converted into a bedroom above and a cafe below.

In the centre of these buildings was the house, which was our living quarters. I think it probably went back to the 1700s. It had an old insurance plaque on the wall. The upstairs landing over the cafe had four bedrooms and at the end of this really long landing was a single toilet. The bedroom at the end of the building was the most troublesome. Underneath this bedroom was the storeroom at the back of the cafe.

When my mum and dad bought the business, they were intending that my youngest sister, her husband and their two children would leave their council house and run the business with them. It was really run down. They decided to convert the storeroom under the end bedroom into a games room. They had only been in the property for about three weeks and my brother in law was decorating it when he suddenly came out in the most dreadful state and said he had got to go back to his parents. We thought he might be home-sick. He was crying and at that point he picked up his youngest child and said that if nobody would take him he would walk, and he started to walk back to Birmingham. He wouldn't talk about what had happened. Later we learned that he had seen a ghost and it had frightened the life out of him. He said that it looked like the man off the Quaker Oats wrapper. After that he wouldn't stop in the house. It took about two years for him to visit for any length of time.

Obviously, you can imagine the chaos. Oh my God! They had bought a place for four people and now there was only two. We all rallied round and helped out, as the holiday season was well under way. My middle brother, who had just left the army, and his wife then moved into the house to help out and see if they wanted to carry on helping mom and dad in place of my sister. She had had to go back with her husband, obviously, to support him. It was a terrible time for both of them.

They often heard this whistling going past their bedroom window, as if a workman was whistling on his way to work. They would say, 'There's that whistler again'. Then one day the whole field was flooded and there was no possibility of anybody human walking down the lane and past their bedroom window. Yet they still heard the same noise. They said, 'There's that whistler again - oooh'.

This didn't work out for one reason and another but mainly I think the influence the house had over everyone.Mom and dad were struggling. My husband and I said we would buy into the business and we bought half. He kept his job in Birmingham and I moved out there with my two children while we sold my house.

My girls were five and three and they shared the middle bedroom. The back bedroom at the end of the house had been used for my youngest brother who had been travelling the world all this time but when he was in England he still 'lived' at home with mom and dad. All his belongings were in this room and he was supposed to sleep in there. He wouldn't stay in the bedroom, he said it wasn't a nice room. He wasn't at home very much. So after few months I decided to have the two children in separate bedrooms so we cleared out the back bedroom and I put my eldest daughter into it. She was a nice little girl, my darling. Slowly from this agreeable, reasonable, lovely little girl she turned into a monster. She was bad-tempered, irritable and disobedient. She was just not herself. When I look back I can say that she was awful. She had terrible nightmares, for example, one night she dreamed that she was drowning. She once told me that she could see someone in her bedroom. When she looked in her mirror she could see that her dressing gown was occupied, not by anything in particular but it wasn't hanging limp in the door. When she turned round and looked, it was hanging limp. One day, a cupboard flew off the wall. You would expect it to fall straight down but they found it in the middle of the bedroom on the floor. It looked as if it had been pushed. I moved my daughter back in with her sister in the other bedroom and she changed into my nice little girl again.

We found that everything we planned to do went wrong. We seemed beset with problems. From repairs going wrong to arguments over petty things. My husband's role was to do the accounts and gradually, over time, he lost nine calculators. He would say, 'Not another one gone missing'. We never found them. Things would go missing and we would find them in the most stupid, illogical places. Things like scissors and sellotape - annoying little things, nothing major. You would just think you were absent-minded.

My husband was always at work and not able to maintain the property easily. We found we had a leak in the downstairs lounge. We called a brother-in-law in Birmingham who was very handy and he said he would fix it so he came out and traced the leak back to upstairs, the pipes come down into the lounge. The floors upstairs were Contiboard and he had to saw through them to get at the pipes. In doing so, he cut through a wire and fused the house. In order to mend the electrics he had to draw all the water off the tank. The tank was a sealed unit surrounded by insulating granules, when we dismantled the tank we filled seven bin-liners with granules. At the bottom of the airing cupboard cavity, we found money that dad had been collecting for years, and which had gone missing - half-a-crowns, florins and so on. No way could anyone have got under all those granules and put it there.

People who lived in the house tended to be ill. Dad knew that he had cancer before they moved but he became very low and died. While dad was ill, the electrics started to play up. One afternoon, dad had gone to bed, my mum was house-hunting and my second sister and I were sitting in the kitchen when suddenly, the whole house fused, 'bump'. To mend the fuses, I would have to go out the back, step on to a chair and climb on to the freezer. As soon as I went out of the kitchen door they all came on again. It was really weird. My youngest sister and I thought it was a sign that my dad had died and we went to have a look at him but he was alright. The electrics used to go all the time, first one room, then another, then the whole house, then they used to come on again. It was really bizarre. I named the ghost George, so I could yell at it every time I had to do the assault course of chairs and freezers to turn the electric back on.

There were the moods and the darkness of the place. Everyone said that as you came down into the dip (the house was below the level of the road and to enter the house you have to go down the to river bank level via some steps) it seemed dark, as if there was an overhanging darkness. It was so dark in there that I was putting my children to bed too early. One day I thought it was eight o'clock so I put them to bed and it wasn't until I climbed up the back place that I discovered it was actually only six o'clock. That was quite upsetting.

Checking through all the other people who have lived in the place that we know of, there seemed to be a pattern of the man being very possessive about the house and the woman hating it and wanting to move. My marriage to my husband had never been brilliant but now it was appalling. Obviously we were all under a strain but it was more than that. My mum and dad had never argued but they had this horrendous row and dad left. He came back later. It was just that sort of place.

The weekend we sold the property I was serving in the shop when an elderly gentleman came in and said he wanted to speak to the owner of the property. He said he and brother had once owned the business. We were chatting when out of the blue he said, 'Have you seen the ghost then?' He told me that his things used to go missing and his wife's make-up used to move from room to room. It was so thrilling to hear a previous occupant had the same experiences. He blamed it on the ghost.

He also told us that where the garage stood at the back of the property was originally a petrol station in the forties. He told us about the petrol station and added that a coach had caught fire on the bridge and the driver had driven into the petrol station, causing a huge fire.

Going back to 'George', I have got a friend who is deeper into ghosts. I was having a number of problems, and this friend said that he knew what was going on. He felt that sometime in the past there had been a love triangle with two men and one woman. Somehow George was on the outside of this triangle, he didn't know exactly how. That's why the ghost particularly affected married couples. It polarised each partner, one left and one stayed.

He decided that we needed an exorcist. My husband didn't believe in these sort of things and he said, 'I'm not having anybody official in' so my friend said that he would give it a go. The spiritual friend, my best friend and I went round the house, holding hands. He held a candle and said in each room, one after the other, to the ghost "that it was making everyone un-happy and that it was time to leave and to follow the light". When we got into the back bedroom, my best friend wanted to run away, I had to hang on to her. The other friend said, 'Don't let her go, it will break the circle'. She felt oppressed and extremely sad and she started crying. Then something clung to her back. You couldn't see anything but you could tell that she was bent under with the weight. It was very frightening. My mother, who was observ-ing said, 'We shouldn't be dabbling in this'. We went into each room and the longer we were, the worse she was getting . My friend said, We need to take this candle and put the candle in the river'. We kept the circle and walked out of the house to the river which was just out side our front garden and managed to throw the candle in the water. Straight away whatever-it-was left her and when we went back inside the atmosphere in the house was lighter. It did help. For a while.

We had been living there for three years when we sold the property. It took us ages to sell the business.We had almost to give it away to sell it, we lost a lot of money. My mum had bought a house with my youngest sister and had moved in.

On the last day, the children were at my mom's new house, I had just completed the stock take with the new owners and my husband was out. I lay on the bed watching the telly. All our furniture was in store as my hus-band and I were moving into a caravan as we weren't sure if we were mov-ing to Preston, leaving just a table, a bed and a portable telly. Suddenly the pipes under the floors started rattling as if the washing machine was run-ning. It kept stopping starting and each time it was worse until it was making a terrible noise. It sounded very angry. I was terrified. I leaped off the bed, I thought I was going mad. I decided to go back into the shop, I took some cans of cider and got very drunk.

When we had been moved for around eight weeks my mother re-ceived an angry phone call from the new owner. She shouted at mom " you didn't tell us there was a ghost!" My mom replied that we hadn't because we were afraid they would think we were mad. And the things that did happen to us were so bizarre that we don't tell many people. Apparently the women's father who had moved out with them to serve in the shop had seen a man dressed like a Quaker. He had refused to stay any longer and after a lot of negotiating and compromise he finally came back but would live in a little caravan at the back of the property and only work in the shop during the day. Mom also had another phone call from the woman to say that things were going missing including a bundle of money. Sound familiar?

While collecting ghost stories for this and other books, we have come across a number of occasions in which an amateur exorcism has been carried out with disastrous results. The editor, Barrie Roberts, adds:

The ritual is an ancient one, devised to drive out evil spirits. If you are not convinced that you are dealing with evil spirits, leave exorcism alone. The major Christian churches will only carry out an exorcism reluctantly if a bishop is convinced that it is necessary. Amateurs may do more harm than good.

The haunted vicarage

Theoretically, the most unlikely place for a ghost should be a vicarage as vicars are those empowered to bless houses and, with the bishop's permission, to perform exorcisms. There was another haunted vicarage at Shrawley:

My family went to live in a Worcestershire vicarage. I never felt that it was a very happy house. It hadn't been decorated for some years, so we renovated throughout, moving from room to room. Upstairs were two rooms and we think one had been a nursery because there were two hooks in the beam as if there had been a swing. We called the room 'The Nursery'.

I slept in the nursery one night and I dreamt that I was being strangled. It was really horrible, but I didn't tell a soul. I just moved into another room. Over the years we had various guests staying who slept in there and nobody said anything. My daughter worked in London and came home periodically. One night, she slept in the 'nursery' and in the morning she said to me, 'I don't like that room'. I asked her, 'Why, what's the matter with it?'. She said, 'I wake up and I feel as if there's something horrible in there and I have to go through it before I can get to the door and I can't bring myself to go through it'.

We have now sold the house and live elsewhere.

HAUNTED SCHOOLS

Poltergeists and other strange phenomena often seem to be attracted to or created by (according to your beliefs) young teenagers and, more often than not, by female teenagers. It is therefore surprising that there are so few 'hauntings' in schools catering for this age range. Various rumours have reached our ears such as 'exploding' libraries, where books and papers shoot in all directions. On Kerrang radio in July 2004 a teacher from a school in Dudley said that doors in the school slowly open and close, the contents of locked cupboards are moved about and items on shelves disappear and reappear somewhere else.

Headmaster pays a visit

In Victorian times, the school was often built with a house for the head-teacher.

A few years ago, I was working as a Classroom Assistant at the local primary school. The old house for the head teacher was still in the centre of the building, downstairs was a kitchen used by the staff and at the top of the stairs was a was a little room used for special projects with children where there was just a small group. I was upstairs, I had had a small knitting class and they had gone to out to play. I was wondering whether to have a cup of tea with the others downstairs, when I heard a man's voice and I could smell a pipe. I decided not to go downstairs because they had got visitors. After the afternoon break, the children came back in and we carried on.

At the end of the afternoon, the staff said, 'Why didn't you come down for a cup of tea?'. I told them that it was because they had visitors and explained what I had heard and smelt. They said, 'Ah, that's the old headmaster, he comes looking for his wife'. The headmaster had died about ten years previously. I knew nothing about the old headmaster until that was said.

The school has now been enlarged and the house has been demolished.

The caretaker returns

The next story comes from one of Worcestershire's High Schools with just under 1,000 pupils aged from 11 to 18. Sue*, a laboratory assistant, says that an old caretaker comes back to haunt the school.

She was a caretaker in the 1970s and 80s and is generally described as a cantankerous old woman, always complaining and off-hand with the staff.

The present caretaker finds floors that have been washed when the school is empty. Things are moved round, for example parcels would be moved and put in different places. He will go round the school switching all the lights off and by the time he comes to the end, some of the lights will be on again.

A personal experience that I had, was that we were in the prep room where there is metal shelving full of chemicals. All of a sudden, this big pool of water appeared underneath the shelving. It wasn't a little bit, it was a bucketful. We tested it to make sure that it wasn't from a leaking jar, then we moved all the racking but there was no sign of anything leaking.

Several people have seen her and that's how she was identified. The caretaker saw her who, of course, knew her and recognised her and she has been seen by one or two other people. When anything happens, they just say, 'Oh, its Mrs C...'. The lady who took over as assistant caretaker was very frightened of her. She won't stay in the school on her own. When something strange happens and someone remarks, 'Oh, it's Mrs C...', she snaps, 'No it's not'.

The Christmas party guest

This narrator works voluntarily at the school with a friend:

We were clearing up after the Christmas party, I was washing the beakers. This school has one kitchen which serves the infants, then there is a narrow corridor leading into another kitchen which has a serving hatch for the Juniors. Suddenly, I went very cold, I looked to my left and saw a woman gliding or floating along. She was medium build and about five feet tall. Her hood was pulled down over her face so that I could only see her nose but I would say from her stance that she was in her fifties. She wore a grey cloak and hood which was down to the ground. She was grey all over but she had little red marks on her cloak, like squares, a bit like noughts and crosses, two lines one way and two lines crossing the other way. I did wonder if her cloak had been patched.

I went to find my friend and said, 'I have just seen a ghost'. My friend said that she had seen the grey lady in the same place. I mentioned this to the headmaster when he came in and he told me to take more water with it next time!

I don't know if it's anything to do with it but I am told that the school is built over an old burial ground.

The ghost with the technical expertise

We have concluded the book with this story, as it is guaranteed to make your hair stand on end:

I have always believed in the after life but for no reason other than that I found it fascinating but one or two intriguing things have happened recently to encourage my beliefs.

Seven years ago I started work at a local residential school which caters for children from four to eighteen. The children are there during the week but go home at weekends, when the school is empty, so I'm in the building quite a lot on my own, especially during the holidays. I have felt very uncomfortable in the school for a long time, I often had the feeling that I was being watched. Sometimes I would be working in one of the classrooms or dormitories, I would turn round to speak to someone behind me and, to my surprise, find that nobody was there. Occasionally, I would hear a door slam and when I went to take a look, no-one would be there. I would just take a deep breath and carry on.

The intruder alarms go off at night and we can't find the reason why. The experts say that perhaps spiders or moths have been running over the PIR system, but we had a total refurbishment recently and there are few, if any, spiders or moths in the building. I lock all the doors carefully on a Friday night and when I arrive on a Monday morning, they are unlocked. You have to unlock them from the inside and the intruder alarm has not gone off.

Then I heard that the night staff were talking about a leg. They would say, 'I saw the leg again last night'. Evidently, they would get a glimpse of a leg as someone disappeared into a bedroom or round the corner of a corridor. They would have to go and investigate in case one of the children had got out of bed. I was my belief that they were just winding each other up, putting the frighteners on.

Now, the Matron is a very level-headed woman and she said that several times, when the school was closed, she had heard somebody walk past her door and a shadow had gone past the doorway. She had been so frightened that she had locked the door and phoned for someone to keep her company.

The headmaster lives in a separate building on the site. One morning, a group of girls told him that someone had left the light on in one of the empty bedrooms. He said, 'How could this be, when no-one has been in there?' He sent staff to investigate, the door was locked and the light was not on. Again, I assumed that the girls were winding him up.

During the last Christmas holiday I went in on my own early one morning, at 20 to 8. Now I am the one and only key holder and when I open up I have to switch off all the alarms. I distinctly heard a door slam. I thought, 'One of the cleaners has come in early' and then I had a second thought, 'That couldn't be a cleaner, because I told them I wasn't getting in until 9.30 or 10.00'. I walked round and nobody was there. That's one occasion when I actually felt frightened. I left the building and returned at half past nine. When the cleaner came in she said, 'You look dreadful, have you seen a ghost or something?' I told her 'No, but I have heard one!'

One night between Christmas and the New Year, the alarms went off at 3.00 am so I had to go and investigate. Now, the doors in the middle corridor are held together by magnets and you have to give them a really firm pull to open them. The alarm had gone off from that area, next to the computer room. When I shut the magnetic doors I heard a door slam. I thought 'Oh Blimey, somebody has got in'. I searched the building but I had entered on my own and as it was the Christmas holiday no-one else had come in and no-one had been working on the computers.

Our computer system is maintained from a central station. If anyone tries to key in it shows up on the computer log and the analytical equipment. The technical manager can see the computer site, the time that it's used, the name of the person using it, and if something is printed off, the number of copies and whether its in black and white or colour. Our technical manager is a very level-headed person, he came to see me and said, 'We have a problem, we keep getting electrical spikes so that the whole system crashes. We put a test on the electrics and a problem showed up on the computer log. The spikes always occur between midnight and 3.00 am and usually during the weekend and holiday periods. This went on for about 12 months. All the computers were taken out and sent back to the manufacturer. Nothing was wrong. They sent an expert to the school to check the installation. There were no faults.

Then something happened that frightened me. The technical manager said, 'Who was in at the weekend? Somebody tried four times to log on to the Internet in one of the classrooms'. If anybody had broken in, they would have set the alarms off. An hour later he came to me, his face was ashen. He said that a member of staff wanted to know who had been messing with her laptop. On Friday night she closed her laptop down and shut it in the office drawer but at 12.30 am it was opened up and the user's name had been changed.

The technical manager wanted to know what we could do about it. My only suggestion was to call a paranormal expert in. We were recommended to a lady in Stratford. She didn't know the school at all, I had to send her instructions on how to get here. I asked her, 'How much is this going to cost us?', because as you know, with a school, price is everything. Her answer was, 'Absolutely nothing, I have a gift and I like to help those who are trapped'. She came all the way from Stratford and didn't even ask for her petrol costs. She said, 'Don't tell me anything, show me round the school and I will tell you what I feel, then you can tell me what has happened here.'

She came on a Saturday afternoon with her partner who was a non-believer and came purely in a scientific role. As soon as we walked in she had her head on her chest and as we went round she kept saying, there's a lot of activity here. Now, this is a complicated building on two storeys with bits added on and corridors running in opposite directions and it takes weeks for someone new to find their way round. However, she picked out two areas of prevalent activity, the one on top of the other. I noticed that these were the places that are perpetually cold. In fact, we have had the heating engineers in and no-one can understand why it is so cold because the radiators are working. She identified the activity as emanating from the one bedroom where the headmaster was told that the light was on. The room below that was the computer room, where we had been having all the problems.

She asked me how old the building was and when I said that it only went back to the 1960s, she wanted to know what was here before. She said 'Is it anywhere near a graveyard?'. There is a church with a cemetery not far away and about 300 yards distant is said to be an old Saxon burial ground. Again, head on chest. She said it wasn't either of those. She didn't know what it was. I said, 'Well, what are we to do about it?' She said, 'Shut your eyes and try to talk to it physically or mentally'. Well, I wasn't into that.

She told me to get some candles and some salt. She put the candles round and sprinkled the salt. She was there for about two hours, then afterwards she said, 'Can you feel any difference?' I told her, 'Well I am loth to say it, it does feel different but perhaps its because I'm not here on my own'. I didn't feel cold but that could have been because I had become acclimatised. However, when I went in the following day, Sunday, it did feel different, I didn't feel as if I was being watched and I didn't get the chest rushes.

Our technical manager was keen to know what had been done and when I told him about the candles and the salt, he laughed, but since that time we have had no problems with the computers.

By 10.30 on Monday, several members of staff had said, 'Thank goodness you've had the heating fixed, but I'm too hot now, could you turn it down a bit?' and I told them that I hadn't done anything! When word got round that I'd had a ghost buster in, it was amazing the number of people who said something like, 'I always felt spooked but I didn't like to say anything in case people thought I was mad'.

The paranormal expert warned us that sometimes things became worse after her visit and in that case, she would need to come back again. But that was three months ago and since then the building has remained warm and we have had no problems with the computers. It has been an incredible experience.

BIBLIOGRAPHY

Amphlett John, *A short history of Clent,* republished by Clent History Society, 1991

Darnet Janet, *Pershore Pubs Past and Present*, privately published 2002

Fraser Maxwell, *Companion into Worcestershire,* Methuen & Co Ltd, 1939 and 1949

Friends, *The Quaker Meeting House, Evesham*, (leaflet obtainable from The Friends)

Gwillam Bill, *'Old Worcestershire Inns'*, privately published, available from libraries.

Havins Peter J Neville, *A Portrait of Worcestershire*, Robert Hale 1974

Hunt Michael, *Seven locals studies in Worcestershire*, with contributions from Michael Hunt

Leatherbarrow J S, *Worcestershire*, B T Batsford Ltd, 1974

Mee Arthur, *The King's England - Worcestershire*, The Caxton Publishing Co Ltd, date unknown.

Pevsner Nikolaus, *The Buildings of England - Worcestershire*, Penguin 1968 and 1985

Roberts Barrie, *Midland Murders and Mysteries*, published by Quercus 1997

Weaver Cora and Osborne Bruce, *Springs, Spouts, Fountains and Holy Wells of the Malvern Hills*, Aldine Press, 1992 and 1997

Weaver Cora and Osborne Bruce, *Aquae Malvernsis, The Springs and Fountains of the Malvern Hills,* privately published 1994

Weaver Cora, *The Priory Gateway of Great Malvern,* Aldine Press 1993

Weaver Cora, *A short guide to Malvern as a Spa Town*, privately published 1991 and 2003

White Alan, *Worcestershire Salt, A History of Stoke Prior Salt Works,* Halfshire Books 1996

Worcestershire Federation of Women's Instutes, *The Worcestershire Village Book,* jointly Countryside Books and WFWI.

Details of other books have been given in the text.

A great deal of information has been obtained from the four volumes plus index of the *Victoria County History*, published for the University of London Institute of Historical Research in 1913.

Books featuring ghost stories by Anne Bradford, published by Hunt End Books.
Out of print books may be available from libraries and second-hand shops.

Haunted, ghost stories from round and about Stratford, Redditch, Bromsgrove and Alcester, 1992, out of print

Haunted Worcestershire, 1996, out of print.

Haunted Pubs and Hotels of Worcestershire and its borders, 1998, out of print.

Unquiet Spirits of Worcestershire, 1999, out of print.

Worcstershire Ghosts and Hauntings, 2001, out of print.

Haunted Holidays, 2002, written in conjunction with paranormal expert David Taylor.

and still available from Hunt End Books.

Oral history books by Anne Bradford:

Royal Enfield, Amulree 1996, out of print.

Stourport-on-Severn, Hunt End Books, 2002, out of print.

Old Redditch Voices, Hunt End Books, 2005. Still available from Hunt End Books.

Books by Anne Bradford and Barrie Roberts, published by Quercus

Midland Ghosts and Hauntings, 1994

Midland Spirits & Spectres, 1998

Strange Meetings, 2002

THE AUTHOR

ANNE BRADFORD has been collecting eye-witness accounts of strange events since 1992, when she was inspired by a Victorian collection of ghost stories in the archives of the local library. This is her seventh collection of weird tales, another three were co-authored with Barrie Roberts: A retired secretary and schoolteacher, she is married to a graphic designer and has three adult children.

THE ILLUSTRATOR

GLENN JAMES drawings have a Gothic interest with a Bohemian streak. He has always had a tendency towards folklore and the Gothic side of art. It seems to run in the family as a great, great grandfather was a sculptor who built tombs in Wales during the Gothic revival. He has a love of horror films and our rich cultural heritage in England has inspired him to move in that direction. He is best known for his creation of Skaler, a new Romantic vampire. The name dates back to the 12th century.

ACKNOWLEDGEMENT

Barrie Roberts, writer, lecturer and consultant on the paranormal, has very kindly copy-read the book.